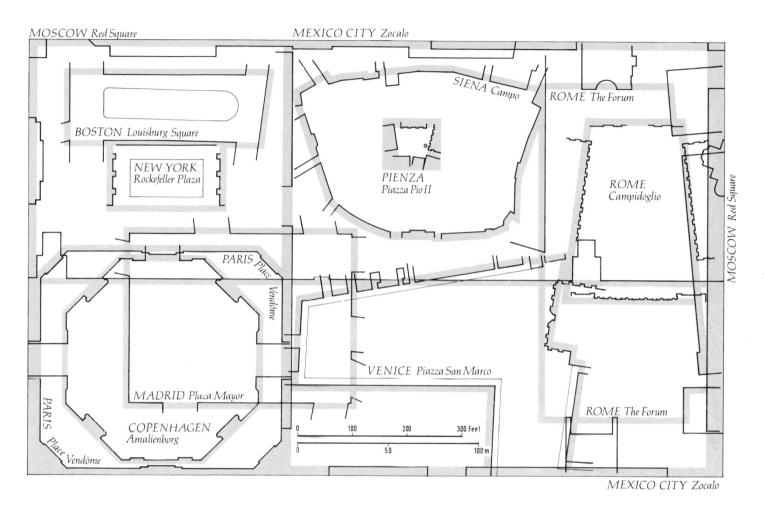

MOSCOW *Red Square*

MEXICO CITY *Zocalo*

SIENA *Campo*

ROME *The Forum*

BOSTON *Louisburg Square*

NEW YORK
Rockefeller Plaza

PIENZA
Piazza Pio II

ROME
Campidoglio

PARIS *Place*

Vendôme

MOSCOW *Red Square*

PARIS

Place Vendôme

MADRID *Plaza Mayor*

COPENHAGEN
Amalienborg

VENICE *Piazza San Marco*

ROME *The Forum*

| 0 | 100 | 200 | 300 Feet |

| 0 | 50 | 100 m |

MEXICO CITY *Zocalo*

Twelve city squares to scale

Piazza San Marco, Venice: drawing by Saul Steinberg, 1951.

A HISTORICAL EVOLUTION
THE CITY SQUARE

MICHAEL WEBB

WHITNEY LIBRARY OF DESIGN
an imprint of Watson-Guptill Publications / New York

First published in 1990 in the United States and Canada by
Whitney Library of Design,
an imprint of Watson-Guptill Publications,
a division of BPI Communications, Inc.,
1515 Broadway, New York, N.Y. 10036

Library of Congress Cataloging–in–Publication Data

Webb, Michael, 1937–
        The city square   /   Michael Webb.
              p.   cm.
        Includes bibliographical references.
        ISBN 0–8230–0636–0
        1. Plazas—Social aspects.   I. Title.
HT153.W39   1990
307.3'42—dc20   90–33356
                                        CIP

Manufactured in Singapore

First printing, 1990

1 2 3 4 5 6 7 8/95 94 93 92 91 90

Contents

Acknowledgments

The City Square was made possible, in part, by a grant from the Graham Foundation for Advanced Studies in the Fine Arts.

Many friends, old and new, have shared their insights and offered their hospitality in the progress of this book; the author is solely responsible for its shortcomings. My greatest debt is to the librarians of the University of California, Los Angeles, especially Anne Hartmere and Bonnie Beduhn of the Architecture and Urban Planning Library, and to the Getty Center for the History of Art and the Humanities. Mildred Friedman, Richard Koshalek, Jon Jerde and Richard Wurman were early advocates of the project. I thank Donald Richie for his wise counsel on Japan, Eduard Maynes for briefing me on Barcelona, and Jean Feray for his witty observations on the royal squares of France. In Berlin, Marianna Feuwagen introduced me to her favorite squares, as did Georg Schmid in Vienna and Rolf Muller in Munich. Jiri Hruza revealed his wealth of knowledge and deep love for Prague, besides providing illustrations, and I am most grateful to Carl Schmidt for the thoroughness of his revisions, and to Wendy Luers for her introductions. In Milan, Benedetta Barzini provided warm hospitality and provocative conversation, as did Verena Zollikofer in Nuremburg. Librarians and curators were unfailingly helpful throughout Europe, but I must single out Celina Fox at the London Museum, Emiliana Ricci at the Museo di Roma, and Magarida Duque Viera in the archives of Lisbon. Ullrich Zollikofer in Zurich and Piotr Mikucki in Warsaw went out of their way to secure illustrations, and Oswald Drobinc of Kodak Laboratories in Vienna rendered services beyond the call of duty. In Mexico City, Carol Miller made her house mine; Milou de Reiset and Cristina Lans were unfailingly resourceful. My gratitude for help and ideas go to Carter Brown in Washington, D.C.; Robert Weinberg, Kenneth Brecher and Nancy Robins in Boston; Renato Danese, Stephen Davies, Karen Alschuler and Jeanne Giordano in New York; Steven Bingler in New Orleans; and to Patrick Macrory, Katrin Adam, Betsey Brown and Adolfo Nodal for their many kindnesses. In Los Angeles, Diane Favro got me started, and Rudy and Francesca Bianchi arranged things in Italy. Arnold Schwartzman, Fritz Neumeyer, Fernando Juarez and Frank Dimster patiently answered questions; Ellen Curtis and Stefanie Pierantoni translated letters and foreign texts. The book would not have appeared without the expertise and enthusiastic support of Stanley Baron, Jamie Camplin and their colleagues at Thames and Hudson.

MICHAEL WEBB
Los Angeles, February 1990

Foreword

EVERYBODY LOVES A GOOD SQUARE, and this book explores, in words and pictures, how people have shaped squares and used them. From thousands of interesting examples around the world, I have chosen to describe a hundred — for their beauty, history and vitality. About 150 more are mentioned in passing; also included are some instructive failures. This is a sampling of the famous and unfamiliar, large and small, quiet and animated, mostly in Europe and the Americas. The first chapter tries to define a square, illustrate its diversity, and explain its origins in the ancient world. The last asks the question: what kinds of squares will enrich the cities of today? In between, the book chronicles their historical evolution, as medieval market, princely showcase, parade ground, residential enclave, symbol of worldly glory and pedestrian precinct.

For much of 1989, they were stages for revolution. In Beijing, Warsaw and Bucharest, Leipzig, Prague and Sofia, the people lost their fear and dictators lost control. As the world watched, the battle for democracy was fought, lost or won on city squares.

Squares have a family likeness, but, as in a human family, each has a distinctive shape and personality. That is what makes them so rewarding to experience, and so difficult to create. Vintage squares remind us of an era when good design was instinctive and cities had a rich street life. We cannot bring back the past, but we can learn from it. An older square that is an organic part of its community usually serves present needs better than a new space ordained by a planner or developer. Cities are learning to preserve, improve and adapt the squares they have, rather than opening up more. People have always enjoyed coming together, and this survey celebrates the different ways in which that impulse can be fulfilled.

Marckt in Bremmen

Schutting oder Kauffmans Hauß

S. Stephani Thurn

S. Anschari Thurn

Ra

Mathias Merian's engraving of
Bremen's market square in 1653.
The city hall on the right and
the outsized statue of Roland
survived wartime bombing; the
other buildings have been
restored.

8

S. Mariæ Thurn

Variations on a Theme

AT THEIR BEST, squares are microcosms of urban life, offering excitement and repose, markets and public ceremonies, a place to meet friends and watch the world go by. They have been shaped by popular needs and rulers' whims, by topography and architectural fashion. Some grew piecemeal; others were planned at a stroke, as a symbol of power or the foundation stone of a new development. A small city may have a single square that serves as traffic hub and as a distillation of its character. Great cities boast squares of every size, style and purpose, demonstrating the varied ways in which space can be contained and manipulated.

Squares have risen from humble origins to become rich and famous; others started out with a flourish only to fall on hard times. Asia and the Islamic world have their own distinctive kinds of urban space. Here we explore the great family of European squares from their beginnings in ancient Greece and Rome, through their rebirth in the trading cities of the Middle Ages, their translation to the New World, and their changing fortunes, from Madrid to Moscow, Boston to Buenos Aires over the past seven centuries.

Reduced to basics, a public square can be as simple as a child's drawing: an outdoor room, with walls to enclose space, doors to admit traffic, the sky as ceiling. The walls can be straight or bowed, high or low, continuous or fragmented. Space can be defined without walls; trees or a railing will do the job, as will a central point of focus like a fountain, column or equestrian statue. The points of entry can be concealed – by an arcade, perhaps – or establish a bold axis, a cord upon which the square is strung. The surface may be paved or planted, left open or filled with trees. Scale, shape and function are infinitely variable.

Throughout Europe and the Americas, labels are applied with cheerful abandon. Every rent in the urban fabric, from a traffic intersection to a park, can be called a square or platz, piazza or plaza, praca or place. But, just as the original theme remains discernible in the most complex of fugues, so can the essence of a square be defined through all its mutations. Public access and activity distinguish it from college quadrangles, palace courtyards and religious cloisters. Residential squares may be parklike at their core, but when winter strips the leaves the enclosure is revealed. Often the test is more subjective than scientific. Stand in a public space, walk about, sit at its edges. Does the space itself have a presence, a definition, a quality that adds significantly to the architecture and the features that it embraces?

The square as a public room, with the sky for ceiling: the late medieval marketplace of České Budějovice in Czechoslovakia.

Nature at the heart of the city: New Square, a secluded enclave of lawyers' chambers, built in 1685–97 and now part of Lincoln's Inn, London.

Exuberant and sober: a stormy day in the cathedral square of Orvieto, an Umbrian hill town, and Georgian doorways in Fitzwilliam Square, Dublin.

In Mexico, everything happens in the plaza: puppet theater in Guanajato's Jardin de la Union.

The square as resort for young and old (below): children playing in the Campo Santa Maria Formosa, Venice; the Plaza de la Borda in the Mexican colonial city of Taxco.

11

Living chess game, presented in the Septembers of odd-numbered years in the walled town of Marostica, near Venice. It recreates a medieval contest in which the winner married the ruler's daughter.

And if you decide that, yes, it is a square, does it work well? Does it take your breath away as you enter, and lift your spirits as you stroll around? Is it a place in which you want to meet your friends and observe strangers? Is it the first choice for community celebrations? Does it offer a sense of place, a feeling of historical continuity, a vision of what urban life should be? Is it maintained with respect or vandalized; does it serve as an oasis or for parking? Ask another question: "If not, why not?" Actors and decor have changed over the centuries, but the need for a stage has remained a constant.

Robert Browning expressed the ideal when he wrote: "Oh, a day in the city square, there is no such pleasure in life!" The best squares have distinctive characters and rhythms, which can change dramatically with the seasons and the time of day. Sometimes these can be precisely plotted. As the shadow of the Mangia tower sweeps around Siena's Campo like that of the gnomon on a sundial, it marks the shifting tempo of everyday life, and heralds, twice a year, the tumultuous spectacle of the Palio. For six centuries, whenever the sun has shone, this shadow has performed the same daily sweep.

Every square in the historic cities of Europe and Latin America shares some of the same daily events. The stillness of dawn, disturbed only by the pigeons fidgeting for a foothold on the ledges, is broken by the clean-up crew with its mechanized sweeper, the clang of garbage bins and the clatter of bottles and barrels as trucks replenish restaurants and bars. The pigeons are up and wheeling in synchronized arabesques, accelerated by the pealing of church bells. The sun lights the towers and gables, then the façades; casts a mirror-sheen off the newly washed cobbles, and bars of shadow within the arcades. The bakery and bars draw their first customers; later, cafés unstack chairs and unfurl umbrellas to lure tourists in search of breakfast and locals taking a mid-morning break.

The day follows its predictable course. Commuters and shoppers crisscross the square or hug the arcades in foul weather and the blaze of noon; cars and cyclists make the circuit; the tables fill up for lunch and empty as people return to work or drift off for a siesta. In those fortunate plazas from which cars have been banished, voices dominate: shrill cries of children at play and of mothers summoning them home, the hum of adult chatter as old men and women gather in knots to exchange gossip, the gurgling of a fountain, a snatch of music from an open window, or the wheeze of a mechanical organ. There may be a daily or weekly market to fill the square with the colorful clutter of produce stalls, cheese, antiques or cheap clothes; with odors and aromas that linger after the debris has been abandoned to cats and foraging pigeons.

At least once a year, the square is likely to host a special event: Bastille Day celebrations in every town and village of France, the May Day parade through Red Square, and the human chess game in the Piazza Castello of Marostica are unique to one country or city, but every European has gone to his local square to cheer a winning team, a political rally or the parade of the local saint's relics; to listen to a band concert or watch summer theater. A few squares have become symbols: of faith (St Peter's in Rome), protest (Tiananmen in Beijing), urban sophistication (New York's Rockefeller Plaza), and mass tourism (St Mark's in Venice).

In northern cities, only teenagers haunt the squares past twilight, unless the night is warm or the illuminations unusually seductive. As these cooler places fall asleep, southern squares come alive. Everyone is welcome to join the party, which spills out from the arcades and surrounding streets. The carriage parade survived as a nightly ritual until the beginning of this century in Spain and Latin America. And in the smaller Mexican towns you can still see the traditional *paseo*: young women and men circling in opposite directions, arms locked, flirting and sizing up prospects; elders observing from a bench or café table; small children scurrying underfoot late into the night.

These are rites of spring, summer and fall. In winter, when the arcades become wind tunnels, when the outdoor tables are stacked away and the trees are bare, the square can have a melancholy beauty, enhanced by darkness and lamplight. Undistracted by the human bustle, by the seduction of leaves and water, you can appreciate the shapes and textures of the buildings: the pediments and colonnades, trophies and reliefs of a Roman piazza, or the sober black-and-white classicism of a London square, with its polished brass plates and windows aglow. The medieval marketplaces of central Europe host Christmas fairs, with pinewood toys and mulled wine and fresh gingerbread. Soon, another year will bring back the crowds, spectacles, and the changing, yet changeless patterns of life in the city square.

Gubbio (above) comes alive for its Race of the Ceri — three images of saints which are carried from the Piazza della Signoria to a convent above the town.

Christmas market in the Gothic Hauptmarkt of Nuremberg: a month-long offering of traditional food, toys and music.

In Greve (top), center of the Chianti region south of Florence, the Saturday market is for locals — to meet and stock up on necessities.

Music students in Munich's Marienplatz, once a market, now the hub of the midtown pedestrian zone.

The Friday cheese market in the Dutch town of Alkmaar is a staged event, with carriers in guild costumes; on other days, the cheeses are sold indoors without ceremony.

These patterns, of stone and human activity, are but the visible part of a square's magic, suggesting but not always revealing the richness of its past. The Old Town Square in Prague is a spectacular showpiece of Gothic and Baroque, a magnet to visitors from all over the world; but for Czechs it enshrines a thousand years of history and the soul of a nation. If you approach it, as you should, down the steep hill from the Hradčany castle, across the statue-lined Charles Bridge and through the narrow lanes of the Old Town, you are following an ancient trade route and retracing the coronation procession of Bohemian kings.

As early as AD 965, the merchant and traveler Ibrahim ibn Jacob described Prague as a rich mercantile community with stone buildings and a wooden bridge over the Vltava. Soon after, the city became the largest trading center in Europe, the commercial and political hub of the kingdom of Bohemia. By royal decree, all goods had to be brought here for customs inspection and payment of taxes. To accommodate the crowds, a large square was laid out, surrounded by stone houses where merchants lived over their stores. Close by was a walled trading enclave with a customs house. German and Jewish merchants and craftsmen were encouraged to settle here and teach the Czechs industrious behavior; so well did they succeed that Prague evolved into a complex of four walled cities, each with its central square and local government, clustered together between the two royal castles of Hradčany and Vyšehrad. In 1348, Charles IV, King of Bohemia, embarked on a massive building program. When he was elected head of the Holy Roman Empire in 1355, he made Prague the imperial capital — the Rome of the North, and a mecca for artists and scholars from all parts of Europe.

Like Venice and Bruges, Prague peaked early but preserved its heritage through long centuries of decline. The imperial glory was shortlived; economic power shifted to newer centers; Bohemia's political authority waned until, in 1648, at the end of the Thirty Years War, it became a vassal state of the Habsburgs in Vienna.

The Old Town Square is a mirror of these changing fortunes. Much of its prewar vitality has ebbed. But on a fine summer weekend it can be one of the most exhilarating places on earth: sensuous and expansive; an interweaving of needle-sharp Gothic spires and exuberant Baroque and Rococo gables; a swirl of color and ornament anchored by gray stone towers and cobbles and by the Expressionist monument to radical preacher Jan Hus. To enter from the narrow lanes is like bursting upon a sun-dappled clearing in a dark wood; the sense of release affects every visitor. All but a few official cars are banned, and those are allowed only to skirt one corner. The pedestrian is king: open space and café tables are jammed, a crowd awaits the hourly procession of painted figures emerging jerkily from the old astronomical clock, young people cluster on the steps of the Hus memorial.

By six, the invading armies are leaving, and the square is repossessed by the residents of Prague. A brass ensemble plays Baroque music from atop the old Town Hall, and the harmonies drift across the square as hauntingly as the interrupted bugle call that marks the hours in the marketplace of Cracow, Poland. Shadows lengthen and the sun becomes a theatrical spotlight. As the painted surfaces fade to dark, the sharp-etched profiles of Týn church and Town Hall assert their presence in this most Gothic of cities.

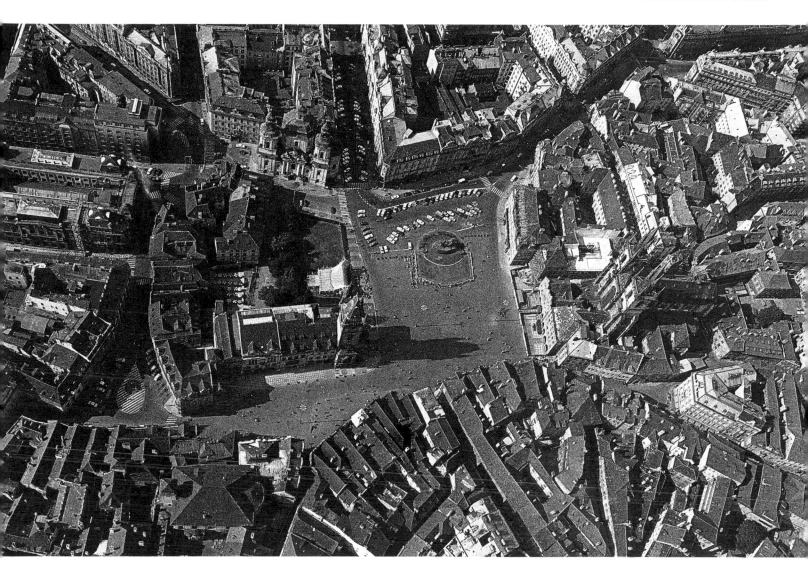

How did the square look in its heyday? Every medieval city was repeatedly burned or bombarded, so that its present appearance represents the latest phase of improvement, enhanced by carefully restored or reconstructed fragments of older buildings. Prague's Old Town Square retains its irregular medieval plan — a 100,000-square-foot trade mart — but the level of the square was raised in the 13th century after repeated floods, and Gothic houses and stores were built on the Romanesque foundations.

The oldest surviving building is, appropriately, the 14th-century nucleus of the Town Hall, now used for weddings and cultural events. As the square lost its role as a market, gentrification set in; Gothic houses acquired new façades in the latest fashion. The Baroque church of St Nicholas was built in the 18th century, as well as the Rococo Kinsky Palace, from whose balcony Klement Gottwald proclaimed the communist party's seizure of power in 1948. In the mid 19th century, the Town Hall was enlarged; later, the north side of the square was rebuilt and entry streets widened as part of a program of slum clearance in the Jewish ghetto. Resistance to

Prague's Old Town Square in the 1970s, before cars were banned and the barrier around the Hus memorial was removed. The three broad streets at the top of the photograph were driven through the maze of the Old Town in the 19th century.

17

Prague's Old Town Square in an 1825 watercolour by Vincenc Morstadt; the view is from the tower of the Týn Church. It shows the since demolished Virgin column, guard house, and the buildings that formerly screened the domed church of St Nicholas.

the Habsburgs found expression in the Hus memorial of 1915, and the destruction of the Virgin column, erected in 1650 to symbolize the defeat of the Protestant armies.

After just two decades of independence, came the brutality of the Nazi occupation, and — on the last day of the war — the vengeful destruction of the city archives and municipal offices along the west side of the square. The four competitions to complete the city hall held since 1946 have yielded proposals that range from the mundane to the monstrous. Happily, none has been approved, and the empty space is grassed over. The rest of the square has been lovingly restored — most recently in 1987. Purists consider the choice of colors too bright and busy — more appropriate for a town in Austria or Bavaria than this somber city. But the harsh climate should soon tone down any excesses.

Darkness harbors ghosts: of medieval rioters and victims of the gallows that stood here until 1840. Crosses in the pavement mark the place where twenty-seven leaders of a Protestant rising were executed in 1621. Rabbi Low, legendary creator of the Golem, and Franz Kafka, who chronicled the city like no other, both lived on or near the square, reminding us that Prague was enriched by its Jewish community for a thousand years before the Final Solution.

The Soviets, acclaimed as liberators in 1945, snuffed out the Prague Spring of 1968. Protestors gathered in the Old Town Square, and renewed their protest here on the twentieth anniversary of the invasion, after marching from the Wenceslas Square. No wonder the authorities nervously discouraged public assembly — fencing the Hus memorial with greenery to restrict access until 1987, and allowing cafés to open only in the last few years. A symbol so weighty is a treacherous thing to have in your midst.

Prague rates high for civic pride, but restoration is barely keeping pace with industrial pollution. The city's one advantage — a byproduct of economic stagnation

— is the absence of cars. In contrast, the center of Vienna is clogged with traffic. Its historic buildings are superbly maintained; its public spaces are shamefully abused. The Am Hof with its exuberant Baroque Arsenal, Jesuit Church and mock medieval castle, has been cut in two by the ramp to an underground garage, with a filling station above. No square so well embodies the spirit of Imperial Vienna as the Josefsplatz, with its equestrian statue of Joseph II as a Roman Emperor, flanked by the Spanish Riding School, State Library, Pallavicini and Palffy Palaces. It is now a parking lot.

Both squares were filmed as locations in *The Third Man*. Harry Lime's death was staged in the Josefsplatz, and he disappeared into the sewers from a kiosk in the Am Hof (though the staircase he descended was located beside the Danube). These and other images of a war-ravaged city, often shot at night in harsh chiaroscuro, with shadowy figures pursued down echoing streets and fragments of sculpture emerging from rubble, seem infinitely more alluring than the sleek and prosperous city of today. But, with a little imagination, you can recover that mythic quality on a nocturnal stroll, when darkness shrouds the tawdriness of commerce, and the cobbles gleam in the lamplight.

Prague acquired its squares as part of a rational planning process during an era of peace, prosperity and enlightened rule. The Lesser Quarter, founded in 1257, has a big commercial square, divided into two unequal spaces by a church, and a succession of neighborhood plazas. Charles Square, laid out by the Emperor in the mid 14th century as the centerpiece of the New Town, is a vast rectangle, once used as a cattle market and now as a park.

A sun-dappled clearing in a dark wood: looking across the square of Old Town Prague (left) towards the Týn Church and Kinsky Palace from beside St Nicholas.

Recently restored façades (right) on the Old Town Square, looking from the steps of the Hus memorial.

Austria, on the other hand, was weak and divided in the late Middle Ages, and Vienna was a border fortress subject to attack from the Magyars and the Turks. "East of Vienna, the orient begins," declared Prince Metternich, and the old city remained imprisoned in the straitjacket of its fortifications until 1857. Its squares reflect the intolerable pressure on space. The Neuer Markt and Hoher Markt, laid out in the 13th century, have the proportions of wide streets. The Stephansplatz, though clumsily restored from wartime devastation, retains an authentically medieval sense of claustrophobia. When the walls were leveled and the defensive area beyond developed as the Ringstrasse, huge open spaces were created between the new civic buildings. But in contrast to the enclosed, harmoniously proportioned squares of Prague, they remain mere vacancies, unshaped and banal.

Why could Vienna, so long trapped in the past, not learn from it, and make better use of this unprecedented opportunity, asked Camille Sitte in his pioneering *City Planning According to Artistic Principles* (1889). Sitte's protests against the growing obsession of his age with traffic flow and geometrical plans have shaped the thinking of preservationists and urbanists down to the present, but his proposals for reform went unheeded in his native city.

Open space is a necessity of urban life. Traditionally it has been shaped by commerce and defense, political systems and cultural traditions, climate and topography. Each society has its distinctive patterns, and the fortunate ones — like medieval Bohemia and the communes of Italy and Flanders — combined utility and beauty. Some of the most glorious squares were located in the trading centers of northern Germany.

Bremen's Marktplatz is a showcase of the city's history: as a leader of the Hanseatic League in the Middle Ages, an Imperial free city, and a prosperous city-state of modern Germany. The square has retained its character despite wartime devastation. Defining the irregular space at the center of the old town are the Gothic Rathaus (city hall) with its Renaissance façade; gabled houses; the Schutting, built in the 16th century as a merchants hall and restored in 1951 as the Chamber of Commerce; and the glass-fronted Parliament, constructed in the 1960s on the site of the old stock exchange. The stone statue of Roland, dating from 1404, is a symbol of the freedom granted the city by the Emperor.

The Romanesque cathedral and Church of Our Lady stand back behind subsidiary spaces and close the vistas. The cathedral's height makes it a participant — not a spectator — like the Týn Church in Prague. It steps forward to conduct a dialogue with the Rathaus: God speaking to man, austere to ornate, vertical to horizontal. The jagged green copper roofline and spires all around the square suggest weather-beaten sails, set in motion by the sharp northern light — a merchant fleet, about to weigh anchor. The fantasy finds an echo in the banqueting hall that overlooks the square, where model sailing ships are suspended alongside brass chandeliers.

Trams rattle past the Rathaus, and steel barrels are unloaded with a dull resonance on the cobbles from horse-drawn drays. The rest of the square is reserved for pedestrians, who step briskly across, from corner to corner, throughout the day. Executives chat on the steps of the Schutting. *Hausfrauen* in felt hats gossip over

Bremen's history as a prosperous city-state in northern Germany is mirrored in its marketplace, the city hall (left), cathedral (center), and postwar parliament building (right).

pastries and coffee with whipped cream at the *Konditorei*. Young people quaff beer at a sidewalk café whose tables extend across the pavement. The elderly and those without the price of a drink contemplate the scene from benches beneath the Rathaus portico. Guides tell tourists everything they were afraid to ask about the statue of Roland. There's even a place for punks, who smash bottles and try to provoke a response from passing burghers, on the terrace of the Parliament.

Around the corner, stalls do a lively trade in flowers and hot sausages. In late May there is a three-day fair, with food and entertainment beneath white canopies that resemble medieval tents. And the square is jammed for its Christmas market, for concerts and political demonstrations. It is a four-ring circus that never flags.

Little disturbs the languid Karlsplatz in the old Bavarian town of Neuburg on the Danube. Like Salzburg in Austria, it was a medieval river crossing, and was rebuilt from the 17th century on by its princely rulers. The square was laid out at the top of a steep hill, as a public forecourt to the palace and to set off the court church. Streets drop away at each end, which increases the sense of isolation. The Pfalz-Neuburg family is no more; the Princes von Thurn und Taxis have moved away, but the plain

Bremen's marketplace (left) bustles all day long, with pedestrians and brewers' drays replenishing the bars.

Virgin column and fountain (right) in the square of Neuburg on the Danube in Bavaria, once a princely seat, now a languid backwater.

and fancy Rococo façades remain. On a summer evening, the loudest sounds are a burbling fountain, conversation on the shady benches and the pious murmur of evensong. Later, there is laughter from the tables set out before the inn, and a trumpet fanfare as locals assemble to rehearse a performance of *Everyman* on a rough wooden stage. The setting sun transforms the intimate space into a theater of light, sparkles in the fountain jets, and gives the yellow-washed church a heavenly glow.

Italy offers many variations on the theme of the square as salon and crossroads. The Piazza San Carlo of Turin is a long rectangle of three-storey, 17th-century façades, as elegant as a dress uniform, trimmed with gold braid. Twin Baroque churches frame an axial street, as straight as the Roman road it followed, which bisects the square and links the railroad station and the Piazza Castello. Traffic speeds past the equestrian statue of Filiberto Emanuele, a warrior king of Savoy. But, so handsome are the proportions of this square, so refined yet assertive is its ornament, that it comfortably accommodates the traffic and the cars that park on both sides. All this is backdrop to the arcades, where fashionable Turin still comes to bank, buy its suits and patisserie, and linger in the warmth of an 1890s café.

The Piazzetta of Capri, shaped in the Middle Ages from a space that existed in Roman times, is a triumph of organic design: one of the smallest, most perfect of squares. It is a miniature of the Piazza San Marco in Venice: a front doorstep to the city, combining an open-sided belvedere and a tightly walled room (65 × 100 feet) with a bell-tower as pivot between the two spaces. The tables of four cafés reach into the room, compressing the foot traffic to a narrow corridor between. In contrast to the ordered symmetry of the Piazza San Carlo, Capri's Piazzetta (or Piazza Umberto I as it is called on the signs) is as irregular and picturesque as the community it serves. The Neapolitan Baroque cathedral flourishes its cupolas and arched buttresses at the blunt medieval campanile, whose oversized clock accentuates the sense of fantasy. In between are low white blocks with roof terraces. Locals and visitors flood in from the

funicular station on the belvedere, from a nearby bus stop, several arched passageways and, most satisfyingly, down a broad flight of steps that cascade into the square like a lava flow from nearby Vesuvius. One hopes that a lunatic proposal to put a plastic dome over the Piazzetta in winter will succumb to the ridicule it deserves.

Tradition flourishes in Turin (above): square and equestrian statue are mirrored in the window of a traditional men's store beneath the arcades.

The Piazzetta of Capri: an open-air theater where everyone takes turns to watch and to perform.

23

From the Baltic to the Mediterranean and through the heartland of Europe, the square in all its varied forms seems an indispensable part of everyday life, the nucleus of ancient cities. What of those countries in which it appears rarely, if at all? Spain is a bridge between Europe and Africa. Its plazas are legend; no country puts them to more intensive use. Yet most of Iberia was occupied by the Moors, and the labyrinth of narrow streets and emphasis on interior patios in many Spanish cities reflect the tradition of Islam, born in the hottest countries on earth.

From Iran to Morocco, the pattern is consistent and eminently practical. As in early medieval towns in Europe, but more for protection against wind and sun than enemy assault, desert cities are intricate networks of alleys that broaden only to accommodate a well or the crowd entering a mosque. Goods are sold in the souk — a shaded street — not in an open square; in Aleppo, Syria, there are ten miles of vaulted souks wrapped around the central citadel.

This maze is the preserve of resident craftsmen; strangers sell their goods outside the city walls. The most spectacular of these extramural markets is the Djema-el-Fna of Marrakesh, Morocco, focus of the city's commercial and social life, bubbling from morning till night with local and itinerant trade, entertainment and refreshment. This unenclosed space has the spirit and much of the variety of a medieval market square. Closer in form and function to our civic plazas are the porticoed courts of the mosques, which serve as church, school and public baths as well as for political assembly and community center. As in medieval Europe, sacred and secular are fused in spaces that serve a diversity of popular needs.

Occasionally, an Islamic ruler ordered the creation of a civic plaza similar to those of Europe. Around 1400, Timur (Tamerlane) began to improve Samarkand, the capital of his state of Transoxiana. His grandson, Ulugh Beg, laid out the Registan (sandy square) as a commercial and religious forum, flanked by a madrassa (university), a bazaar and baths, mosque and caravansery. It is uncertain how regular or open this space was in the early 15th century. Only the madrassa survived the pillage and neglect that followed, and it was the Mughal emperors who gave the Registan its present rectangular form (235 × 200 feet) in the early 17th century, and constructed new madrassas on the north and east sides to create a symmetrical ensemble.

As they were doing this, another visionary, Shah Abbas I of Persia, was rebuilding his capital of Isfahan. At the heart of the city he laid out the Maidan, a rectangular public forum seven times the area of the Piazza San Marco in Venice, to serve as a marketplace and polo field; for archery tournaments and contests of wild beasts. It is enclosed by a two-storey blank arcade of buff brick, with shops below and plaster niches above, penetrated by a few narrow streets. This enclosing wall links the royal bazaar and adjoining caravansary at the north end with the Royal Mosque, 1,700 feet to the south. Facing each other across the 540-foot width are the Sheikh Lutfullah Mosque and the Ali Qapu Palace, with its elevated viewing gallery for the Shah and his companions.

Shah Abbas's capital had a population of half a million — almost as many as today — making it at that time one of the largest cities in the world. A print of 1698 shows the entire square covered with the pitched tents of traders. Shade trees and a water

channel ran down the long sides. At night, according to contemporary accounts, the buildings were illuminated by 50,000 small lamps. Sir Thomas Herbert, a member of the British diplomatic mission of 1628, described the Maidan as "without doubt the most spacious, pleasant and aromatic market in the universe."

Even in its present condition of neglect it offers an incomparable spectacle. The excitement of emerging from the cool darkness of the bazaar, with its lofty stone vaults admitting narrow shafts of sun, into the dazzling immensity of the Maidan is rivaled only by the splendor of its architecture. The repetitive rhythm of the arcaded walls and the restrained exterior of the palace focus attention on the mosques. Their façades are aligned with the square; behind, each is turned at an angle to face Mecca. This shift of axis separates the towering portal and dome of the Royal Mosque, increasing the visual impact of its richly patterned turquoise tilework. The Sheikh Lutfullah Mosque, built as a shrine, is modest in scale but sumptuous in its combination of blue and yellow tiles that flash gold in the westering sun.

On the eve of the 1979 revolution, an Italian firm proposed a renovation scheme that would have revived the flagging energies of the bazaar, repopulated the shops around the square, banished through traffic to an underpass, and restored the original combination of water, trees and open space now occupied by a listless sunken garden. Like so many projects commissioned by the Shah, it seems unlikely that this will soon be realized.

The Maidan offers another parallel with the West: it was created as a unified composition at the command of one ruler, just as 17th-century popes were putting their stamp on Rome, as an act of civic improvement and self-glorification. Very different is the Temple Mount in Jerusalem, one of the most sacred and fiercely contested spaces in the world, which has evolved over three millennia. Here, according to myth or history, Abraham prepared to sacrifice Isaac, and Solomon built the Israelites' First Temple, which was destroyed by Nebuchadnezzar. The Second Temple was built on the site, enlarged by Herod, and demolished by the Romans in AD 70. Islamic armies captured the city in 638, and later constructed the Dome of the Rock over the rock of Abraham, from which, they believed, Mohammed had leapt to heaven. A Christian basilica, dedicated to the Virgin by the Emperor Justinian, was transformed into the El Aqsa Mosque.

An 1867 engraving of the Maidan in Isfahan, Iran. Now a landscaped public square, it was laid out as a polo ground and marketplace by Shah Abbas I, the early 17th-century ruler who rebuilt the city as the capital of Persia.

25

The civic square in the central Asian city of Samarkand was laid out by the grandson of Tamerlane in the early 15th century. Mughal emperors gave it its present form two centuries later.

Western Wall Plaza (opposite above), Jerusalem, looking away from the Temple Wall. Old buildings were bulldozed to create this paved open space after the Israeli capture of the Old City in 1967.

Opposite below: Temple Mount, Jerusalem, which has been occupied in turn by Jews, Christians and Moslems. It may be the world's oldest continuously functioning urban space.

Around these two venerated structures extends the Haram esh-Sharif (noble sanctuary), a raised plaza of ancient stone slabs, seeded with grass, and defined by free-standing colonnades, monuments and pavilions. Steps lead down to a broad terrace and garden. It is easy to sense what a hallowed place this is, not only from the devotion of the worshippers, but from the way it seems to float between earth and heaven, overlooking the honey-colored stones of the old city and across to the Mount of Olives and Garden of Gethsemane. Little has changed since it was made the focus of a woodblock of Jerusalem that illustrated one of the first printed travel books, *Peregrinationes in Terram Sanctam* (1484).

The weakest element today is what should be the strongest: the Dome of the Rock, whose cupola, crudely anodized during the Jordanian occupation, suggests McDonalds' golden arches more than it does a classic of Islamic architecture. The wall mosaics are scarcely more convincing. But the stones have an authentic patina, and the space sings.

That is more than can be said for the equally holy place below. For centuries, Jews came to pray in the narrow space before a fragment of the wall of the Second Temple. When Israel captured Jerusalem in the 1967 war, it was decided to excavate more of the wall and bulldoze a swath of old houses to embrace the crowds that were

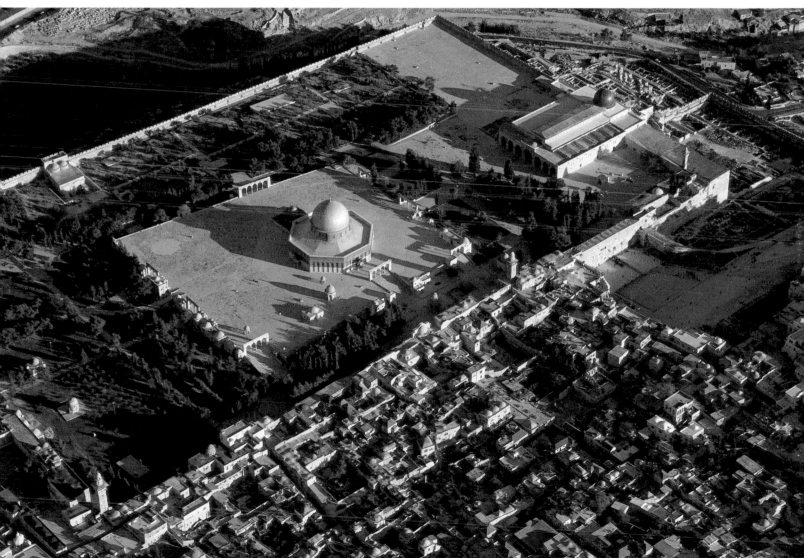

expected to augment the daily worshippers. Aesthetically, the move was as disastrous as Mussolini's insensitive exposure of the monuments of ancient Rome. The 200,000-square-foot Western Wall Plaza (increased from the original 1,000 square feet), is out of character and scale with everything else in the old city; it diminishes the impact of the Wall, and it remains a yawning vacancy on all but a few days of the year.

To fill the void, Mayor Teddy Kolleck commissioned architect Moshe Safdie to replan the entire area, and attempt to reconcile the conflicting demands of religion, archaeology and tourism. Safdie, whose plan was first presented in 1974 and revised in 1983, was inspired by the Jewish historian Josephus Flavius who wrote that, before the Roman destruction, "the city lay before the Temple in the form of a theater . . ."

The architect proposed that the praying area at the base of the Wall be excavated 30 feet to reveal the recently discovered Herodian street, and that the rest of the plaza be transformed into a series of smaller squares, framed by buildings, that would step up the hillside like the bleachers of an outdoor theater. This would create an intimate enclosure for daily prayers, and flexible spaces for the crowds that assemble on High Holidays. The scale of this grid of spaces and structures would be reduced as it moved from the busy areas at the base to the network of residential squares and courtyards in the reconstructed Jewish Quarter at the top of the slope.

Safdie also proposed to divert through traffic past the praying area along an arcaded street that would follow the path of the Roman Cardo Maximus, north to the Damascus Gate. To the south, the courtyard of a recently excavated Umayyad palace could be reconstructed, together with a segment of the grand stair leading up to the temple. Road, palace and stair are the latest finds in a rich layer-cake of history. Unfortunately, this visionary plan is unlikely to be realized as long as Israel remains polarized by religious factionalism and paralyzed by political inertia.

An Indian village in the Amazonian jungle would seem to have little in common with any of the communities described thus far. One similarity, observed by the anthropologist Kenneth Brecher during two years he spent there as a researcher, is the central role of the square in every aspect of daily life. Processions through the plaza offer men and women relief from everyday chores and an opportunity for social intercourse. It serves as an outdoor theater: myths are enacted here in the hungry months of winter, when floods make it impossible to hunt. And it is permissive space, a surrogate house in which to entertain rival tribesmen without compromising the security of the home and exposing personal possessions.

Tribal custom demands that when young people reach puberty they should be locked up for a year or more, with nothing to do but observe the plaza, acquiring the culture through observation. Villagers describe this period of learning in seclusion as the happiest of their lives. How remote this web of ritual and custom seems from our world! And yet we catch an echo of it in the reminiscence of Emilio Ambasz, a visionary architect who divides his time between Bologna and New York. Ambasz explains his obsession with designing urban spaces by recalling how happy he was as a boy playing in the neighborhood squares of his native Buenos Aires.

For Europeans, the history of the square begins in ancient Greece. Lewis

Mumford has described the agora ("place of speech") as a refined version of a village gathering place, irregular and unenclosed, where goods and gossip were freely exchanged. For Greeks of the classical era, the agora was the essential component of a free *polis*, a symbol of democracy and the rule of law. Writers such as Herodotus and Xenophon contrasted the Greeks' good fortune with the lack of an agora in tyrannical or anarchic states.

First came the acropolis: a sacred space that also played a civic role. As it became congested with temples and monuments, its political functions shifted to the agora, a place whose resident deities protected orators. This civic space began to accumulate other uses: buying and selling, the practice of law, government and popular worship. Steadily it overtook the acropolis to become the most vital feature of the city, the focus of its social life and its most important buildings.

Inclusiveness and free access were eroded by social fragmentation and architectural formalism. Aristophanes observed how, in democratic Athens, the landed gentry segregated themselves from *hoi polloi*, preferring the gymnasium to the agora. Later, Aristotle proposed that the agora be restricted to political activity among freemen, and that tradesmen should be excluded unless summoned by the magistrates.

In the classical period, the agora remained irregular in plan and loosely defined by civic buildings. But, as the growth of population stimulated the creation of planned settlements in Asia Minor, the agora was regularized and tightly enclosed on at least three sides by arcades containing shops. Aristotle credited architect-philosopher Hippodamus with designing the first such agora — a perfectly rectangular space measuring 400 by 540 feet, surrounded by stoas (porticoed civic buildings) with a single street entry — in his native city of Miletus, as early as the 5th century BC. Mumford believes that Hippodamus may have introduced this regularity and the grid plan to mainland Greece in his plan for Piraeus, and have "thought of his art as a means of formally embodying and clarifying a more rational social order."

By the 3rd century BC, regularity and enclosure had become the norm. As wealth increased and democracy ebbed, rulers compensated their subjects for the loss of liberty by building ever more splendid agoras — a triumph of form over function that was to be repeated in Imperial Rome, the princely states of Renaissance Europe, and by the totalitarian regimes of this century. In Greek cities that lost their independence and abandoned even the pretense of political debate, the agora sometimes vanished, leaving a marketplace and a series of specialized buildings.

Even before the Greeks began to refine the agora, Roman tribes had established their first forum, as a symbol of union, market and meeting place in the natural depression between the Aventine, Palatine and Capitoline hills. The addition of a temple made it a sacred space and guaranteed the "market peace" essential for trading activity. It steadily evolved, from a linear open space along a main traffic artery, to a built-up precinct. Commercial functions were relocated to smaller, specialized squares, establishing a clear distinction between *fora civilia* for assembly and *fora venalia* for the sale of fish, meat, grain and other essential goods. What is still known, simply, as the Roman Forum belongs to the first category.

Architectural historian Diane Favro describes how, through the five centuries of the Republic, "every Roman's life revolved around the Forum. In this central urban space citizens received schooling, worshipped, conducted business, attended ceremonies, gathered news and took part in history." Every building and monument was steeped in tradition and associations, so that the place became the collective memory of the city, tightening the bonds of past and present, ruler and ruled. For much of this time, Rome retained an intimacy that permitted a single modestly scaled square (measuring about 200 by 600 feet) to serve all its people.

It remained open space, not only to accommodate crowds, but because it served until the construction of amphitheaters as a place for ceremonies and sporting events, which spectators watched from the surrounding colonnades and balconies, exactly as the Spanish *plaza mayor* served (and still does in remote towns) as a bullring.

This traditional pattern can be seen in its purest form in the ruins of Pompeii, a commercial center that became a Roman colony in 80 BC. Its forum survives as an almost empty expanse, 500 by 100 feet, at the high point around which the city grew. It was surrounded on three sides by two-storey colonnades, adorned with statues, which concealed the street entrances and masked the irregularity of the temples and civic buildings, treasury and market clustered behind. At the north end, dominating the entire space, is the Temple of Jupiter, oriented towards Vesuvius which buried the city in volcanic ash in AD 79. The forum was closed to wheeled traffic and was free of commercial bustle except on market day.

In the port city of Ostia, the civic forum is located at the junction of the two principal axes, the Cardo and Decumanus. Close by is the main commercial square, now known as the Piazzale delle Corporazioni, the World Trade Center of its day. It was surrounded by seventy commercial offices representing towns that traded with Rome, each symbolized by a mosaic emblem.

By the end of the 1st century BC, the Roman Forum became, in Diane Favro's words, "a museum of history and art, not a stage for contemporary action", as "the

Ruins of the forum at Pompeii, which was destroyed in AD 79 by an eruption of Vesuvius. Two-storey colonnades masked entrances and the irregular buildings behind, and framed the Temple of Jupiter (left).

Reconstruction of the agora at Assos, a Greek settlement 40 miles south of Troy in what is now Turkey. Porticoed civic buildings frame the space and a temple.

The Roman Forum as it appeared in Giuseppe Vasi's etching of 1765. For centuries in antiquity it was the center of the city's political, religious and social life.

aristocratic Republic was transformed into an absolutist imperialist state with political control concentrated in the hands of one man." The city's population swelled to over a million, outgrowing any one place of assembly. Ceremonies and sporting events were relocated to vast amphitheaters, like the Colosseum and Domitian's Stadium (now the Piazza Navona). Legal and financial affairs were conducted in the basilicas, which became the counterparts of imperial temples, raised on massive bases and approached by flights of steps. Emperors withdrew to opulent villas and constructed new fora, not for assembly or practical use, but as grandiose memorials to themselves. The Palatine hill, with its imperial palace, supplanted the Forum as the city's center of gravity.

But the myth of Rome far outlived its temporal power. Edward Gibbon conceived his masterwork, *The Decline and Fall of the Roman Empire*, in 1764 "as I sat musing amidst the ruins of the Capitol, while the bare-footed fryars were singing vespers in the Temple of Jupiter." As Rose Macaulay remarked, in *Pleasure of Ruins*, "competition for the inspiration of literary works has always been keen among Roman ruins." It was a compulsory stop on the Grand Tour and a favorite subject for view painters and engravers.

After two centuries of archeological exploration, the Forum resembles a building site more than a pastoral idyll. It is hard to discern its original form as a paved rectangle, amid the clutter of imperial monuments, plundered and crudely excavated in later centuries. Yet there is excitement in finding, amid the gaping holes and fallen columns, the *Curia*, last of a succession of buildings in which the Senate met, and, beside it, the *Comitium*, the original place of assembly, whose origins date back to the founding of Rome. In the Dark Ages, when wolves roamed these ruins, and human wolves preyed on the Eternal City's few remaining inhabitants, the memory of Rome stayed obstinately alive, here and in a hundred provincial versions of the Forum.

31

Siena's Campo was designed,
seven centuries ago, as a meeting
ground for three hilltop
settlements, and it remains the
hub of a tight network of streets.
The belltower casts its shadow
across the piazza like the gnomon
of a sundial.

Medieval Hubs

ALL SQUARES are stages for the human drama, but few rival the Campo of Siena, a prosperous Tuscan hill town, in perfection of form and richness of history. Cafés line the high rim of a shallow, semicircular amphitheater, looking across to the backdrop of the Palazzo Pubblico (city hall). A pavement of gray stone ribs and nine tapered segments of brick laid in a herringbone pattern converge on a scallop-shell opening that drains the plaza and draw the eye to the Mangia, a 286-foot campanile, named for its first bellringer. Eleven narrow streets feed into the Campo, but they seem invisible, so tightly is the space enclosed by a wall of five-storey blocks. At the top of the bowl is the Fonte Gaia (fountain of joy), a replica of Jacopo della Quercia's early-15th-century original, now preserved in the civic museum.

Little has changed since the Council of Nine, an oligarchy of leading merchants, planned the Campo, nearly seven centuries ago. Harmony was achieved by consensus and by the ruthless application of what Wolfgang Braunfels has described as "the most precise building code that has been handed down from the Middle Ages." Municipal commissions, headed by lawyers, enforced the regulations and punished deviations. Civic pride was the spur, intensified by rivalry with the neighboring city-state of Florence. The entire ensemble was completed in fifty years, just before the Black Death of 1348 carried off half the population and curtailed such ambitious building projects, here and throughout Europe. (A chapel, dedicated to the Virgin, was added to the base of the tower in 1349 as a thanks-offering for the end of the plague.)

When Siena was a Roman colony the forum had occupied this site. In the centuries of turbulence that followed the fall of Rome, the few remaining inhabitants retreated to the security of fortified settlements on three converging ridges. In the hollow between, the junction of three main roads, a market and meeting place grew up — much like the first Forum of Rome. This campo (field) was divided by a wall in the late 12th century, to create a civic plaza fronting the first city hall (a one-storey wooden structure), with a marketplace behind. In 1297, construction began on the present palace of brick and stone, which combined administration, justice, treasury, and council rooms frescoed by Ambrogio Lorenzetti, one of the city's leading artists, with allegories of Good and Bad Government.

Its location at the low end of the Campo was carefully selected to satisfy the rival claims of the three original settlements, which had by now been divided into thirty-nine contentious contradas (parishes), and to achieve a visual balance between its tower, which symbolized secular pride, and the cathedral. The form of the plaza may have been an allusion to the robe of the Virgin, to which the city had dedicated itself in 1260, and the segments in the paving alluded to the benevolent rule of the Council of Nine, in which a majority of citizens actively participated. The Campo was but one project; streets were paved and the city adorned with private palaces and civic amenities. Work began on a new nave, later abandoned, that would have made Siena's cathedral one of the largest in Europe.

This golden age of commerce and the arts had its shortcomings. Sanitation was primitive. In 1296, a sow and four porkers were officially employed to clear the Campo of rotting vegetables left from the market. The splendor of the fountain celebrated the engineering achievement of piping in fresh running water; until then, the population was dependent on wells. Sporting events in the Campo included bullfights, battles with staves and stones, and a death-defying horse race through the streets to the cathedral, in which the contradas competed for the prize of a palio, a banner carrying the image of the Virgin. Plague was followed by two centuries of fighting, culminating in a bloody siege by the Emperor Charles V and annexation by Florence in 1555.

The Campo of Siena (far left) is a peaceful oasis for most of the year. But for two days in summer it is jammed for the Palio (right, above and below), a parade in period costume that is followed by a horse race, a short and violent contest among the city's neighborhoods. In the past, the Campo has hosted many colorful spectacles, and an anonymous painting of the early 17th century (below) shows a tournament held there in honor of Ferdinand I, Grand Duke of Tuscany.

Siena went into a long decline. In 1909, Henry James described it as "cracking, peeling, fading, crumbling and rotting." In recent years, there has been a dramatic recovery in this town of 60,000, many of whom still live within the medieval walls. It was the first city in Italy to close its historic center to cars, and the Campo remains the undisputed center of social, if not business life. The market is limited to the canopied structure behind the Palazzo Pubblico, and no pigs forage there. Within the Campo, residents and visitors stroll, chat, and (on warm afternoons) sprawl on the paving as though it were still a field. Babies in strollers, kids playing football, lovers locked together like praying mantises, a German pedant force-feeding his flock with facts: the Campo embraces them all as though this really were the Madonna's cloak.

And in the stillness of night, when the restaurants have closed and only cats prowl the space, it still seems inviting. The Mangia Tower "leaps like a rocket into the starlit air", as American writer William Dean Howells observed a century ago. The faded red brick refracts the warmth it absorbed while basking in the sun. The narrow streets all seem to lead to this one great open space; wherever you walk you are bound to end in the Campo.

Twice a year, on July 2nd (Feast of the Visitation) and August 16th (Assumption Day), Siena revives the Palio. Since 1656, it has been run not through the streets, but around the Campo. Books have detailed the months of preparation and elaborate rituals among the seventeen competing contradas (half the medieval total), which can be briefly summarized here. Each contrada has its own church, local administration, precise boundaries and symbol; the loyalty it commands, from birth to death, cuts across all other ties. Alliances and enmities shift and simmer all year to burst loose in the violence and skulduggery of the race.

A week before the race the Campo is covered with earth; hired jockeys ride the horses entered by ten contradas, selected by lot, in a succession of trials. On the great day, bleachers, windows, and every space around the track are jammed. The city's history is reviewed in a colorful two-hour parade; banners are tossed with a skill born of long practice. At sunset comes the race: three circuits of the track, the jockeys shoving and whipping their rivals, horses colliding, sweat and dust. In a few minutes it is all over, bar the cheering, the odd fight and a hysterical celebration for the winners.

Tourists flock to the spectacle but, unlike many folkloric revivals, the passion of the local participants is unfeigned. It is an authentic survival of the Middle Ages, when such races and parades were a feature of saints' days in every European city. In the Palio we can glimpse the energies that created the Campo: as the symbol of a vital, independent community, a masterly balancing of factionalism, and a flexible public arena. Lucid, elegant and complex as a mathematical equation, it is also a work of art whose colors change with the light, casting its spell on successive generations.

Few cities can match this example, and the rebirth of the square that accompanied the 11th-century revival of trade in Europe was decidedly unspectacular. Towns had shrunk and stagnated, reduced to a subsistence economy by the insecurity of the times. Power and wealth were concentrated behind the walls of castle and monastery; outside, the life of man was — as philosopher Thomas

Hobbes described it — "solitary, poor, nasty, brutish and short". To protect their domains, bishops and feudal lords began to fortify those towns that had formerly stood defenceless, creating secure containers that became magnets for trade.

In Italy, where urban traditions had lingered most strongly, the revival had begun among independent city states as early as the 9th century. Venice, impregnable from attack within its treacherous lagoon, pursued an aggressive maritime policy but was soon challenged by the ports of Pisa and Genoa. Wealth and civic pride are clearly evident in Pisa's Campo dei Miracoli, and in the contemporary basilica of St Mark's, Venice.

North of the Alps, cathedral cities were forerunners in urban regeneration, for monasteries were the largest landowners and bishops were (according to the architectural historian Wolfgang Braunfels) among the more enlightened of leaders. By the middle of the 11th century, the situation was fast improving. Norsemen had turned from raiding to state building — in England, Normandy and southern Italy. The Moslem advance in the Mediterranean had been halted. Rulers found it profitable to grant trading privileges to old towns and to found new settlements.

Profits enriched merchants and craftsmen, and soon this emerging bourgeoisie were clamoring for independence. As Steen Eiler Rasmussen noted, "the development of a monetary economy created a commercial boom that disrupted the preordained hierarchy of church, lord and commoners." Towns became self-governing communes, seized control of the market and established the first city halls. In Italy, government came first: Bergamo's Palazzo della Ragione (begun in 1199) has a ground-floor loggia to protect traders, with a council hall above. In northern Europe, as Spiro Kostof has observed, market halls came sooner, and were often built more grandly than the centers of administration. But the distinction between business and politics was blurred, for, as in Siena, rich merchants were leaders in both fields.

The first markets grew organically around a ford, along a trade route, at the foot of a castle or monastery, within the gates of a city for protection, or outside for ease of access and relief from dues. Often, a flourishing extramural market attracted so many new residents that the city extended its walls to bring this *faux bourg* (suburb) into the fold. A new market might then be created outside the walls for the freedom and space it offered, and the process repeated a century later. Medieval town plans — Milan and Moscow are good examples — reveal successive phases of expansion like the rings in a log.

In or outside the walls, trade acted like a stream, carving away gullies and eddies that remain after the stream has changed course. Old cities often include broad streets, or Y-shaped spaces where two roads fork, which once housed markets. Sometimes these have retained their identity as the main squares. In the north German city of Luneberg, which grew rich from the medieval salt trade, the formal market square with its Rathaus is far outshone by Am Sande, so named because it was built on a sand bank. Extending from a Renaissance mansion to the Romanesque spire of St John's Church, and lined with ornate brick gables, it seems like a roofless nave, 900 feet long and only 120 feet wide. At the heart of Munich, the Marienplatz, now overshadowed by the neo-Gothic Rathaus and post-war reconstruction, and

Telč's Gothic buildings were rebuilt in the Renaissance style after a fire, and acquired new façades in the 18th century, when new churches, fountains and the Virgin column were added. The town's arcades are as irregular and varied as the space they surround.

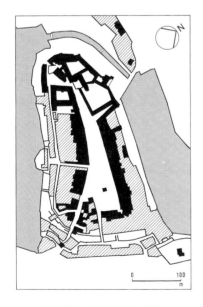

In Telč, lakes flank the old town and a single row of houses encloses the square.

serving as recreational space within a pedestrian precinct, retains the plan of a medieval market, carved out to one side of a through street.

Czechoslovakia has preserved a diversity of market towns, and one of the finest, designated a historic monument by UNESCO, is Telč in Moravia. Peace Square defines the town, for this elongated wedge of space is bordered by a single file of houses, churches and a palace. Beyond, are gardens leading down to the twin lakes that protect the town like a moat.

Established in the mid 14th century, Telč was renewed after a fire two centuries later. The Gothic castle was rebuilt as a Renaissance palace with two arcaded courts; the houses were reconstructed with gables and painted façades. Improvements continued throughout the 18th century: the Renaissance façades were replaced by Baroque and Rococo gables, though much of the Gothic arcade was left intact; two new churches with onion domes were built, and the square was adorned with a column, dedicated to St John Nepomuk, flanked by fountains.

Since then, Telč has become a sleeping beauty. Too small to support a market, it is shielded from modern intrusions by administrative fiat, a stagnant economy, and a new town beyond the gate. A few steps can take you into the intensely green Moravian countryside, and this pastoral isolation gives the square a fairy-tale quality. From a table outside the Black Eagle Hotel, the expanse of cobbles seems framed by dolls' houses, adorned with strapwork, basket patterns, scrolls and *trompe l'oeil* facets in faded colors. Its medieval origins are signaled by the lazy curve of the road that runs the length of the square, by the Gothic church tower that alone survived the conflagration; most of all by the arcade, which ducks and weaves as it switches from pointed to round arches and back, tying the space together like a ribbon around a parcel. By 9 p.m. on midsummer's eve, the space is unnaturally quiet. All cars have gone; a few people lean from flower-decked windows to converse with late strollers; swallows wheel in the twilight.

Something of the same timeless tranquility can be experienced at night in medieval squares throughout Europe, but most hum with life by day. San Gimignano, founded in the 10th century as a fortified waystation between Siena and Lucca, now subsists on tourists, drawn here by a skyline that suggests a medieval Manhattan. Thirteen towers survive from the original seventy or more, built for protection by noble families during two centuries of factional conflict that depopulated the town and compelled its surrender to Florence in 1353. These memorials to violence and vanity are extreme examples of the upward development in medieval towns that were unable to expand beyond their walls. Height conferred status, as in modern cities, but it also became a necessity.

It is this compressed, perpendicular quality that makes San Gimignano's twin squares seem much larger than they are. Narrow streets lead up from city gates to meet in the triangular Piazza della Cisterna, named for its central well, and the trapezoid Piazza del Duomo (cathedral), opening out of one corner. There is a sharp contrast between street and square, between the lucid plan and the pleasing irregularity of the 13th- and 14th-century buildings and paving. Every urban planner should set aside his ruler and rule book, and spend a week here to experience the subtly shifting perspectives and the irresistible pull these spaces exert on residents and visitors alike. It is a relevant lesson, for the plot-height ratios must be as great as in any modern city; indeed, the relationship between cathedral square and its seven towers recalls Rockefeller Center. Cafés stimulate social activity in the Piazza della Cisterna, which also hosts a market and enjoys its finest hours as an outdoor opera house on summer evenings.

Similar in plan and date to this piazza is the Haidlplatz in the ancient Bavarian city of Regensburg, site of a Stone Age settlement and Roman camp, which flourished as an Imperial free city in the 12th and 13th centuries. According to a legend perpetuated by a relief in the Ratskeller, a citizen called Dollinger slew Krako

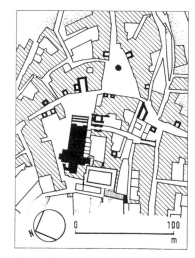

Plan showing the twin squares at the heart of San Gimignano, which evolved from the street plan and topography.

Above: San Gimignano's cathedral square and two of its seven towers, from the arch that leads into the Piazza della Cisterna.

The Piazza della Cisterna, named for its medieval well, viewed from the tallest of the 13 surviving towers of San Gimignano.

The wedge-shaped Haidlplatz in Regensburg is part of a linear sequence of market and civic squares extending through the old Bavarian city.

the Hun in the Haidlplatz in 930 before the German King Henry I. From its organic shape we can deduce that it was an early marketplace, linked by a narrow lane to the Rathaus, from where a sequence of small, specialized market squares lead on to the cathedral. Farmers' wives still sell long white radishes in the Watmarkt, but the Haidlplatz has been gentrified. Gothic, Baroque and neo-classical buildings in color-washed stucco frame the cobbles. Cafés extend out towards the Fountain of Justice with its spiky iron parapet and scarlet geraniums.

Much earthier is the organically shaped Markt in the Dutch city of Gouda. Best known for its cheeses, which are carved into the façade of the Renaissance weigh-house, it also hosts a crowded general market. At the center of the triangular square is the picture-book Gothic Stadhuis (town hall, 1449–59). It has lost its moat and gained a Renaissance portal; unchanged are the stepped gables and sprouting pinnacles, and the trim red-and-white shutters that enliven the gray stone.

All squares benefit from serendipity, and Gouda's enjoys the felicitous juxtaposition of heaven-ascending Gothic (the Stadhuis and looming Grote Kerk, largest church in Holland), dynamically angled plan, and sensible merchant houses to serve as a foil. As the market packs up, seagulls swoop in to forage among the remains; just as rapidly, cars fill the emptied space. Every historic Dutch square seems to be under assault — if not from the automobile, then from fast-food stands and litter, unsightly store fronts and graffiti. This slovenliness reminds us how overcrowded (and permissive) the Netherlands are, but it also evokes the Middle Ages as they probably were, rather than as we would like to romanticize them.

Medieval towns spent their limited funds on what they considered essential to survival: walls for protection in this world, churches as insurance for the next. Open space had to be justified by its utility; later, if the town prospered, it might be beautified. Streets were for access and defence, narrow and circuitous to impede an invader and give residents time to retreat to a fortified church or keep. Historians have speculated that most were formed from the space occupied by the scaffolding used in construction. A market place might be laid out just inside the gate, conveniently accessible both to burghers and to peasants. More often it occupied a central location, for the entire city was a market, trading within itself more than with outsiders. The richest citizens lived on or near the square, over their store, workshop or warehouse.

Initially, the space was elastic, expanding to accommodate more stalls, contracting as more people sought a privileged building site. It took its form from the street pattern: regular in grid-plan cities, long and thin in linear settlements, irregular in towns whose topography interrupted orderly development. It stabilized as the town's government began to exercise greater authority and to replace houses and stores with city and trade halls, belfries and palaces. But the authorities often fought a losing battle against encroachment; unauthorized buildings attached themselves like barnacles to cathedrals and fortresses and to the grandest civic buildings. It is to the 19th century that we owe our sanitized vision of medieval squares: paved, opened up and painstakingly restored, with elaborate fakes to fill any gaps. All too often the soul vanished with the squalor. The devastation of the Second World War and subsequent reconstruction augmented the loss, especially in Germany.

In Gouda, a Dutch city best known for its cheeses, the lively marketplace is dominated by the ornate town hall.

One notable exception is Goslar, a Saxon mining town that survived the war unscathed. It was founded by Henry the Fowler in 920. Soon after, rich silver mines were discovered, making Goslar the "treasury of the German Emperors" and a seat of the Imperial court. Later, merchants asserted control; in the mid 14th century it became a free town and joined the Hanseatic League. In the 18th century, the mines gave out and growth ended. Streets lined with handsome medieval and Renaissance timbered houses lead to the irregular Marktplatz, unified by its cobbled pavement which is patterned as a sunburst in black, white and brown, radiating from a 13th-century fountain with a gilded eagle that symbolizes the town.

The arcaded Rathaus and merchant tailors' guildhall (now a hotel) were rebuilt in the 15th century on older foundations; the other buildings, half-timbered or faced with slate shingles, are more recent. But there's a pleasing harmony of spacing and proportion that does justice to the town's rich heritage, and to the handsome market church that rises behind the Rathaus. The square has been cleaned up but not spoilt, and on market days — especially around Christmas — its spirit is infectious.

Markets were the principal space generator in the Middle Ages, but not the only one. Some squares formed the parvis (forecourt) of a church, others set off a castle; some were, from the start, civic plazas. Arras, near the French border with Belgium, has two squares: the aptly named Grand' Place (525 × 300 feet) and the Petite Place (renamed the Place des Héros). They are set at an angle to each other, a block apart, and linked by a continuous arcade that runs around each square and along the narrow Rue de la Taillerie between. Devastated in both World Wars, they have been restored in the spirit of an ordinance of 1711: "brick for brick and stone for stone."

Arras flourished as a medieval cloth town (giving its name to a tapestry wall hanging, best remembered from *Hamlet* in the scene where Polonius spies on the Prince and is stabbed to death). The Grand' Place was formerly a monastic cloister, secularized in the 12th century to create a public plaza for tournaments and fairs, military parades and the reception of visiting celebrities. The Place des Héros has always served as a marketplace; not until 1517 did it become the setting for the late Gothic Hôtel de Ville (city hall), with its splendid 250-foot belfry.

The French took the town from the Habsburgs in 1640, and in 1692 decided that every house on the two squares should conform to the height and ornament of the Maison de l'Ecu d'Or, the finest of the traditionally gabled houses of that century. And so, in a style that was archaic and alien, the squares were rebuilt. No two houses are quite alike, but the consistent use of brick and stone, the round gables and steady rhythm of the arcade, and the unbroken expanse of cobbles unify the two squares and bind them together.

In late May, the town celebrates its three-day Festival des Rats; advertised attractions include a circus, clowns, actors, craftsmen, horticulturists and "artistes en liberté." Pennants flutter from lamp standards; the Place des Héros is turned into a garden, and the circus pitches its tents on the Grand' Place. Late into the evening, on an outdoor stage, country musicians play gigues and rounds on fiddle and accordion, bagpipes and fife, as families dance on the cobbles. A huge stall dispenses beer and *frites*, and the paper cups drift across the plaza like an early snowfall. A donkey brays — or is it the circus llama, penned in one corner? The ghostly backdrop of gables strengthens the feeling that you have strayed into a Breughel painting.

Across the border, the Flemish city of Bruges is still centered on the Markt, with its cloth hall and towering belfry. But the spiritual heart of the city is around the corner in the Burg, a smaller square named for the Castle of the Counts of Flanders,

The Burg in Bruges, spiritual heart of the medieval Flemish city, as it appears from the belfry of the nearby marketplace.

Medieval and neo-classical buildings, rebuilt from the wartime devastation of Brunswick, enclose the Burgplatz and its lion statue.

which stood close by until it was demolished in 1434. The Saturday market, with its painterly array of the finest produce, has moved here, but for the rest of the week the Burg sees nothing more animated than horse carriages awaiting their fares.

An anthology of architectural history surrounds the cobbled space: the exuberant Baroque Landhuis (once a priory), subdued classical law courts, gilded Renaissance Recorder's House and soaring Gothic Stadhuis. The Chapel of the Holy Blood is Romanesque below, late Gothic above. There are even a few step-gabled houses; Genoese and Florentine merchants lived here when Bruges was one of the richest cities in Europe. The one gap, now filled with trees, was formerly occupied by the cathedral of St Donaas, founded in 900 and destroyed by Napoleon's troops.

Another Burgplatz, in the Saxon city of Braunschweig (Brunswick), still has a vestige of its castle, recreated from wartime rubble. In the 12th century it was the residence of one of the most colorful of medieval rulers, Henry the Lion, Duke of Bavaria and Saxony. Henry consolidated the town, built the huge Romanesque cathedral at an angle to his castle and erected the statue of a lion in the square as a symbol of his power. When he died and was buried here in 1195, Braunschweig comprised five distinct towns, each with its own constitution, town hall, market and parish church. Almost leveled by wartime bombing, it has made a remarkable recovery, but it is the Burgplatz, not the more celebrated Altstadtmarkt, that best enshrines the city's past.

As in Bruges, the eclecticism of the frame is a source of strength. A Gothic aisle makes a graceful step up to the mountain face of the Romanesque cathedral; a bridge links it with the Burg Dankwarderode, the remnant of Henry's fortress, now a museum of medieval art. Beyond, you can glimpse the bustle of the post-war town and the ornate cliff of the neo-Gothic Rathaus. Timbered Renaissance and mock medieval buildings carry the eye round to the neo-classic Landesmuseum, whose collection includes the original of the lion statue. Closing the open corner is a pleasing 18th-century printing house.

What gives the Burgplatz such a strong presence? Above all, its balance: of high and low, massive and tiny, open and enclosed. It is a peaceful enclave that is plugged into the rest of the city; bikes whizz around the perimeter, cars are limited to one corner, pedestrians have total freedom to wander or linger beneath the lime trees. There is a café, a miniature corner bookstore and, for children of all ages, new stone benches adorned with playful variations on Henry's lion. The domed pavement of large cobbles pulls the composition together; tufts of grass soften the stoniness. In every kind of weather, and at every time of day, it is a magic place.

Many of Italy's finest medieval piazzas have been preserved by their remote location and inaccessible sites. Bergamo is a short drive from Milan, but the old hilltop town feels as separate from contemporary Italy as Venice. A funicular railway leads up from the modern city, reshaped during the fascist era; you emerge into streets that have scarcely changed since the 15th century, when the Venetians made it the western bulwark of their mainland empire.

A loose grid of narrow lanes and irregular marketplaces leads up to the Piazza Vecchia, the social hub of the upper and lower towns. Created in the 13th century, when Bergamo was an independent commune, it was enlarged by the Viscontis of Milan and given final form (together with its pavement of brick framed with white stone) by the Venetians in the 15th century. From the start, it was a civic square, the setting for Italy's first city hall (Palazzo della Ragione, begun in 1199, rebuilt in the 16th century), and counterpart to the adjoining Piazza del Duomo, which may occupy the site of the Roman forum.

The Piazza Vecchia displays the history of the town: from the 12th-century belltower, built to celebrate independence, to the Lion of St Mark's that symbolized subjection, to the 18th-century fountain with its whimsical lions, snakes and sphinxes, which children love to ride as though they were horses on a carousel. The Palladian Palazzo Scamozziano of 1610 houses a library. Above and between these buildings you can glimpse tantalizing fragments of the town, with its blunt stone watchtowers, spires and domes. Beyond are the green foothills of the Alps.

The open loggia at the base of the city hall draws you through to the Piazza del Duomo, which is tightly framed by a Romanesque church, 18th-century cathedral façade, octagonal baptistery and, squeezed between, the sumptuous chapel that commemorates the greatest of Renaissance mercenary leaders, Bartolomeo Colleoni. The loggia once sheltered market stalls; now it's the place to enjoy the last of Bergamo's puppeteers. In his sketches of Italian cities, Paul Hofmann describes these dialect plays, starring such traditional characters as Arlecchino and Gioppino, which were earlier incorporated into the *commedia dell'arte* of Venice. On Sunday afternoons the square's four cafés and *gelaterie* are thronged; the fountain boasts more children than animals. A concert, with free balloons, draws an even larger crowd, and everyone cheers as the balloons are suddenly released as an airborne bouquet.

Umbria, which likes to call itself the green heart of Italy, is studded with hill towns. History repeats itself, from one to the next. Most were founded by the Etruscans, conquered by Rome, and fought over by a succession of invaders. They achieved a brief moment of glory as independent communes in the 12th and 13th

The Gothic city hall, begun in 1199, and fanciful 18th-century fountain in the Piazza Vecchia of Bergamo. Beyond the arches is the tiny, lightly enclosed cathedral square.

centuries, before degenerating in factional strife, falling prey to tyrants and being swallowed up among the Papal States. The largest of these, now the regional capital, is Perugia. Like Bergamo, the upper and lower towns are separated by a road that snakes up the hillside in a succession of switchbacks. Or you can make the ascent by escalator, following the path of several thousand university students who flock to class five days a week. The broad Corso Vanucci has become a pedestrian walkway, leading from the 19th-century Piazza d'Italia (which replaced the papal stronghold after unification) to the Piazza Quattro Novembre, a monumental Gothic ensemble that is the heart of the old city.

The Piazza Quattro Novembre is a dynamic composition in a state of arrested motion. The irregular space is tightly framed but eddies out around the cathedral and into a succession of steep, cobbled minor squares. The cathedral turns its side to the Piazza, an unfinished barn of rough brick rising above steps (which students use as bleachers) and a dado of patterned marble. Guarding the entry from the Corso is the Palazzo dei Priori, a massive crenellated block of white marble, with a pulpit from which rulers could harangue the people, as St Bernard did from a pulpit on the cathedral. Both are rough, tough piles that recall the years when conspirators were hung from the walls, noble families battled to the death, and a nephew of Pope Innocent VIII was stabbed in broad daylight. Between is the 13th-century Fonte Grande, its marble reliefs carved by Nicolo and Giovanni Pisano.

47

Even more austere is Gubbio, known as the "City of Silence". Few towns better dramatize the vertiginous quality of medieval Umbrian settlements. It comprises five streets, each on a different level and linked by steep alleys. The Piazza della Signoria, halfway up, seems to have been sliced through to expose the structure of the town, like a cutaway model. Arched vaults support a platform, open on one side, and flanked by the Palazzo dei Consoli (now a museum) and the Palazzo Pretoria (now the courthouse). The fourth side is occupied by a handsome classical range, above which the hill continues its dizzying climb to the cathedral and ducal palace.

As a belvedere from which to admire the Apennines and marvel at man's determination, it is matched only by its role as a stage for the Race of the Ceri on May 15. The Ceri are three huge wooden hourglass forms, topped with wax figures of saints, which the young men carry uphill from the piazza to a convent 900 feet above, in celebration of a famous victory in 1151. Later in the month, there is a crossbow competition; sculpture is trucked in for an annual arts festival; but the greatest appeal of Gubbio's piazza is its customary languor.

Orvieto's Piazza del Duomo demonstrates how space can be compressed to dramatize the impact of an extraordinary building. The cathedral was begun in 1295, to shelter relics of the Miracle of Bolsena (the origin of the Feast of Corpus Christi), and its façade of gaudy mosaics within a Gothic marble frame suggests an oversize jeweled reliquary. Behind this façade is a vast zebra-striped church that would have been even larger had the force of gravity not overtaken medieval building technology. As you turn into the square from the ascent, or approach it down a narrow lane, your eye is seized by this gorgeous apparition. The space, wrapped tightly around three sides of the cathedral, makes it seem even larger and more arresting. Geometrical patterns in pink, black and white form a decorative border to ease the transition between structure and surface.

Lombardy is as flat as Umbria is precipitous, and Mantua owes its isolation to the lakes which surround the walled town on three sides (a moat once protected the fourth). Like the hill towns to the south, its early history ran the familiar course, until, following the collapse of communal government, the Gonzaga family seized power from the Bonacolsi (in 1328) and held it for almost 400 years. They transformed the city and created the largest palace in Italy after the Vatican, hiring the finest artists and architects (including Andrea Mantegna and Giulio Romano) to immortalize their name. It lives on; busts in the ducal garden mark the graves of two recent scions, a soldier and a priest.

Before the Gonzagas, life in Mantua revolved around the Piazza dell'Erbe, a modestly scaled marketplace flanked by city hall, courts, a clock tower and a round Romanesque church. On each side are the parvis of the church of San Andrea, and the Piazza Broletto, forecourt to the palace of that name. The Piazza Sordello, now the main square, had an equally modest beginning as a narrow space fronting the cathedral.

When Pinamonte Bonacolsi was named Captain of the People in the late 13th century, he bought up and cleared the houses clustered around his palace, across from the cathedral, to create an impressive Piazza del Capitano. When the Gonzagas murdered the last Bonacolsi captain, they renamed his seat of office the Ducal Palace,

Patterned paving creates a decorative border between the cathedral and the square in Orvieto.

The Piazza della Signoria of Gubbio (opposite) is supported on arched vaults that are built into the steep hillside.

49

concealing their extensions behind the old façade to achieve a semblance of legitimacy. To improve the square, they demolished a church, and renamed it for a local poet who had been acclaimed by Dante. And in subsequent centuries, they constructed arcades tying together a sequence of squares to create a processional route between the Ducal Palace and the new Palazzo del Té.

A fondness for lighting bonfires in the Piazza Sordello (it was reported that 7,000 bundles of wood fueled the blaze of 1576) created even greater opportunities for improvement than the Gonzagas' ambition; the cathedral was rebuilt twice. In its heyday, the Piazza was the setting for tournaments and the rituals of church and state. Its physical appearance has scarcely changed in the past two hundred years: a cobbled rectangle framed by medieval brick, Baroque and neo-classical stone façades, up to 60 feet high. When the exterior of the Ducal Palace was restored in 1940, the primary source was the great painting that showed it as it looked in 1328. But the spectacle that animated this space has vanished with the Gonzagas. There is little traffic; the square is too remote from present activities, barren and lacking in amenities to draw residents. The Piazza Sordello has the same melancholy grandeur as Mantua itself.

The Gonzagas' act of will in shaping public space as a setting for their power and glory anticipated what was to occur all over Italy during the Renaissance. But the idea that medieval man had a preference for picturesque irregularity is an invention of the Romantic era. Quite the opposite: the Middle Ages had a strong sense of order and, whenever possible, translated this into regular plans. No Renaissance square could be more precisely plotted than the cloister of a monastery, built for one purpose, at one time on virgin ground. Irregularity was the product of circumstance, not choice. The survival of a Roman grid plan encouraged cities all over Italy and

The cathedral and civic buildings surround Bologna's main square, which occupies the site of the former Roman forum.

Mantua's Ducal Palace on the Piazza Sordello was restored in 1940 to conform with its appearance in this painting of 1494, which shows the Gonzagas battling the Bonacolsi family for control of the city in 1328.

The Piazza Sordello was given its present form by the Gonzagas, the family that ruled Mantua for four centuries.

beyond to create orthogonal squares, sometimes in the footprint of the forum.

No city has more successfully adapted its Roman plan than Bologna. Its central square, the Piazza Maggiore, is built over the forum at the junction of the two original axes; its basilica occupies the site of a Roman temple. The square fuses antique grandeur, the symbolic elements of a medieval commune, and a Renaissance aesthetic. The Gothic Palazzo Comunale (city hall), the free-standing Palazzo del Podestà (governor's palace) and the rugged brick nave of San Petronio (all that was realized from a 14th-century plan to create the largest basilica in Christendom): everything is on a heroic scale.

Linking these monuments and Vignola's Palazzo dei Banchi (an arcaded commercial block, built to house banks) is the Piazza Maggiore, which flows around the Podestà to become the Renaissance Piazza Nettuno (with its Neptune fountain by Giovanni da Bologna) and the subsidiary Piazza di Re Enzo behind. The space is enclosed and enclosing; it can be read as three contiguous squares, of different proportions, flanking the governor's palace, and linked by a broad commercial street, or as a single space that the palace dominates.

Bologna's Piazza Nettuno draws its name from its fountain of Neptune.

The Piazza Castello in Turin (another Roman grid) attempts a similar feat but fails to achieve a coherent relationship of mass and space. In Bologna, the parts work together to create a complex unity. The space swells and contracts to hold Gothic and Renaissance, towers and façades in equilibrium. The Piazza is enhanced by its location, at the center of one of Europe's most civilized cities, which generates a constant bustle, and from its rich textures. "The square of San Petronio with its colour as if sunset were built into the walls," noted Freya Stark in her *Traveller's Prelude.*

Cremona's Piazza del Comune is smaller and simpler but no less impressive. Around a cobbled rectangle with white stone markers are deployed two solid 13th-century brick palaces, a Romanesque cathedral with a springy Renaissance portico, a freestanding octagonal baptistery and the Torrazzo — at nearly 400 feet the tallest campanile in Italy. It has been the town center since Cremona became a free commune in 1098, and the feisty marble lions that guard the portals of the cathedral and baptistery have been worn smooth by 800 years of affection. Everything soars: towers, turrets, lanterns; even the chimney pots on the modern bank that completes the enclosure. Cremona's wealth comes from agriculture, but it is celebrated as the home of Stradivarius and Guanieri, families that made the world's finest violins. The Piazza mirrors that tradition of craftsmanship and sense of harmony.

The Lombard city of Cremona is celebrated for its violins, and the tradition of solid craftsmanship is mirrored in the harmonious Piazza del Comune.

Cremona's main square finds an echo in the Piazza del Duomo of Pistoia, which occupies the site of the Roman forum, flanking the Cardo, in this old walled town. The forms are similar, the spirit entirely different — which is what makes a voyage through Italy so rewarding. Here, it is church not secular authority that dominates. The L-plan piazza exposes the façade and a side of the Romanesque cathedral. The freestanding campanile, a blunt watchtower topped by three tiers of delicate columns, counterbalances the striped marble baptistery. This is Tuscany, and the source for the Romanesque architecture of these three sacred structures is Pisa, not the Lombard north. Each has a light-hearted, lyrical quality; in contrast, the civic buildings are the plainest of Gothic, an admirable foil.

Pistoia's piazza feels more dynamic than Cremona's; there is a brisk diagonal flow of pedestrians and cyclists; intriguing vistas open up between the buildings. The weekly market fills the space with a patchwork quilt of awnings. And in July the city hosts its version of the Palio: the Giostra dell'Orso, a medieval joust performed almost continuously since the 13th century as a competition among the city's four districts.

In Arezzo, a lively Tuscan hill town, the annual fiesta is the Giostra del Saraceno held in September. But almost as entertaining is the antiques fair that fills the Piazza Grande on the first weekend of every month but September. The contents of a hundred attics spill out in disorderly profusion from the Renaissance loggia, across a sharply tilted expanse of brick and travertine, to the Romanesque apse of Santa Maria della Pieve: a surreal juxtaposition of the monumental and the ephemeral.

Todi is the connoisseur's favorite among Umbrian hill towns, cited in a dozen books as a model of inspired spatial drama. Again the ground plan is Roman, the buildings medieval, the achievement timeless. A farming town of 16,000 inhabitants, isolated on its high crag, Todi remained entirely enclosed by its medieval outer wall until the 1970s. Its center, since Roman times, has been the long rectangle now called the Piazza del Popolo.

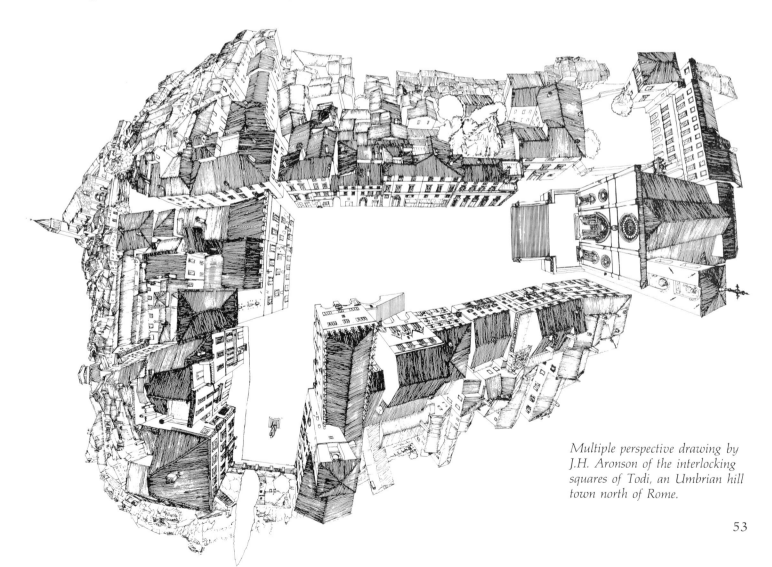

Multiple perspective drawing by J.H. Aronson of the interlocking squares of Todi, an Umbrian hill town north of Rome.

Chance encounters (above left) in the Piazza del Popolo of Todi.

Pistoia's Piazza del Duomo (above right) is animated by a lively flow of pedestrians and cyclists.

A monthly antiques fair (right) fills every corner of Arezzo's main square, as though a hundred attics had been ransacked.

The Piazza Grande of Arezzo (opposite), a Tuscan hill town, is bordered by a Romanesque church and Renaissance loggia.

At the north end is the cathedral, its 13th-century white marble façade rising high above steps, as did the Temple of Apollo that once stood here. At the south end is the 14th-century Palazzo dei Priori, built to house the papal governor after the town lost its autonomy in 1368. But the counterpart of the cathedral in date and significance is the Palazzo del Capitano, the former seat of communal government, which also rises above steps to emphasize its importance. At the portal created by these two Gothic palaces, the square makes a sharp left turn into the stubby Piazza Garibaldi, with its panoramic view over the Umbrian hills.

There is something immensely satisfying about these interlocked spaces: the closed, self-sufficient medieval forum, with its balance of church and civic authority, and the open, outward-looking administrative square, adorned with a cypress tree and statue commemorating the hero of Italian unification. Around this hub, streets drop away to the gates and passages step down steeply to arches that frame vistas of green. On an early spring morning, mist swirls up from the valley, filling the space with miniature clouds. As the sun emerges, men gather at the junction of the squares to chat, or stroll unhurriedly up the gentle slope of grey flagstones; strangers meet and exchange addresses, familiar characters emerge on cue to play their preordained roles. Parking in the Piazza del Popolo has recently been banned, but cars still buzz around like angry insects, searching for a place to settle.

In Verona, the medieval Piazza dell'Erbe evolved as an elongated oval in the footprint of the Roman forum. As its name suggests, it was, and remains, the market square; a forest of distinctive white umbrellas shades flower and produce stalls within the perimeter of imposing palaces. Beside the Gardello Tower an arch leads into the arcaded Piazza dei Signori, known as the salon of Verona. This was the civic center during the city's brief heyday as an independent principality and the four centuries of Venetian rule that began in 1405.

One more example of creative adaptation, but a piazza only in name, is the Roman amphitheater in the walled Tuscan city of Lucca. In the turbulent 9th century, houses were built into the ruins, facing into the oval arena and out over a street that followed the line of the galleries. For centuries the space was used to grow vegetables, then a public market was constructed here; finally the market buildings were relocated, to create a recreational space for the community. You enter through one of four arches, and feel you have strayed into a Neapolitan back yard. Five-storey tenements rise sheer from the paving, adorned only by washing hung out to dry; this is found space, raw and uninflected.

The Romans created models for medieval town planners that proved as valuable as the foundations they left for builders. We have seen how the Middle Ages liked to create order and, as in every age, a new town on an empty site offered the best opportunity. As the Romans extended their Empire across Europe, North Africa and the Middle East, they developed standard plans for their settlements. The most basic and adaptable was the *castrum*, a grid-plan military camp, with a small central square for the mustering of troops. In origin, the plan is no more than a built-up version of a tent encampment, and the Romans merely refined a fundamental concept. But for medieval rulers, it was the most familiar example and a reminder of the long-vanished stability of a great empire. From the 12th century on, the *castrum* influenced the layout of the new towns that were established in newly settled or disputed lands all over Europe.

English kings built them along the Welsh border and in Aquitaine; French kings resettled the territories of the Count of Toulouse, devastated by the bloody crusade against the Albigensian heresy. Where the Spanish regained territory from the Moors, and the Teutons rolled back the Tartars, new towns were created to lure settlers. Their foundation was a mark of growing stability and the expansion of trade. These were not military strongholds, designed like castles to withstand the assault of invading armies, but economic colonies, protected by walls and a fortified church against the depredations of local raiders.

The Roman *castrum* was peopled by legionaries, the new towns by farmers. Settlers were lured by the promise of free building plots, exemption from military service and taxes, and by the right to hold markets. The Germans had a saying, "City air makes men free," and a runaway who could spend a year and a day in a new town without being apprehended became a free citizen and could remain. Settlers had obligations: to construct a house and live there, to build the walls and defend them in case of need. Few of these communities flourished. Amenities were few. Created as an act of policy on inaccessible hilltops, far from existing trade routes, most languished with the impetus that gave them birth.

An exception to this pattern is Montauban, a prosperous town in south-west France, founded in 1144 by the Count of Toulouse. For a hundred years its large regular central market remained a unique innovation in this area, and the historian Charles Higounet believes it may have been inspired by a settlement the crusaders had seen in the Middle East, and that it served as a regional prototype for the *bastides* (fortified planned towns) that proliferated in the following century. More typical is Aigues-Mortes, built by Louis IX in 1246 to defend the harbor in Provence from which French armies departed for the Seventh Crusade. Its walls were strengthened by twenty-eight towers, but little thought was given to how its inhabitants would sustain themselves once the armies had gone. Today it is a museum city.

The French and English built about 300 *bastides* between 1220 and 1374. Most comprised a rectangular grid of identical building plots, though standard plans were varied to accommodate irregular sites. At Forcés, houses are ranged in a rough circle around a large central place. According to a study by Higounet, about a third of the *bastides* have regular central market squares, which became centers of communal life. Charters regulated market days and hours, special fairs and religious festivals. The first houses were built on the square for the convenience of being close to the market, civic offices and church, though nobody was more than a few blocks away. Arcades were added from the 14th century on, by allowing homeowners to extend their upper storeys, leaving a public right of way below.

A textbook example, and one of the most appealing small towns in France, is Monpazier ("peaceful hill") in the Dordogne. Founded by the English King Edward I in 1285, it has lost its walls, but has preserved much of its original flavor. One of the twenty rectangular blocks is occupied by an arcaded square, about 210 × 190 feet; the church and a smaller square open off the north-east corner. Along the south side is an open-sided market hall, a tiled roof supported on weathered timbers, with the counter on which stood standard weights and measures.

The massive arcade is lightened by openings at each corner, as though curtains were being parted to allow a glimpse of the stage. The points of contact are aptly described as *cornes* (horns), and the square is thus known as Les Cornières. What was planned to be as spartan as a barracks square has acquired a delightful set of variations through the accidents of history. Not everyone took the opportunity of extending over an arcade, and so the building line steps back and forward unpredictably, like recruits learning to drill. The arcades frame the shifting composition, and you can look in any direction and see — as though through a telescope — a gate at the edge of town. Benches beneath the arches serve as a barrier to cars.

Monpazier has discovered the secret of zero growth without decay. Within the boundaries almost every plot is occupied; open fields begin just below the grassy promenade that replaced the walls, with no suburbs to blur the dividing line. At 7 o'clock on a summer evening, only a handful of visitors remain, for there is a single small hotel and nowhere else to stay for miles around. The square seems like an old but contented cat, drowsing in the sun. Roses and bougainvillea brighten the honey stone. The last rays reach deep into the arcades, casting long shadows. Locals throng to Le Ménestral, a newly opened restaurant on the south side of the square. It is run by a young woman, helped by her mother and other family members, who cheerfully offers a complimentary glass of vintage Montbazillac with which to toast her success. A set menu includes fresh foie gras, omelette aux cèpes, magret de canard and more, all for the price of a main course in a Paris bistro. The lights and conversation spill out into the darkened, deserted square late into the night.

At the other end of Europe, a similar pattern was emerging. As the Teutonic Knights pushed east against the Tartars, they secured their advance with a succession of fortified, grid-planned towns, such as Chelmno and Toruń, whose central squares framed town halls. The Polish kings did likewise. The town hall in Warsaw's Old Town Market Square was demolished in 1817, but the central square of Poznań is dominated by a handsome structure that was remodeled during the Renaissance by an Italian architect.

Grandest of all these East European markets (670 feet square) is that of Cracow, which was rebuilt on a grid plan in the mid 13th century after the old city had been destroyed by the Tartars. E.A. Gutkind has shown that, as late as the 18th century, the square (like that of Poznań) was crammed with buildings and permanent market stalls, leaving only the periphery as open space. This is why the square is called *rynek* (ring road). Today, three buildings survive: the Romanesque church of St Adalbert (which predates the square), the surviving tower of the Town Hall, and the 360-foot long Cloth Hall, which bisects the space like a wall.

Miraculously, the square escaped the Nazis' planned destruction, but it has become inexpressibly forlorn. Pollution from a nearby steelworks has erased the features of medieval carvings. Façades are begrimed and in urgent need of restoration. So depressed is the Polish economy that only flower sellers animate the vast expanse of paving. The mood of sadness is caught in the bugle call that sounds

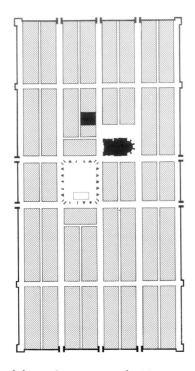

Monpazier was one of 300 fortified towns created by French and English rulers to buttress their conquests in south-western France.

Massive arcades are delicately joined at the corners like horns (cornes), giving Monpazier's square its name, Les Cornières.

on the hour from the Church of Our Lady, and ends abruptly in mid-phrase. It recalls the medieval watchman who sounded an alarm that the Tartars were approaching and was silenced by an arrow in the throat. It seems characteristic of a romantic, quixotic race, that this broken tune should be broadcast on state radio daily at noon, much as the BBC uses the chimes of Big Ben.

New towns were established all over Bohemia and Moravia in the 13th and 14th centuries. Out of thirty-five that have been designated "historical reservations" by the Czech authorities, nearly all have central markets. About half are grid-planned, with large orthogonal squares. Ceské Budějovice has one of the most symmetrical, Miesian in the precision of its angles. Tábor's, with its distinctive late Gothic and Renaissance façades, is less regular but more picturesque. Other towns, like Domažlice, Litomyšl and Telč have squares that suggest organic growth along a street or around an intersection.

The Christian reconquest of Spain extended over centuries, culminating in the final defeat of the Moors at Granada in 1492. As the kings of Aragon and Castile pushed south, frontier areas were fortified. New towns were founded on the high plateau of New Castile, south from Madrid, but many were extensively rebuilt during the Renaissance. It is in the remoter regions of Old Castile to the north, and Extremadura to the west, that you can best capture the distinctive flavor of medieval Spain. So isolated are some of these towns that life has almost dried up, and the Arab heritage lingers on in the whitewashed arcades and black-shrouded women.

La Alberca, a Castilian mountain village 40 miles south-west of Salamanca, has preserved its traditional architecture, customs and styles of dress. The Plaza Publica seems carved from rock, so hard and austere are its arcades, benches and cobbled pavement. By comparison, the two upper storeys, constructed of wood and plaster, seem delicate and airy, with their balconies and tiled roofs. The plaza is everyone's front yard: a place to gather, in sun or shade, on Sundays; a stage for traditional songs and dances on August 15, and for elaborately costumed mystery plays on Assumption Day.

The same contrast of stone base and graceful half-timbered superstructure characterizes the Plaza Mayor of Penaranda de Duero, a town built for defense at the furthest limit of the Moslem conquest. It still has its medieval pillory, well and cross, together with the Miranda Palace, one of Spain's greatest Renaissance mansions.

Extremadura is famous as the province of the conquistadores, driven to adventure in the New World by the poverty of the Old. Garovillas gives a sense of what they left. Villagers still ride mules through the cobbled streets; the Plaza Mayor has a two-storey arcade supported on delicate champfered columns that suggest the courtyard of a mosque. Trujillo, birthplace of Francisco Pizarro, the conqueror of Peru, has been transformed by the wealth his captains brought home. Its arcaded Plaza Mayor was begun by the Moors and adorned by Renaissance mansions. But in its irregular plan, stepped up on one side, it remains medieval.

Isolation has preserved the buildings and patterns of use in these remote Spanish towns, but even in the great cities of Italy traditions linger on. Every day but Sunday, from early morning till lunchtime, market stalls fill Rome's Campo dei Fiori. Flowers and produce, fish, meat and cheese mingle colors and aromas against an

unchanging backdrop of ragged stucco façades, in faded reds and browns, a simple fountain, a corner church. The past is omnipresent. Julius Caesar was assassinated at Pompey's Theater, just around the corner. Lucrezia Borgia owned several hotels, when the neighborhood was as fashionable as the Via Veneto is today. A statue recalls Giordano Bruno, the monk who was burnt here for heresy in 1600. And the families who buy and sell have been doing so for generations.

Our brief tour of medieval squares ends in Venice, the forerunner of urban revival in the Middle Ages. As Spiro Kostof has noted, by the end of the 11th

The Plaza Mayor of Garovillas in the remote Spanish region of Extremadura.

Once a fashionable hotel district, the Campo dei Fiori has long flourished as one of Rome's liveliest markets.

century "parish churches and open spaces with cisterns to collect fresh water flecked the dense townscape." A hundred years ago, W.D. Howells observed: "Each campo in Venice is a little city, self-contained and independent. Each has its church, of which it was in earliest times the burial-ground; and each within its limits compasses an apothecary's shop, a blacksmith's and shoemaker's shop, a caffe more or less brilliant, a green-grocer's and fruiterer's, a family grocery — nay there is also a second-hand merchant's shop where you buy and sell every kind of worn out thing at the lowest rates. Of course there is a copper-smith's and a watchmaker's, and pretty certainly a wood carver's and gilder's; while without a barber's shop no campo could preserve its integrity or inform itself of the social and political news of the day . . . the buildings are palaces above [housing tradesmen and noble families] and shops below." Howells had plenty of opportunity to study the subject: in return for a favorable campaign biography, President Lincoln had made him Honorary U.S. Consul in Venice.

Campi began as open fields, created from drained marshes around the first churches, which were cultivated, used as pasture and for burial grounds, just like the village greens of New England. In both, the church was the center of community life, which spilled over into the field, an island of sociability in a watery wasteland. Throughout the Middle Ages, the campi were built up and linked by street and canal. The Piazza San Marco was always the city's main square, and it moved with the times, becoming a Renaissance showpiece, where Venetians are now far outnumbered by tourists. The campi have changed, too, losing much of their commercial significance, but preserving their local flavor. In recent years, efforts

VENICE

A council of war (above right) beneath the statue of mercenary leader Bartolomeo Colleoni in the Campo SS Giovanni e Paolo.

The rhythms of daily life (above) and the exoticism of a fashion boutique (right) in the Campo San Stefano.

A diagram plan of the heart of Venice showing the network of streets and campi between (1) San Stefano and (2) the Piazza San Marco.

have been made to revive traditional outdoor theater, with productions of Goldoni's comedies on outdoor stages. Films have been shown for residents during the annual festival that is held out on the Lido. There are summer concerts, dancing under the stars, and a share in the city-wide Carnival. But the campi bubble with life every day of the year.

San Stefano, also known as Francesco Morosini, is the largest of several campi located like beads on a cord along the busy route between the Accademia and Rialto bridges. There is a dynamic tension between its two interlocking wedges of space which together are almost as long as the Piazza San Marco. All around are ranged Gothic and classical palaces, two churches, a walled garden and a canal, punctuated by ten streets. All day there is a lively flow of people taking the direct route between the two bridges over the Grand Canal. Students hang out after school, children play on the cistern and around the statue of Niccolo Tommaseo, a hero of the Risorgimento. One main entry is tightly framed by a café and newsstand, and the stores range from basics to boutiques.

The most spectacular square in Venice after San Marco, for its buildings and history, is the Campo SS Giovanni e Paolo. It comprises two interlocking rectangles that hinge on a masterpiece of Renaissance sculpture: Andrea Verrochio's idealized equestrian portrait of Bartolomeo Colleoni, the *condottiero* whose chapel is located in his birthplace, Bergamo. Colleoni offered his Venetian employers a large bequest if, after his death, they would erect his statue outside San Marco. The war lord meant the basilica on the Piazza San Marco; the authorities, greedy for the money, but unwilling to celebrate an outsider in so important a location, placed the statue here, facing the Scuola San Marco.

Everyone has gained from this shameful duplicity. What would be lost in the huge piazza is here the unchallenged focus, anchoring space that would otherwise float away over the flanking canal — a distinctive presence for the past 500 years. And the setting is distinguished: the huge brick barn of the Dominican church, a pantheon for political and military leaders; the Scuola, with its intricate marble façade; and the harmonious context of fading stucco and weathered stone.

From Siena's Campo to the modest Campo Santa Maria Formosa in Venice, the medieval square was indispensable and multi-purpose. Religion, politics and commerce were tightly interwoven in the Middle Ages; a market or church festival involved everyone in the community. For lack of theaters, mystery plays were performed on the church steps and watched from the plaza; ribald entertainment was staged on a scaffold. Admission was free to bullfights and football games, for they were held in the square, not the ruined Roman stadium. Executions were major social events; the square was the only place for celebration or protest.

Prosperity strengthened civic pride. Art works showed donors holding their city as though it were a reliquary; woodcuts in early travel books idealized earthly cities as they had the celestial city of Jerusalem. Yet, even as communities began to think of themselves and their squares as works of art, they were losing their social cohesion. Society had been stratified through the era of the communes: rich merchants dominated government; small traders and artisans enjoyed limited benefits; the growing proletariat was disenfranchised and rebellious. By the 14th century, nobles were gaining power at the expense of the bourgeoisie, tyrants and oligarchies had supplanted the communes, free cities were swallowed up in princely states. Residences and businesses grew apart, as merchants sought more opulent and exclusive places to live, and became commuters. The square was starting to lose its universal appeal.

Classical Ideals

WHAT Le Corbusier's Villa Savoie is to modern architecture, Bernardo Rossellino's Piazza Pio II is to Renaissance planning: a seminal mix of innovative theory and individual genius. Located in the remote Tuscan hill town of Pienza, which is no bigger than a village, this square shows that the best things often come in small packages. As with the Villa Savoie — a white stucco box on a recessed base — the elements could not be simpler. Two palaces fan out past a church and frame a tiny trapezoid forecourt, with a porticoed town hall closing the fourth side. Compressed within this frame are the visions of patron and artist, and a new ideology of building, in which one man imposes his will on public space.

The patron was Pius II, and few popes have enjoyed a more colorful career. Enea Silvio Piccolomini was born here in 1405, in what was then called Corsignano, to a noble family that had been driven into exile from Siena, 30 miles to the north. As a young man he wrote an erotic novel in Latin, practised diplomacy and was crowned poet laureate by the Emperor Frederick III. Not until he was 40 did he become a priest; at 53 he was elected Pope. His first thought was to transform his birthplace into an ideal Renaissance town, as a rebuke to Siena by a local boy who made good, and as an expression of the belief that perfect form symbolized wise rule. Rome would take centuries to perfect: Corsignano was malleable clay.

In a later, more authoritarian era, Pius might have rebuilt the entire town as a unified whole. Lacking the means, he focused his efforts on the town center, enlisting the services of Leone Battista Alberti, a man as many-faceted as himself, who had written the first great Renaissance treatise on architecture. Alberti passed the commission to Rossellino, a sculptor who had worked as his assistant on the Palazzo Rucellai in Florence, and for Pope Nicholas V on St Peter's in Rome. Rossellino had to shoehorn a cathedral, papal and bishop's palaces and town hall onto an irregular plot about 250 feet square, working quickly and on a tight budget.

To maximize the space, he pushed the church apse to the brink of the hill, from which it has been threatening to topple ever since, and turned its axis to the north. Like Michelangelo, who later remodeled the Campidoglio in Rome by exploiting what he found there, Rossellino retained the divergent lines of existing structures in building the Piccolomini palace and refacing a Gothic courthouse (at the expense of a Borgia Cardinal) to balance it. Cleverly, he concealed the much greater bulk of the papal palace (modeled on the Rucellai) which runs past the church, then drops down the hillside as an airy triple loggia framing the countryside beyond.

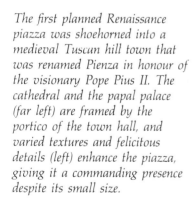

The first planned Renaissance piazza was shoehorned into a medieval Tuscan hill town that was renamed Pienza in honour of the visionary Pope Pius II. The cathedral and the papal palace (far left) are framed by the portico of the town hall, and varied textures and felicitous details (left) enhance the piazza, giving it a commanding presence despite its small size.

The cathedral has a Florentine Renaissance façade; within, Pius insisted it be as luminous as the hall churches he had seen as a papal legate in Austria. When it was finished, he proclaimed: "No one shall deface the whiteness of the walls and columns. No one shall draw pictures [or] change the shape of the church . . . If anyone disobeys, he shall be accursed."

The piazza, a mere 100 feet wide at the cathedral steps and 75 feet deep, is an early Renaissance painting of an ideal city come to life. Its white travertine grid is a study in linear perspective which pulls the whole composition together. The divergent façades of the palaces amplify the modestly scaled cathedral. The lines are crisp, the textures varied, the details felicitous. Bracketed to a wall is a stone well, a homely touch that is echoed in a stone circle set asymmetrically in the paving. Distant hills can be glimpsed between the buildings. The project was completed in just three years (1459–62), to the delight of Pius, who forgave his architect a 500 per cent cost overrun, saying: "If you had told us the truth, you could never have induced us to spend so much money . . . Your deceit has built these glorious structures." He renamed the town Pienza.

Muriel Spark observed that "Walking around the square of Pienza, I often have the illusion of being in a roofless temple, as in the Parthenon." Murray Kempton caught the spirit when he wrote: "Having been denied space for the scenic, Rossellino found rescue in the scenographic: Pienza is a theater, the plaza is its stage and the cathedral is the garden outside. Inside the cathedral we are almost in the open air, and in the plaza we have a sense of enclosure made stronger if anything by the cunning and careful workings with perspective."

The Piazza Pio II is a stage in form but not in function. There was no play and few players. The market remained where it had always been, behind the town hall. When Pius died in 1464, the papal connection lapsed, and it seems unlikely that the worldly Rodrigo Borgia made much use of his palace, before or after he became Pope Alexander VI. The piazza endures, not as useful space, but as a celebration of power and a demonstration of aesthetic principles.

Pius II was one of the first popes to revive the tradition of Imperial Rome, when Emperors created fora to buttress their fame and beautify the city. He set a lead that other rulers would later follow. Medieval squares evolved from competing pressures and collective decisions, and always in response to practical needs. In Florence and Venice that tradition continued through the Renaissance, though with increasing emphasis on individual artistic expression; in others it lapsed.

The link between art and power is as old as civilization, but it achieved a fresh significance in 15th-century Italy. There was a revival of scholarship and a surge of intellectual curiosity and experimentation in the arts. The study of nature and man generated rules to govern scale and proportion, form and space. "Renaissance architecture was conceived as an image or mirror of a pre-ordained, mathematical harmony of the universe," wrote Rudolf Wittkower. The ancient world was mined for its theories and its practice. Vitruvius's *Ten Books of Architecture*, the one surviving Roman architectural treatise, was universally studied, first in Latin, later in translation. Versatility and erudition were prized. Filippo Brunelleschi (1377–1446), who helped formulate the laws of linear perspective and employed them in his own

buildings, began as a goldsmith and sculptor, and proved his skill as a structural engineer in creating the dome of the cathedral in Florence. Enlightened rulers shared in and supported these activities.

In the first architectural treatise of the Renaissance, *De re aedificatoria*, published in 1452, Alberti set out his pragmatic vision of an ideal city. He argued that some streets should wind like rivers to avoid the monotony of a regular grid, and that varied open spaces should be provided for markets and recreation. Quoting from Vitruvius, he recommended that a square should be twice as long as it is broad, and that surrounding buildings should be between a third and a sixth as high as the square's width to achieve a pleasing harmony of proportion. And he urged that it be surrounded with porticoes, "under which the old men may spend the heat of the day, or be mutually serviceable to each other; besides that the presence of the fathers may deter and restrain the youth, who are sporting and diverting themselves in the other part of the place, from the mischievousness and folly natural to their age."

For a ruler who wanted to assert his authority and his humanist values, this and later treatises provided a blueprint for action. But no prince wanted to risk bankruptcy or rebellion by rebuilding a functioning community, and there was no good reason to do so, for cities were still recovering from the population loss of the Black Death a century before. Thus, like Pius II, they settled for a square, which could serve as a symbol and as a practical way of developing a new quarter or improving an old.

Perugino's Sistine Chapel fresco of c. 1480, Charge to St Peter, is set in an ideal square and exemplifies the fascination of Renaissance artists and architects with linear perspective and harmonious composition.

Ludovico Sforza, Duke of Milan, created the first arcaded Renaissance piazza in Vigevano, his birthplace, 20 miles south-west of the capital. Known as Il Moro (the Moor) for his swarthy complexion, Ludovico had a short and violent reign, and is chiefly remembered for his patronage of Leonardo da Vinci and Bramante. A marble tablet on the castle tower celebrates his improvements: "After quieting external and internal disorders, Ludovico . . . turned the old, squalid residential quarters of the populace into an ornament of the community. Finally, after the old buildings surrounding the forum had been torn down, he made the square more beautiful by enlarging it and surrounding it with an arcade. In the year of grace 1492." Wolfgang Lotz, who reconstructed the history of the square, concluded (on grounds of style) that it was designed by Bramante, who had also remodeled the castle.

The Piazza Ducale marked a decisive advance towards the age of absolutism. "Quieting disorder" was a polite evasion; the Sforzas had suppressed a free commune to enlarge their dominions. The piazza was planned less as an "ornament of the community" than as an outer courtyard of the castle — to which it was linked by a ramp — and as a decorative façade to screen the town from the castle. Opposite the ramp was a painted triumphal arch (now vanished); elaborate frescoes and ornamental paving served as tapestries and carpet for ducal ceremony, though a sanitized town market was permitted to use the space. The urban historian E.A. Gutkind states that the arcades were reserved for the workshops of craftsmen and artisans brought from Milan to supply the court.

The Piazza Ducale in Vigevano, from the tower of the ducal castle. The cathedral was given a concave Baroque façade to align it with the piazza two centuries after the other sides were completed.

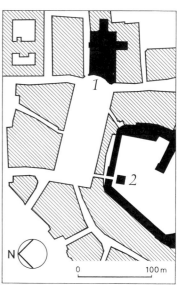

Vigevano: the piazza was created by Ludovico Sforza as a public forecourt for his castle (2), with the cathedral (1) to its right.

Anonymous painting of the burning of Savonarola in Florence in 1498, showing the Piazza della Signoria with its medieval buildings and a perspective grid.

The Piazza della Signoria (below) in a mid-18th-century painting by Bernardo Bellotto, showing the fountain and statue that created an illusion of regularity in the medieval L-plan square.

The Sforzas survived for only a few decades more, but their final gift to Vigevano was a charter, and the town became a bishopric. Deprived of political significance, the piazza changed — from a trapezoid outer court, to the present symmetrical 450 × 160 foot enclosure. Alberti would have applauded the harmony of proportion, the uniform three-storey buildings and seductive rhythm of the arcades which mask the street entries as effectively as the colonnades in a Roman forum. Two centuries after the piazza was laid out, a bishop removed the ramp — which became a public nuisance when children used it for winter sledding — and sealed the piazza's east end by giving the cathedral a concave Baroque façade. In 1900, the façades were repainted in a style that — according to Lotz — owed more to romantic historicism than to the fragments of 15th-century decoration that the restoration disclosed.

Today, the piazza mirrors the leisurely rhythms of a small provincial town, whose inhabitants bike or stroll slowly through it, the better to observe the passing scene and chat with friends. Cars are excluded and the loudest sound is of voices. On a fine Sunday morning, after mass, there is a steady hum, broken only by the cries of children and the fluttering of pigeons chased by dogs.

Florence did things differently. More than any other city it was the birthplace of the Renaissance, an innovator in the arts from the late Middle Ages, but unlike other Italian cities it preserved its democratic constitution until 1532. Leading citizens took votes on how to replan the city in the 14th century, extend the walls, and make their cathedral worthy of the republic's wealth and fame. The Piazza della Signoria had been created as a civic forum in the late 13th century by clearing houses and a church from property owned by the disgraced Uberti family. The space complemented the Palazzo Vecchio, a Gothic fortress built in 1299–1314 to protect the city's magistrates from violence in the streets, with a 308-foot watchtower that allowed surveillance of the entire city and surrounding country. Its bell tolled for danger and summoned citizens to general assemblies.

During the 14th century, the piazza was enlarged four times to assume its present L plan. The most notable addition was the Loggia dei Lanzi, built in 1376–82 from designs by the artist Orcagna to house public ceremonies. Its graceful round arches and entablature anticipated the Renaissance, and it soon acquired new uses as a sculpture gallery and as a guardhouse for mercenaries. Commercial traffic was banned from the piazza as early as 1385, and an annual cloth fair was relocated to enhance the dignity of this political stage and the great events of state.

But the improvements were made piecemeal with no master plan. A painting of 1498 that shows the burning of Savonarola (the monk who had terrorized the city, incinerating those works of art he judged immoral) depicts the medieval piazza with its new brick pavement, framed by a white stone grid. Not until the mid 16th century was an attempt made to update the space. The Neptune fountain (1557) and the statue of Cosimo I served, like the Colleoni statue in the Campo SS Giovanni e Paolo of Venice, to articulate the L plan as two interlocking rectangles. A proposal by Michelangelo to extend the arches of the Loggia dei Lanzi as a unifying arcade around the piazza was rejected. But Vasari was inspired by Michelangelo to create a dramatic perspective in the long narrow piazza of the Uffizi Palace, which links the

Arno with the Piazza della Signoria, and frames the cathedral dome and palazzo tower as though they were on a single axis.

The purest Renaissance square in Florence, the Piazza SS Annunziata, took two centuries to build, and was the product more of luck than planning. Its church was established in 1234 and the square reached its present size in the 14th century. Its transformation began with the construction of Brunelleschi's Ospedale degli Innocenti (1419–26), with its wide-arched loggia and cloister that express the springtime freshness of the Renaissance. (It still serves its original purpose as a refuge for orphans). Michelozzo rebuilt the church with a central portico; Antonio da Sangallo reproduced the hospital loggia a century later on his building for the Servite confraternity, and the piazza was completed in the early 17th century, when the church portico was extended to the full width of the building. Giovanni da Bologna's equestrian statue of Duke Ferdinand de' Medici and the twin fountains form a triangle that complements the elegant rhythms of the loggias, and accentuates the axis of the Via dei Servi which frames the cathedral dome.

It is hard to enjoy these squares today. For decades, Florence has endured the assault, as destructive as a medieval siege, of cars and tourist coaches. Commercial greed and political infighting have impeded reform and diverted the profits of tourism from the restoration of the monuments that draw six million visitors a year. Only recently, with Brunelleschi's dome in danger of collapse, the air fouled, and the façades begrimed, have the authorities come to their senses and banned traffic from the historic core. Here, as throughout Italy, major buildings are likely to remain shrouded in scaffolding for many years to come. Florence compounded its problems in the 1980s by turning the Signoria into an archeological dig, while prevaricating over whether and how to display the Roman and medieval remains that were excavated. Soccer ranks high above scholarship in Italy, and the impending arrival of fans for the 1990 World Cup put an end to the debate. The piazza was restored, but a great opportunity was lost: to repave its surface in brick and thus recreate a harmonious balance with the gray stone buildings, as in other medieval Tuscan squares that were improved during the Renaissance.

The elongated piazza of the Uffizi Palace (left), created by Giorgio Vasari about 1560 to link the Arno with the Piazza della Signoria, frames the tower of the Palazzo Vecchio and the cathedral dome beyond.

The Piazza SS Annunziata (right) is the purest Renaissance square in Florence, even though it was built by different architects over two centuries and with no master plan.

In contrast to Florence, spoilt by its popularity, the handful of new towns built according to Renaissance theory have too few people. But isolation and torpor have preserved them intact. Perhaps the most appealing is Sabbioneta, a princely folly created by Vespasiano Gonzaga in the forty years before his death in 1591. Though fortified, it had no defensive role; and with Mantua just 20 miles away, the Duke had no need to build another city. But, just as Pius II was able to express himself more freely away from the Eternal City, so Vespasiano determined to create his own "new Rome" where he could hold court as a patron of the arts. Deserted streets and a few blocks of completed buildings surround the rectangular Piazza Garibaldi (an absurdly inappropriate name for so patrician an undertaking) with its rusticated arcades, church and Ducal Palace.

Sabbioneta was an aristocrat's dream of an intellectual retreat. Palmanova, a defensive outpost of Venice, designed in 1593 by Vicenzo Scamozzi, was a textbook example of Renaissance military theory. For the impetus to plan new towns was fueled by the practical need for fortifications that would withstand artillery. Leonardo da Vinci was one of many artist-engineers who devised elegant combinations of earthworks and projecting bastions. These were grafted onto existing cities; Palmanova was planned from the outside in, with a radial street plan and polygonal central square that allows the defenders a clear field of fire down six straight avenues. The plan is as beguiling as a snowflake, and the town, as built, remains a spectacular sight from the air because it has not grown beyond its original boundaries.

Exactly one hundred years later, the Sicilian town of Grammichele was laid out on similar lines, also with a polygonal central square but lacking the fortifications, to accommodate the victims of an earthquake. By then, the plans of Italian theorists, including Filarete's "Sforzinda", and the writings and paintings of Francesco di Giorgio, had begun to inspire ideal cities in northern Europe.

No city is such a fruitful mixture of planning and serendipity as Venice. A thousand years ago, much of the Piazza San Marco was an orchard, the Piazzetta was cluttered with butchers' stalls, and horses were tethered to trees in the parvis of St Mark's. The Piazza was doubled in size around 1176, possibly to accommodate the stonecutters who were rebuilding the basilica and campanile. During Venice's centuries of growth, architects and artists had looked to the East for inspiration, emphasizing gorgeous surfaces over perspective, and conspicuous show (often of looted treasures) over piety. Theophile Gautier aptly described St Mark's as "a pirate cathedral enriched with the spoils of the universe." Gentile Bellini's celebrated *Procession of the True Cross* shows the Piazza as it appeared in 1496, with irregular brick arcades flanking the freshly gilded St Mark's.

Around 1500 came a decisive shift, from utilitarian to ornamental. A planning commission decided that the Piazza should be rebuilt in the currently fashionable High Renaissance style and become the ceremonial gateway to the city, with the Piazzetta as a functional link with the Grand Canal, the city's prime artery. As Venice began her long decline, she strove to catch up with the taste of the rest of Italy.

Along the north side, Mauro Coducci built the Procuratie Vecchie to house high government officials, and the Clock Tower that arches over the Mercerie, Venice's

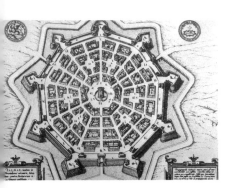

Plan of Palmanova, designed by Vicenzo Scamozzi in 1593 as a defensive outpost of Venice. The city survives in its original form, though its fortifications were leveled and the central tower was never built.

The Piazzetta of St Mark's, Venice, with San Giorgio Maggiore beyond, by Francesco Guardi, c. 1770. The square served as a gateway to the city from the Grand Canal.

Main Street. To the south, the Florentine Jacobo Sansovino built a library (to replace a bakery), pushing the building line back to widen the piazza and expose the campanile, which now became a hinge on which the axis of the piazza turned into that of the Piazzetta. Vicenzo Scamozzi, a pupil of Palladio, who had designed Palmanova, continued the project, and Baldassare Longhena completed the south side in 1640.

Four very different architects working over a span of 150 years created a unified ensemble, which was enhanced by the geometric paving of black and white stone that replaced the earlier brick surface in 1722. In the early 19th century, Napoleon — who had threatened to treat Venice as though he were Attila the Hun — was seduced, and added a final touch in the form of a ballroom (now the Correr Museum) to replace a church at the far end of the piazza. The campanile, begun in 888, rebuilt in brick in 1329, collapsed in 1902, and was rebuilt "as it was, where it was" in 1912.

This brief summary of the Piazza's building history does little to evoke the spirit of what may be the most familiar and best-loved square in the world. In *Italian Hours*, Henry James deplored "the infestation of tourists and peddlers" around the basilica, which he described as "the biggest booth in a great bazaar." It was always so. By the year 1000, pilgrim hostels were clustered around the parvis; Venice has always been a mecca to visitors and everyone has voiced an opinion. "I don't know that there can be anything like it on this earth," declared Petrarch in the 14th century. In the 19th, Ruskin idolized St Mark's; Mark Twain thought it resembled "a vast warty bug taking a meditative walk."

Everything is freighted with history or legend. The granite columns that define the Piazzetta were brought from the Levant in 1172, and were originally used as mooring posts and for the execution of traitors, who were strung up between. The statues that crown them are impostors. St Mark's lion is Chinese; a pagan god has been transformed into St Theodore, Venice's first patron saint. The four Greek

Francesco Guardi painted the Piazza San Marco for a number of 18th-century tourists.

The fashionable crowd at Quadri's in 1869, soon after Venice became part of united Italy, in a detail from Michele Cammarano's painting of the Piazza San Marco.

As Venice continues to sink, winter floods in the piazza become ever more frequent.

horses of gilded bronze that once crowned the façade of St Mark's were brought here as spoils from Constantinople in 1204. The pigeons trace their ancestry to doves that were released, from 877 on, after Palm Sunday service. According to W.D. Howells, those that were caught were fattened and eaten; those that escaped acquired protected status and were fed, first by the Republic, then by the bequest of a pious lady, and since by visitors.

Bullfights were held in the Piazza to honor important guests as late as 1782, and it remained a stage for the spectacles of church and state until the end of the Republic in 1797. During the Austrian occupation, Venetians patronized Florian's cafe on the south side, leaving Quadri's on the north to the enemy. Today's visitors tend to arrive in the summer, when the piazza is as full as Times Square on New Year's Eve, the bands are playing and every seat is taken. The landscape architect Lawrence Halprin experienced it in winter, recalling it as his "greatest urban experience":

> It was cold and foggy and the top of the Campanile barely showed sunlit above the low hanging sea mist. The tide was in and the black and white stones of the intricately laid pavement were covered with a thin film of water. There was no sound – no automobile exhausts, no buses. Absolute quiet in the very heart of a great city. In the distance you could hear faintly some young people singing. All of a sudden the air became dark with birds, the square filled with the beating of thousands of wings, the noise increased and increased until it was deafening, and the deserted square became absolutely filled with pigeons. The noise was incredible – even frightening. They had come to feed, and when they had finished, they left just as quickly, and the great square was empty and quiet again.

Bullfights link Venice's Piazza with the plazas of Spain. During the Counter Reformation of the 16th century, the plaza was inserted (often by royal decree) into

Madrid's Plaza Mayor was imposed by royal fiat on the medieval labyrinth of the city in 1617–21.

Tarantellas on the cobbles in Madrid's Plaza Mayor during the spring fiesta of San Isidro, the city's patron saint.

the inherited labyrinth of Moorish streets to create a solemn stage on which the rituals of church and state could be performed. Here everyone could witness royal fêtes and proclamations, tournaments and poetry contests, canonizations and autos-da-fé, and tremble at the execution of heretics (common criminals were despatched outside the city walls).

In Almagro, a handsome Renaissance town 90 miles south of Toledo, plays have been performed since the 16th century in the Corral de Comedias off the south portico of the Plaza Mayor, and the custom survives in the late-August theater festival. Bulls were fought in Madrid's Plaza Mayor until 1846, and in August they still are in the elliptical Plaza Mayor of Chinchon, 25 miles south of the capital. Here, and at Tembleque, 40 miles south-east of Toledo, the tiers of galleries around the plaza inspired the purpose-built bullrings, the first of which were built in Ronda and Seville in the 18th century.

The first regular, unified *plaza mayor* was laid out on the orders of Philip II as a symbol of royal authority in the Castilian city of Valladolid in 1561. It remained unique until his son, Philip III, commissioned the Plaza Mayor of Madrid on the site of a medieval fairground in 1617–21. Juan Gomez de Mora's design draws on Philip II's monastery-palace of El Escorial to achieve an austere grandeur, incorporating its steep-pitched slate roofs and dormer windows above an unbroken arcade that sharply separates the plaza from the cramped and tortuous streets beyond. Like the contemporary Place Royale (now the Place des Vosges) in Paris, its dominant feature was a royal pavilion, the Casa de la Panaderia, from which the king could watch such spectacles as the canonization of Santa Teresa (in 1622) and the reception of Charles Stuart, Prince of Wales, the following year. Today, the Plaza feels like a relic of the era of absolutism: stiff, formal and official, cut off from the bustle of the nearby Puerta del Sol, and out of touch with the uninhibited spirit of post-Franco Spain. But it serves as a peaceful retreat at the heart of the old city, and it still has the capacity to surprise. For ten days in May it is jammed, as families celebrate the festival of San Isidro, Madrid's patron saint, with music and fireworks and dancing on the cobbles.

Salamanca's Plaza Mayor seems always to be festive. Created over a century later than Madrid's, in a more relaxed era when Spanish power had begun to crumble, it has a happy, lyrical spirit. "It hums, swirls and sings," declared the Soviet writer Ilya Ehrenburg during his stay in 1931, observing that the inhabitants "lived on the plaza and grew old there." Conceived during a visit by Philip V in 1710, it was designed by members of the Churriguera family, who created lavishly ornamented altars and gave their name to a florid style of architecture that achieved its greatest popularity in the New World. Here, from 1728 to 1755, they created a surprisingly disciplined, yet elegant composition in the same sharply carved, yellowish stone that is used for churches and palaces throughout this ancient city.

The plaza is as unified as a single building ranged around a great courtyard. The space, not quite a perfect rectangle, is contained by a consistent three-storey range rising above a continuous arcade. The façades are articulated with shallow window mouldings and shutters, and crowned with parapets and finials. Roundels celebrate heroes and rulers; King Carlos and Queen Sofia have recently been added. The dominant feature is not the King's Pavilion, but the Ayunimento (city hall), which

The elliptical Plaza Mayor of Chinchon. The tiers of galleries which surround it are supplemented by temporary wooden seating and barriers in readiness for the August bullfights.

Similar tiers of galleries also overlook the Plaza Mayor of Tembleque (left). It was galleries such as these which inspired purpose-built bullrings.

steps boldly forward from the north range. Wider arches mark the entries of eight streets. Set-backs at the corners allow the plaza to be seen as a three-dimensional structure, and create visual links with smaller flanking squares. A wide arch and steps lead down to the covered market. Madrid's plaza seems brutally imposed on its neighborhood; Salamanca's is spatially integrated. The square is to the city what the city is to the surrounding country: a major focus of social, business and cultural activity.

From all over Europe students throng to Salamanca's university as they have since the 13th century, and they animate the cafés and restaurants that eddy out from the porticoes. A lucky few can scramble up rickety staircases to rooms that overlook the Plaza. A book fair creates its own square of stalls within the square, and at 10 p.m. it is full of browsers. Around them swirls a dense mass of strollers, enjoying a Sunday evening *paseo*. Children are tireless as their parents, and the porticoes echo to the shrieks of the little angels who received their first communion that afternoon in the cathedral. Lamps cast a soft glow across the façades. Lost in the darkness is the Plaza's guardian spirit: a stork that makes its nest in the Romanesque tower of San Martin.

The Plaza Mayor of Salamanca is as unified and distinct as a single building ranged around a great courtyard.

Spain imposed a similar pattern on all its wide-flung possessions. In the Netherlands, it polished the gems created in the Middle Ages by free trading cities. From the 15th century, the dukes of Burgundy, and then representatives of the Spanish king, collaborated with city magistrates to transform market squares into fit settings for civic ceremonies. As Pierre Deyon has written, showy festivals and royal entries dazzled the masses, absorbed the ambitions of leading citizens, and consoled both for their loss of political power. Medieval festivals had often been an unruly mixture of the pious and bawdy. From the 16th century on, the élite asserted control, creating symbolic *tableaux vivants*, triumphal arches and other elaborate decor as a setting in which the prince could receive his subjects' homage and formally pledge to respect their rights.

Brussels' Grand' Place, which Victor Hugo described as "the most beautiful square in the world," was embellished by a succession of rulers. It began as a market on a drained marsh beside the 10th-century castle that formed the city's first nucleus. Brussels became a prosperous trade and textile city, and a seat of the court of the dukes of Brabant (in 1383) and later of Burgundy. Civic pride found expression in the Gothic Hôtel de Ville (city hall), with its 300-foot spire (1402–54), and the Maison du Roi (begun 1515, now the communal museum). As the city lost its economic importance, the square was transformed from a workplace to a showcase of luxury. Markets were relocated to neighboring streets and squares.

A band plays in front of the city hall in Salamanca's Plaza Mayor.

Everything but the tower was destroyed in a French bombardment of 1695, but in four years the Place was rebuilt, more splendidly than before. City authorities exercised right of approval over the additions, demanding that they be built of stone, evenly and without projecting storeys. Thirty-nine guild houses surround the square; most are gabled in a Flemish version of Italian Baroque, and adorned with statues of virtues, trade signs, gilded columns and allegorical reliefs. The parade of rich fronts suggests a gathering of burgesses, their velvet doublets trimmed with gold lace, standing around the edge of a great hall. The last addition was the Maison du Roi. An earlier reconstruction collapsed, and in the late 19th century a second attempt was made, based on the original Gothic designs. While work was still in progress, it was dressed up to resemble a medieval fortress as backdrop to a knightly tournament that was presented in 1891.

The Grand' Place revives its medieval glories on the first Thursday of July, when it hosts Ommegang, a costumed procession that was initiated by the Guild of Crossbowmen in 1348 to honor the Blessed Virgin. Almost as magical is the summer sound-and-light show. The trickle of cars around the square is halted and, as the music begins, a hush settles over the Place. Cafés provide orchestra seats for the spectacle. In the Hôtel de Ville, the dormer windows glow scarlet, as though in memory of the bombardment, and lights glint off leaded panes, infusing the over-restored façade with a sense of mystery. The floodlit Gothic spire stands out against the darkness like a space shuttle poised for lift-off. The moon rises over the roof, misty and remote. As the entertainment ends, lights glow from within the upstairs restaurants; then every façade is illuminated, highlighting fantastically intricate surfaces and a fretted roofline that ripples around the square.

Sunday Market in Brussels, *a mid-19th-century painting by Charles Dommershuyzen, shows the Gothic city hall in the Grand' Place.*

Every night in summer, the façades of the Grand' Place are illuminated, following a sound-and-light show.

On the first Sunday in July, the Grand' Place hosts the Ommegang (below), a procession in honor of the Blessed Virgin Mary which dates back to 1348.

Brussels' Grand' Place and the Plaza Mayor of Salamanca are as classical in spirit as they are Baroque in ornament. Together with the piazzas of the Italian Renaissance, they are balanced and enclosed like palace courtyards. The 17th-century *places royales* of France belong to that same tradition, and were created for a similar purpose: as symbols of power and glory in a disorderly world.

In 1600, Paris had a population of half a million, and just two public squares: the parvis of Notre-Dame and the Place de Grève (now the Place de l'Hôtel-de-Ville), both much smaller than they became in the 19th century. Open space was reserved for the use of church, crown and the nobility; the rest of the population was crammed into an insanitary warren of tenements and alleys within the medieval walls. From the compressed triangle of the Place Dauphine on the Ile de la Cité, which Henry IV began in 1606, to the expansive Place de la Concorde, inaugurated by Louis XV in 1763, the professed intention of honoring the monarchy also served to develop the city and create usable public space.

The first planned square in Paris was the Place Royale (now Place des Vosges), which Henry IV commissioned in 1605 as a setting for royal fêtes and as the center of the Marais, an aristocratic faubourg that had supplanted religious foundations

The Place des Vosges in the Marais district of Paris was inaugurated as the Place Royale in 1612, an exclusive residential enclave with an open space for royal fêtes.

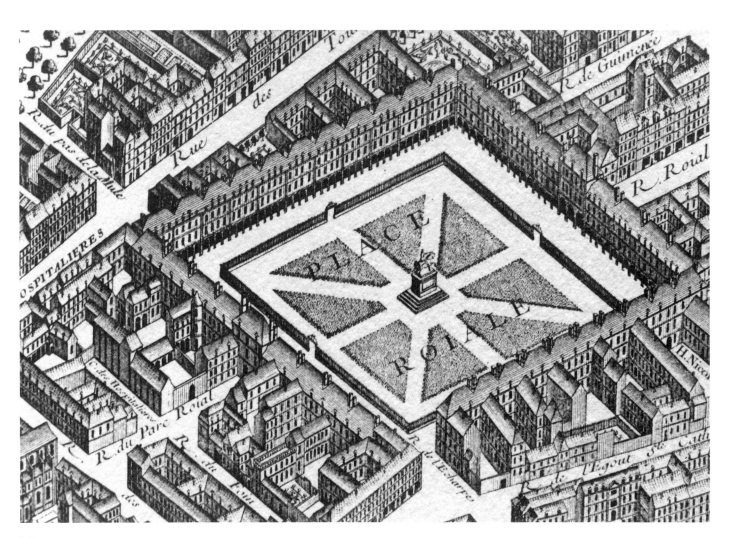

established in the 12th century on drained marshland. It was built over a horse market that occupied the site of the Hôtel de Tournelles, where Henry II had been killed in a tournament fifty years before. Mark Girouard suggests that the symmetrical arcaded square was inspired by the recently completed piazza of Leghorn, a planned Florentine port city. Italian influence in France was strong, and Henry's wife was Marie de' Medici. The first plan was utilitarian: there was to be a silk workshop along one side, in place of Leghorn's church, and the other sides would have shops in the arcades and houses above.

The square was designed by Clément Métezeau, who had worked on the royal palace at Fontainebleau, to become an exclusive residential enclave, with no commercial tenants. It comprised thirty-six houses with uniform three-storey brick and stone façades, a continuous arcade, and dormer windows in steeply pitched slate roofs. Each side is about 450 feet long and the square can be entered through arches beneath the King's Pavilion on the north side and the Queen's Pavilion directly opposite. Originally, there was one corner entry; by 1765 a through street ran along the north side. The Place Royale was an immediate success. It was inaugurated in 1612 with a three-day fête and tournament to celebrate the marriage of Louis XIII to Anne of Austria. Cardinal Richelieu, Molière, Corneille, ministers and nobles were among the first residents, and the graveled expanse of the square became a promenade for fashionable carriages and riders, a must-see for visitors. Richelieu commissioned an equestrian statue of Louis XIII in 1639; the space was fenced and later planted with geometric parterres.

The Place began to lose its status as soon as Louis XIV established his court at Versailles in 1686. Madame de Sévigné was born at No. 1, and Victor Hugo lived at No. 6 (now the Hugo Museum) but, by the end of the 18th century, the Marais had become a district of artisans' workshops and poor immigrants. During the

The Marais has made a spectacular comeback after a long decline, and restaurants (left) now flourish in the arcades of the Place des Vosges.

Trees (above) were planted in the Place des Vosges during the French Revolution; later a statue of Louis XIII was erected to replace the one that had been torn down in 1792.

The Place Ducale is the centerpiece of the planned city of Charleville in north-eastern France, designed within a few years of the Place des Vosges by the same architect.

Revolution, the statue was torn down, a walk of limes was planted, and the square changed its name with every shift of faction: Fédérés, Indivisibilité, Vosges (for the *département* that first paid its taxes); then back and forwards from Royale to République as the monarchy was restored and dethroned.

In 1966, the Marais was declared a historic district, and much of its 17th-century splendor has been restored. The Place des Vosges (or the Square Louis XIII, as the authorities are trying to call it) has made a spectacular comeback. Its arcades, until recently deserted, are filled with restaurant tables, including the three-star L'Ambroisie and an outpost of the Tour d'Argent. Galleries and antique dealers are flourishing and the façades — of real and imitation brick — are being carefully restored. The chestnuts that cluster around the restored statue have grown so large that they obscure the sweep of the square, the landscaping is 19th-century, and the roadway is cluttered with parked cars. Despite these flaws, it is a special place.

As the Place des Vosges neared completion, Clément Métezeau designed the Place Ducale as the centerpiece of Charleville, Charles de Gonzague's grid-plan town adjoining Mézieres in north-eastern France. The elements are similar, but the effect is dramatically different. In the Place des Vosges, the street entries are concealed; here two axial streets intersect at the central statue. The four angled sections of arcaded houses are articulated by slate roofs as sharply angled as witches' hats. An ugly town hall has replaced the ducal palace that formerly closed the west side. The brickwork is covered with painted trade signs and the square has the character of a battle-scarred mongrel, missing an ear, one foot bandaged, but full of life and character. Still more battered, from wartime devastation and clumsy restoration, is the Place Royale of Rheims (1755–60), with its restored statue of

Louis XV serving as the focus for one cross axis, and for the street that links the Préfecture with the Hôtel de Ville, three blocks to the north.

Charleville and Rheims demonstrate how the French reinterpreted Italian principles, emphasizing the straight line as an expression of human reason and will, with a statue of the ruler at the center as a symbol of his authority and to terminate the axial vistas. These royal squares were a creation of 17th-century France that inspired a succession of 18th-century squares in provincial capitals, and as far afield as Lisbon and Copenhagen.

Noble landowners were encouraged to dedicate a square to the king as a way of evading restrictions on new development. Thus the Duc de la Feuillade provided the land in Paris for the circular Place des Victoires, designed by Jules Hardouin-Mansart in 1685. Pierre Lavedan described it as "a sanctuary of royalty . . . day and night torches burned before the statue [of Louis XIV]." The same architect designed what is now the Place de la Libération in Dijon (1688–1725), with its semicircular screen creating a public forecourt to complement the outer courtyard of the ducal palace. Mere fragments survive from the Place des Victoires; Dijon's has lost its statue and is submerged in traffic.

Proposal of 1688 by Jules Hardouin-Mansart for a royal square facing the ducal palace in Dijon. It survives, though without its statue, as the Place de la Libération.

The masterpiece of Hardouin-Mansart and still the noblest square in France is the Place Vendôme, inaugurated in 1699 as the Place Louis le Grand, on land formerly owned by the Duc de Vendôme, north of the Tuileries Gardens. It was proposed by the Superintendent of Buildings as a focus for the westward development of Paris into the open country beyond, and few speculations have proved so far-sighted. The architect created a sequence of palatial façades on a 420 × 440 feet rectangle with chamfered corners. Like the Place des Vosges, the square was sequestered from through traffic, and the short vistas to north and south were terminated by convents. François Girardon's equestrian statue of Louis XIV was inaugurated with a magnificent fête in August 1699, but it was another twenty years before the building plots behind the façades were filled.

This royal shrine and residence of dukes was used, in June 1792, for a bonfire of the king's title deeds. Heads from the guillotine were displayed on spikes. The statue was replaced in 1808 with a 130-foot column, cast from captured guns, and crowned with a statue of Napoleon. It is faced with copper reliefs of the victorious Austerlitz campaign that spiral up, as on Trajan's Column in Rome. In 1871, the painter Gustave Courbet incited the Communards (who had seized control of Paris) to topple the column — for aesthetic and political reasons. Regrettably — for it is out of scale with the Place — the column was restored, and the expense bankrupted the iconoclastic artist.

Hardouin-Mansart's masterpiece was the Place Vendôme in Paris. Its original appearance, as the Place Louis le Grand, is shown in this 18th-century engraving by Aveline.

The 130-foot column of the Place Vendôme, erected in 1808 to celebrate Napoleon's victory at Austerlitz, appears in its original form in this engraving of 1830 by Berger.

Since then, the Place has been the resort of the rich, of literary lions from Proust to Hemingway, and several odd characters. The charlatan Franz Mesmer and the publisher of Henry Miller's *Tropic of Cancer* both lived here. Chopin died at No. 12 and the Prince of Wales (later Edward VII) bought his cravats at Charvet's (No. 28). The Ritz has occupied No. 15 since 1896, alongside the Ministry of Justice; Schiaparelli and Chaumier set the tone for the stores. The snobbery of wealth has displaced that of birth, but the most damaging change dates from the Revolution, when the convents that blocked the Place from through-traffic were demolished. Now, there is a ceaseless stream of tourist buses, cars and trucks, which fatally compromises its intended tranquility.

Two of the least-known royal squares in France are located side by side in Rennes, the capital of Brittany. The town is charming, if sleepy; however, lacking a Gothic cathedral, castle or mountain view, it is abruptly dismissed by the Blue Guide. The Place du Parlement de Bretagne (formerly the Place Louis XIV) combines the mid-17th-century Palace of Justice, with its broad slate roof, and, on the other three sides, Jacques Gabriel's four-storey range with its Ionic colonnade rising over a high rusticated base. Begun in 1720, its south side was not completed until after the First World War. The French architectural historian Pierre Lavedan considers this "among the most perfect works of French architecture". The central area has been pitifully landscaped and has lost the central statue that gave it a point of focus.

A block away is the larger and livelier Place de la Mairie, originally dedicated to Louis XV, in which Gabriel's Hôtel de Ville (1734–43) faces the theater (1856) across a cobbled expanse. The two buildings, separately conceived, are a perfect match, male and female reaching for an embrace. The city hall comprises two angular and

In Rennes, the capital of Brittany, the firemen's band, L'Harmonie Municipale, celebrates its 125th anniversary. After parading triumphantly round the town, it returns to the Place de la Mairie (above left), where it takes up its position in front of the theater. Crowds of people wander in the square (above right), while a carousel revolves gaily beside the theater.

severe blocks, with a recessed central tower; the theater is rounded and sensual. In between are varied but compatible classical blocks, mostly faced with pale stucco. The well-trafficked roads that run down the sides and the broad cross axis are all terminated with buildings that preserve the square's sense of enclosure.

On a cloudless Whit Sunday the entire population seems to have turned out to celebrate its good fortune. Fanned tricolors and banners flutter at every window. Harmonie Municipale, the firemen's band, celebrates its 125th anniversary from a dais before parading around town and returning, red-faced and footsore, for speeches and refreshments. Small boys are in heaven, darting from carousel to ice-cream stand, before joining the band on its final triumphal entry into city hall.

In France, tradition demands that a square be open to the public; even the elegant Place Vendôme used to host an annual fair. This is why, according to Mark Girouard, few Parisian squares became or long remained fashionable places to live. The upper classes demanded a town house that was separated from the street by a

Rennes acquired two royal squares in the 18th century: the Place Louis XIV (now the Place du Parlement de Bretagne) and the Place de la Mairie.

St James's Square, London, in an aquatint of 1812 by Thomas Ackerman. It was developed in the 1670s by the Earl of St Albans as an enclave of plain but fashionable houses, minutes from the royal court.

forecourt and sheltered entry. Lacking such amenities, the houses of the Place des Vosges and Place Vendôme were soon divided into apartments. Girouard points out that in London, the rich and well-born were quite content with a plain row house opening off the sidewalk, with a rear mews for horses and carriage, because society regarded the city as a temporary retreat from a country seat — a place to spend a month or two each year, attending to business.

From a hesitant start in the 17th century, squares soon became the building blocks of London's westward expansion, and the most desirable places to live. With the exceptions of Trafalgar and Sloane Squares, all were created as residential enclaves, facing onto open space which later became railed gardens. A survey of 1907 describes a hundred such squares, most of them laid out between the mid-18th and mid-19th centuries. Many were surrounded by the same modest row houses that lined the neighboring streets. The best were very stylish. An 18th-century observer described Grosvenor Square, begun in 1695, as "the very focus of feudal grandeur, fashion, taste and hospitality."

In Oscar Wilde's *The Importance of Being Earnest*, Jack Worthing cites his residence at 149 Belgrave Square as evidence of his worth. The mother of the girl he seeks to marry is only slightly impressed:

> Lady Bracknell: "The unfashionable side. I thought there was something. However, that could easily be altered."
> Jack: "Do you mean the fashion, or the side?"
> Lady Bracknell (sternly): "Both, if necessary, I presume."

The social center of London, like that of Paris, has moved steadily west over the past three centuries. Its squares have flourished by giving their residents the illusion of living in a palace and looking out on a private park — the romance of the country allied to the convenience of town. It helped that England's monarchs held court in London during the season, rather than exiling themselves to a Versailles. St James's

Square was developed in the 1670s by the Earl of St Albans, a favorite of Charles II, only minutes from the royal palace. In 1721 its residents included six dukes, seven earls and assorted ambassadors. Yet, as Sir John Fielding commented in 1776, "the houses are built more for the convenience of their opulent and noble Possessors than for causing surprize in the Beholders", and residents judged the houses along the south side "scandalously rude and irregular". Lavish interiors were concealed behind plain and uniform facades.

The great squares of London's West End have fared poorly in this century. As taxes eroded private fortunes and noble families were forced to retrench, the London house was sold to pay for the upkeep of the country seat. The aristocratic estates that first developed the squares, giving them their family names, exploited their ownership in the land as the ground leases fell due, replacing houses with offices that were twice as large and much less distinguished. Leicester Square was an early casualty, becoming the Times Square of London; since the 1930s, Berkeley and Hanover, Russell and Cavendish Squares have lost all but a few of their original houses. Grosvenor Square is dominated by the American Embassy and an eight-storey wall of neo-Georgian apartment houses. The roar of traffic around St James's Square makes it hard to imagine that, in 1899, the Trustees' greatest concern was Lady Strafford, who "continually used the Square for cycling."

It is well known that the English value trees above buildings, just as they prefer dogs to people. The gale that felled the ancestral oaks of southern England in 1986 was mourned as a national tragedy. Londoners have tolerated the desecration of their architectural heritage while fiercely preserving the gardens that conceal or distract from new construction. Foreigners have long delighted in this uniquely English arrangement. In 1791, an Italian visitor expressed surprise "to see wide squares containing a garden in which the inhabitants of the surrounding houses, who possess a key to it, may go to stroll."

That connoisseur of cities, Steen Eiler Rasmussen, rhapsodized over Blooms-bury in the 1930s, when it was still a settled community, with a strong literary and artistic flavor. In *London: the Unique City*, he wrote:

> On a summer day when the sun is shining you can walk for hours from one square to another under fresh green trees and see thousands of little circular spots cast by the sun on the green lawns. But in the dark season the old squares are no less attractive. In the afternoon, when the lights begin to appear in the houses, when the tea is served — a rite so sacred to the English — when London is being swallowed up in the moisture and fog of the same yellowish color as the tea, the London square appears to be at the bottom of the sea under branches whose indistinct outlines form a pattern like seaweed floating overhead.

This has been the image of the London square for two centuries, since the first plane trees were planted within an iron fence, but the earliest models were as bare as those of France. The first improvements were also inspired by the example of Paris: Sutton Nicholls' engravings of the 1720s show neatly fenced parterres and shrubs with axial walkways in the French taste. Either they were indifferently maintained or

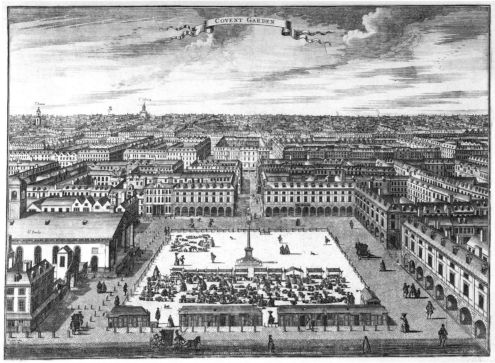

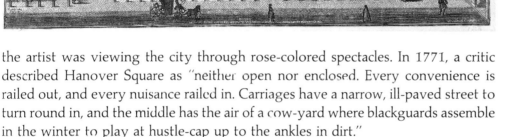

the artist was viewing the city through rose-colored spectacles. In 1771, a critic described Hanover Square as "neither open nor enclosed. Every convenience is railed out, and every nuisance railed in. Carriages have a narrow, ill-paved street to turn round in, and the middle has the air of a cow-yard where blackguards assemble in the winter to play at hustle-cap up to the ankles in dirt."

The enclosure in Berkeley Square had "gone to ruin" by 1766, and residents resolved to appoint trustees and raise money to pave, light, clean and adorn the space. In its most fashionable era, St James's Square was criticized as "a receptacle for rubbish, much utilised for the display of fireworks . . . and not unknown to footpads." Only in the 1820s was the space railed, planted and enhanced with the present statue of William III.

The earliest London squares were laid out as commercial speculations: Covent Garden in 1631, Leicester Square in 1635, and Lincoln Inn's Fields in 1638. Covent Garden took its name from the orchard of the Convent of St Peter, Westminster, which had been appropriated by the crown and given to the Russell family. A century later, the Earl of Bedford applied for permission to develop these lands to the north of his mansion on the Strand. To fulfill Charles I's requirement that it be an ornament to the city, the Earl commissioned Inigo Jones, Surveyor of the King's Works and the greatest English architect of the age, to plan London's first and only Italianate Piazza. Jones, who may have delegated the architectural detailing to his French assistant, Isaac de Caus, drew on the models of Leghorn and the Place des Vosges for the two rows of houses with their rusticated arcades, and for the temple-like church with its flanking pavilions. The garden of Bedford House bounded the south side.

Planned to house "Persons of the greatest Distinction", Covent Garden immediately veered off course. The Civil War eliminated the royalists who were

Engraving (left) by Sutton Nicholls c. 1728 of Covent Garden, London. Designed by Inigo Jones "for Persons of the greatest Distinction", it rapidly became a vegetable market and lost its social standing.

It was the arcades (right) — a novelty imported from Italy — that became known as the piazzas of Covent Garden; engraving of 1768.

meant to live there. Traders set up stalls under the arcades and against the garden wall; in 1670, the Earl secured a royal charter to hold a flower and produce market and the stalls steadily spread across the piazza. The arcades became a popular meeting place, and taverns and coffee houses flourished on the custom from the Drury Lane Theatre, which opened in 1663. Public bath houses followed, and the square was later described as "the resort of abandoned rakes and shameless prostitutes." A Hogarth painting of 1738 lovingly details the debauchery.

Society painters had been among the earliest residents. More popular artists moved in as the gentry moved out; Bedford, now a Duke, relocated to Bloomsbury in 1700. Historian Celina Fox identifies a "Covent Garden Group" of artists, mostly immigrants working in the realistic Flemish tradition, who satisfied a demand for urban views by painting the market, documenting its vibrant life and color. Through the 18th century, it became increasingly crowded; Thomas Rowlandson depicted an election meeting of 1808 as a near riot. Houses were rebuilt piecemeal, without porticoes, and occupied by tradesmen and cheap hotels. By the 1820s, the area had become a slum. In response to complaints, the Bedford Estate bought up and rebuilt neighboring streets, and effectively obliterated the square by commissioning a market hall that filled the space and became London's principal flower and vegetable mart.

Covent Garden Piazza and Market *painted by John Collet, 1770–80. The market was a favorite subject for the many artists who lived in or around the square.*

Bloomsbury was developed by the Bedfords to be everything that Covent Garden was not: respectable, discreet and tightly controlled. Donald Olsen describes how the Estate created a visually uniform upper-middle-class suburb across the pastures of north Bloomsbury, beginning with Bedford Square in 1776, and ending with the completion of Gordon Square in 1860. Elsewhere, sober Georgian architecture gave way to heavy and flamboyant Victorian, and society moved west. The Bedfords maintained an unwavering course, insisting on the finest materials and the largest houses the market would bear, excluding such undesirables as tradesmen and taxis by gates and by strictly enforced regulations. Around the squares and down the broad streets ran the plain row houses. Around 1800, the custom began of painting the window reveals cream to contrast with the soot-blackened brick — a fashion Rasmussen has compared to the understated elegance of Beau Brummel, with his bleached linen stocks and dark cloth suits.

Before this, most squares had been developed in different styles, by independent builders, foiling plans for a grand design. In Bedford Square, two builders worked closely with Thomas Leverton and the Estate office to create four identical sides, in which the individual houses are treated as parts of a palatial façade, with white stucco central pavilions and dark brick wings set off by cream doorways and keystones. The pavilions are rusticated, pedimented and adorned with Ionic pilasters, but the grandeur is skin deep. A froth of cast-iron balconies at one corner, and the brightly colored doors relieve the sobriety.

No. 1 has a sumptuously stuccoed Adam interior with decorations by Angelica Kauffmann. No. 6 was rescued by soldiers from an angry mob that was after the blood of an unpopular Lord Chancellor. These are the exceptions: most of the interiors are reportedly as unremarkable as their occupants. The City merchants and

The private garden (left) of Bedford Square, London, to which only tenants hold the key; one of the many green oases that give London its special character. The square was designed in 1776 as a unified whole in which individual houses were treated as parts of a palatial façade (right). The first of many such planned squares in the Bloomsbury district of London, it is the last to remain intact.

lawyers who raised their families here were briefly augmented by the Bloomsbury Group, a tentatively avant-garde coterie of artists and writers. Today, they have all been displaced by the offices of international trading companies, public relations consultants, and publishers. The square remains unspoilt: an oasis of civilized taste in a city that is rapidly becoming one of Europe's ugliest. Few prospects are more enticing than the chiaroscuro of Bedford Square on a stormy day, as rain alternates with sunlight of startling clarity. Within the moist green womb of the garden, little has changed in the half century since Rasmussen strolled here; the muffled sounds of traffic seem to belong to another world.

Bath also remains another world, though high-speed trains have made it accessible to London commuters. After its first heyday as a Roman spa, it languished in obscurity until an 18th-century promoter, Beau Nash, made it England's most fashionable resort. Alone among provincial towns, its public spaces rival those of the capital. They were created by two talented architect-developers. John Wood, who had gained experience on London squares, launched an innovative sequence of parades, squares, circus and crescents, and this was extended by his son. It marches from the medieval core into the hills with ever longer and looser strides, as it progresses from closed to open forms, from classical to picturesque taste.

In *Heavenly Mansions*, John Summerson describes the senior Wood's first, fanciful proposal for a revival of the Roman spa, with a Royal Forum for assembly, a Grand Circus for sporting events, and an Imperial Gymnasium for exercise. This elaborate program was soon abandoned in favor of incremental residential development. First came Queen Square (1728–35), whose palatial north side was far grander and more unified than any in London. From here a broad street leads uphill to the Circus, a pivot in the great design, comprising thirty-three houses in three symmetrical arcs. The façades of warm Bath stone have a classic nobility, inspired by Inigo Jones, their three storeys adorned with Doric, Ionic and Corinthian columns, and topped by a parapet with acorn finials. The ground floor has a shallow relief frieze of fruit, animals and musical instruments; at the top are richly carved masks and swags.

Tobias Smollett shared Wood's romantic misconceptions of ancient Rome; in his novel, *Humphrey Clinker*, a character remarks: "The Circus is a pretty bauble and looks like Vespasian's amphitheatre turned outside in." Today, its sweep can be perceived only from the air, for the original expanse of cobbles has been replaced by a grassy mound from which rise five huge plane trees that block much of the view. This softening of Wood's scheme is much appreciated by the residents, and although the houses have been divided into apartments, they have retained their status. Through-traffic is discouraged, and it would not be too great a surprise if a carriage were to trundle in from the Assembly Rooms, or a sedan chair were to appear around a corner.

From the Circus, the axis leads off at an angle to the Royal Crescent, begun in 1767 to the design of John Wood, Jr. The Circus is an enclosed space and can be seen as an outgrowth of the square; the Crescent breaks the mould, achieving a balance between man and nature that has proved a popular model for residential development ever since. In the year construction began, Edinburgh launched its

New Town, a romantic sequence of landscaped spaces, whose buildings are as dour as Bath's are sensual.

Bath has never been matched, and Summerson explains why:

> The Woods were at the same time practical and romantic; they had their feet on the ground and their heads in the clouds. They never tried to make Bath into a grand pattern because they knew that the man in the street never sees a town as a pattern but only as a perspective from the point where he happens to be. On the other hand they knew that buildings, even when they are groups of quite ordinary houses, are capable of that heightened effect which constitutes monumental architecture.

That lesson was applied in Bloomsbury and throughout the West End of London, in squares, and in the sinuous openness of John Nash's Regent's Street development. Privacy and restraint were the key elements, even as the rulers of continental Europe strove for ever grander and more authoritarian stage effects.

The Circus and Royal Crescent of Bath, which the John Woods, father and son, designed as part of a speculative development in the mid 18th century. The detail (above) shows the elegant sweep of the façades of the Circus.

The main plaza in Mexico City, painted by Antonio Gualdi in 1835, soon after the country secured its independence from Spain.

New World

EVERY MORNING at 6 a.m., troops march out from the National Palace of Mexico City to form an open square within the Zócalo, the largest plaza in the Americas. There, in the deserted, lamplit square, a huge flag is raised. A band blares, swords flash, troops salute and march away. Rockets explode from the roof of the Palace. "Oh say can you see/In the dawn's early light". . . the symbolism is universal. On this same site, Aztec priests and Spanish conquistadores performed equally solemn rituals, for this has been the heart of a nation since the city was first established, six hundred years ago.

When Hernan Cortés and his troops arrived at the Aztec capital of Tenochtitlán in 1519, they were dazzled, for here was (in all but name) an ideal Renaissance city, laid out in orderly fashion on islands in a lake, with a ceremonial central plaza approached by causeways. It was twice the size of Seville, then the largest city in Spain. Palaces and temples soared above the polished stone plaza. An idea of its magnificence can be gained from the Zapotec ruins of Monte Alban, near Oaxaca, with its enclosed 900 × 450 foot plaza. Cortés's lieutenant, Bernal Diáz del Castillo, estimated that the Tlatelolco marketplace held 60,000 traders, far outshining that of Salamanca. Within three years, the Spanish had obliterated this city and had begun to construct their own from its stones.

At first, it was a military cantonment of sixteen blocks, surrounding a Plaza de Armas (parade ground); as basic as a Roman *castrum*, or the fortified town of Santa Fe, from which the Spanish king had launched his final attack on the Moorish stronghold of Granada. The Plaza was laid out over that of the Aztecs', the cathedral beside their chief temple; Cortés built his palace on the site of Moctezuma's. The first permanent Spanish settlements in the New World, beginning with Santo Domingo in 1502, were largely improvised. Panama City (1513) was laid out according to official guidelines, sent from Spain, which became ever more detailed over the next sixty years. But the soldiers of Cortés were chiefly inspired by what they found, and by the necessities of defence and shelter. Practical concerns more than theory shaped Mexico City.

For three centuries of Spanish rule, the plaza remained the hub of political, religious and commercial life. As Robert Payne has noted, it introduced the amenities of Western civilization. Here, or close by, were built the first cathedral, hospital, school, university, printing press, library, mint and military barracks in the

New World. To celebrate the accord of 1538 between the Emperor Charles V and François I of France, a forest was created in the plaza. Animals roamed wild, naked Indians battled, jeweled Negroes rode in procession. Then the trees were uprooted and replaced by a wooden replica of a fortress, with a canal to simulate the sea. Cortés defended the fort against an infidel attack (supposedly of Suleiman the Magnificent) and, after much jousting and mock battles, was declared the winner.

Fortified buildings were rebuilt in a more gracious style after 1570. Other improvements came slowly. The Viceroy's Palace was replaced after it had been torched by rioters in 1692; construction of the cathedral stretched out to the eve of Independence in 1819. The dusty expanse of the plaza, once a place for fashionable carriage parades, became an increasingly squalid market. In the 1790s, the stalls were banished, the plaza drained and paved, and new porticoed buildings were erected across from the cathedral and palace. The Emperor Maximilian (1864–67) transformed it into a park. By now it had acquired the nickname of Zócalo (pedestal) – an ironic reference to the base that stood here from 1843 to 1920, awaiting a monument to Independence.

Its official title is the Plaza de la Constitución, but everyone calls it the Zócalo – and the name was picked up by almost every provincial town. But Mexico City's Zócalo is different from the others. It sags under the weight of history. The trees were removed in 1956 to permit huge assemblies; a half million people gather to hear the President's address on Independence Day, 15 September, or to attend political rallies. Its vast expanse of unshaded paving, about 830 × 500 feet, demands crowds just as the Aztec temples extorted their quotas of sacrificial victims. Other cities have turned their squares into gardens; the capital's has returned to its original role – a place where the populace can be awed by the expression of power and the aura of history.

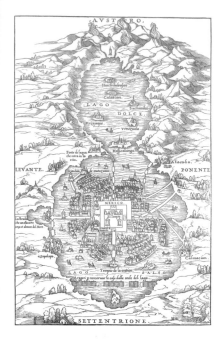

Plan of Tenochtitlán, as the Spanish conquerors described it; from Ramusio's Delle Navigationi e Viaggi, *1556.*

Professional letter writers have plied their trade in the arcades of Mexico City's Plaza de Santo Domingo since the early 18th century.

This reversion to the past is doubly significant, for life in the metropolis has moved on; the Zócalo and the historical center that surrounds it arc being transformed into a museum-shrine. Traffic has been limited to one corner to protect the monuments from destructive vibrations. The Zócalo is too solemn to accommodate everyday activity. Vendors of trinkets and tortillas gather in a subsidiary plaza between the recently excavated Aztec Templo Mayor and the Sacristy. The Alameda offers shady walks and bubbling social life just a few blocks away. And around the corner is a truly popular gathering place: the Plaza de Santo Domingo.

Mexico City has plazas to suit every taste and purpose. It has swallowed up outlying villages like San Angel and Coyoacán, with their rustic squares. It has created new ones, like the monumental Plaza de las Tres Culturas which marks the Aztec center of Tlatelolco. The Plaza Garibaldi is the gathering place for mariachi musicians, and the square that fronts the church of Santo Domingo is where you go to get a letter written. That tradition began in the early 18th century, when clerks from the neighboring Customs Office sought help in composing inventories of goods to be shipped. Today, beneath the portico, a dozen or so professional letter-writers sit at their old-fashioned Remingtons composing romantic epistles, job applications, pleas to officials and after-dinner speeches. Their fees are modest, and they double as psychiatrists, marriage counsellors and protocol experts in their choice of words and forms of address. Alongside, printers turn out invitations and business cards on heavy manual presses.

Crowds throng the Zócalo on 15 September to celebrate Independence Day.

The 17th-century state house of Guadalajara (above left), Mexico's second city, is framed by the kiosk in the Plaza de Armas.

In Taxco (above right), the Plaza de la Borda is named for the 18th-century silver magnate who donated Santa Prisca, the church that dominates the square.

Every spring and fall, traditional plays are performed throughout Guanajato, notably in the Plazuela San Roque (right) whose church serves as backdrop.

City hall, formerly the Spanish governor's palace, in the Mexican port city of Veracruz. It faces over the Zócalo, which buzzes with activity till late at night.

Stray dogs on early morning patrol through Taxco's plaza. As the city comes to life, the square is transformed into a hub of traffic and social activity.

None of this diversity was planned or anticipated by the Spanish. They thought of the plaza as a symbol of authority, and as the seed from which the city would grow. The New World was a blank slate on which they had the opportunity – and the duty to God and king – to write. They were propelled by greed to exploit and fervor to convert, and the building of cities was a means to both ends. For centuries, Spanish kings had been pushing back the Moors, and their last stronghold fell in the same year (1492) that Columbus reached the Americas. Now the crusade could be extended, and the process began with the plaza. Cortés had a foundation to build on; Francisco Pizarro laid out Lima, the new capital of Peru, on bare ground, with cords and stakes.

Soldiers and friars taught themselves the rudiments of urban planning, and by 1573, when the Council of the Indies in Seville issued detailed instructions, most of the principal cities of Latin America had already been established. Just as Alberti summarized medieval practice in creating a prescription for the Renaissance, so did the Spanish authorities codify what had already been tested in the field. Historians dispute how detailed were the first instructions, whether model plans (now lost) were sent from Spain, and how familiar the settlers may have been with Italian cities and theories. Did they read Vitruvius and had they studied the Roman plan of Barcelona?

Two things are clear. In size and regularity, the major plazas of Latin America anticipate, by as much as a century, those of the mother country. And the "Laws of the Indies" of 1573 were tempered by pragmatic considerations. The choice of a healthy, economically viable site, its orientation and defence, take up most of the space. The Laws prescribe a waterfront square in ports; that of Veracruz is set well back from the landing. They recommend proportions of 3:2 (following Vitruvius) "as this shape is best for fiestas in which horses are used"; the most celebrated colonial plazas are square. It is proposed that streets enter the plaza at the corners and the middle of each side; more commonly the sides are unbroken, since the plaza occupies one block of the street grid. In defiance of another Law, the principal church was often located directly on the square, and not set back or raised high above the ground.

But the Laws are full of good sense and often correspond closely to what was actually done. Building lots around the plaza were reserved for church, *cabildo* (royal government), customs house and hospital. Remaining plots were allocated to the city, which made some of them available for shops and merchants' houses. Plazas were surrounded with porticoes, set back at the corners to allow free access, in contrast to the closed arcades of Spanish cities. Smaller, church plazas were distributed through the city, "in good proportion for the instruction of religion." An attempt was made to scale plazas to the expected growth of population.

Rules also governed the use of plazas. Indians were generally excluded from the *plaza de armas* in Spanish-occupied cities, and markets were usually segregated from civic functions, though Mexico City was one of the exceptions. The monuments of the plaza symbolized the rights and duties of the residents, who might be summoned to the plaza to ratify civic decisions. The identification of a city with its plaza is graphically demonstrated in a series of sketches of Peruvian cities done by a native artist, Huaman Poma de Ayala, around 1600. Spain, like Rome, imposed standard forms on alien cultures so forcibly that they endured long after her Empire collapsed.

Nowhere in the world does the plaza flourish more strongly than in Mexico. It can be seen as a distillation of the national character — its love of conviviality and spectacle, its ability to make the everyday seem special, its energy and fatalism, the tight bonds that link friends and family. Fernando Juarez, a Mexican architect living in Los Angeles, recalls how his mother took him to the plaza when he was small, and how he spent every evening there as a teenager, hanging out with the guys and trying to meet girls, in an era when young unmarried women were still chaperoned. He describes the excitement of driving through Mexico and arriving late at night in a plaza that was still brightly lit and crowded, as though he had walked in on a party. A middle-class teenager in today's Mexico City explains that she gets bored with meeting the same crowd every night in the disco, and drags her friends off to join the interesting mix of people in the plaza of Coyoacán.

The appeal of the plaza is eroding in larger cities, as the young find more private places to gather, families move to the suburbs, and the middle classes segregate themselves — as in Europe and the United States. But in the neighborhoods and small towns, it remains a magnet, drawing people from the streets to stroll, chat or snuggle up and feel at home. It achieves a harmonious balance of activity and repose, interaction and separateness. Parents allow children to play freely, secure in the knowledge that each is supervised by his peers. Men and women of different ages form tight-knit groups, then re-form as families. The intensity of social intercourse imparts a vitality to the most prosaic of plazas.

There is nothing prosaic about the Zócalo of Veracruz, the tropical port that has been a gateway to Mexico since Cortés landed here in 1519. Its handsome porticoed *cabildo* (now the city hall) dates from 1600; the cathedral was rebuilt in the 18th century; the other two sides are occupied by hotels, restaurants and bars. The plaza has been tidied up in the last decade, repaved and given a new fountain; it is less raucous since traffic was restricted to one side and the rattletrap streetcars were retired from service. But the atmosphere is still as palpable as the humidity. Graham Greene would feel at home, sipping a rum cocktail in the damp-speckled arcade with the ceiling fan turning lazily and the marimba players moving from one café to the next. Naval officers in crisp whites pass streetwalkers in red sateen; the children seem more hyperkinetic than usual, the grackles (a sleek blue-black bird) more tirelessly shrill. Everything is for sale at your table: food, flesh and cigars; balloons, trinkets and nuts; not to speak of the seafood.

Life on the square in smaller towns is more subdued, but no less engrossing. The Plaza de la Borda is the social hub of Taxco, a colonial hill town 115 miles south-west of Mexico City. Founded by Cortés, it owes its prosperity to two other foreigners: the French Count José de la Borda, who discovered a rich silver mine in the mid 18th century, and the American writer William Spratling, who settled here in 1929 and made silver jewelry a major source of income. The Plaza is the ideal small-town square, ample in contrast to the tight-knit labyrinth of streets, but modest in scale and character. So steep is the site that the Spanish made no attempt to impose a grid plan, and the Plaza is the only level and fairly regular point of arrest on a hard

For the Spanish, the plaza was a symbol of authority and the seed from which a new town would grow. Its importance is graphically demonstrated in this woodcut of Lima, Peru; one of a series done by a local artist, Huaman Poma de Ayala, c. 1600.

climb – a vortex of taxis and jitneys, and a gathering place for locals and tourists.

Overwhelming the space is the sumptuous Churrigueresque church of Santa Prisca, built by de la Borda in the 1750s. Larger and grander than many cathedrals, its west towers soar high above the plaza to dominate every view, blazing gold in the late afternoon sun, and reappearing as an unearthly apparition when floodlit against the night sky. The towers bulge with ornament and would seem top-heavy were the carving of masks and cartouches, putti and saints less refined. The city hall is unremarkable, and the rest of the plaza is filled with restaurants, bars and silver shops. Everything is subordinated to the exuberant gift of the man who struck it so rich that he donated the church and its rich furnishings and gave his name to the square.

A raised pedestrian enclave, shaded by laurels and bordered by cast-iron benches, occupies a third of the plaza. It is tied together with the roadway by a checkerboard pattern of dark paving stones and cobbles, framed with white, like the perspective grid of Pienza. The town rises early, and by 8 a.m. on a cool winter morning old men are taking the first sun, a small boy is sweeping leaves with a birch broom, and another trying to drag a recalcitrant pig to market. A dozen stray dogs patrol the plaza as if they own it. Children hurry to school.

As the tempo increases, so does the sound. Mexicans adore noise. Fireworks explode to inaugurate the fiesta of San Martin at 5.30 a.m.; later come church bells, more explosions and an off-key band. Now an elderly cop lets off piercing blasts on his whistle, not to direct traffic, but to advertise his role as a parking attendant, a key player in the drama. Friends pull over to chat, further tangling the traffic. At 1 p.m., children return from school and fill the plaza before going home for lunch. The plaza becomes a social club, first for old men, then families, and finally, at night, for teenagers.

Similar to Taxco in its steep site and irregular plan is Guanajato, 220 miles northwest of Mexico City, once the richest silver-mining town in the Americas. The university and an annual arts festival keep it alive, and it has preserved its colonial character in a succession of winding hilly streets and tiny *plazuelas*. The Jardin de la Union, which serves as the main square, is as organic a wedge as any medieval market; a thickly shaded promenade faces the neo-classical Teatro Juarez and the richly modeled Church of San Diego. But the town's most distinctive square is the Plazuela de San Roque, a splendidly theatrical space that is used for outdoor drama in May and October. A narrow lane steps steeply up from the main shopping street, broadens to create a forecourt for the church and then branches into narrow neighborhood passages. Bleachers are set up in the neck of the funnel, and short plays by Cervantes and Lope de Vega are played against the façade of the noble but crumbling pink sandstone church.

An hour's drive away is San Miguel de Allende, a colonial town that was declared a national monument in 1926, and has since become the Mexican version of Sante Fe or Saint Paul de Vence, home to artists and socialites from Europe and the United States. Its cobbled streets are as tricky to negotiate as rock-strewn ravines, but for the newcomers the town's greatest appeal is its resistance to change. Nothing could be more traditional than the Jardin de Allende, with its arcades,

Guanajato, like Taxco, flourished as a silver-mining town, and was too steep to acquire a typically Spanish grid plan and central plaza. Its tiny Jardin de la Union functions as the main square.

ayunimento and hotel, and its raised promenade boxed in by pollarded laurels. Only the church stands out: its flamboyant Gothic façade was built in the 1890s by an unlettered Indian mason who based his design on postcards of European churches he had never seen.

The most remarkable thing about the plaza is that it preserves the fast-vanishing custom of the segregated Sunday-evening *paseo*. This is heralded by a sunset chorus of grackles, which swarm in, screaming and chattering as though auditioning for a remake of Hitchcock's *The Birds*. By 8 p.m. every bench is full, and the mating dance begins. Young women and girls parade counterclockwise around the plaza, arm-in-arm and three abreast, gossiping but watchful, in a progress as brisk and stylized as a cotillion. The boys make a perfunctory clockwise movement, but most dart into line to walk with the girls or draw them aside. The young or shy pretend not to be interested. Foreigners and couples thread in between; the balloon sellers work the families on the benches; a band blasts away from the kiosk. Nothing slows the youthful carousel, which revolves late into the night.

Oaxaca, 330 miles south-east of the capital, no longer has a *paseo*. Aldous Huxley describes, in *Beyond the Mexique Bay* (1933), how the flappers, "high-heeled, in every tender shade of artificial silk . . . stroll giggling under the electric light. There is a rolling of eyes, a rolling of posteriors. The young men stroll in the opposite direction. In the roadway, the most correct of the *correctos* circulate very slowly in their automobiles — round and round and round." Now the city sprawls far beyond its Zócalo, and since 1981 chains have been strung across each corner to exclude cars.

It remains one of the most enchanting and imposing of Mexican plazas, retaining the plan it was given in 1529: a square within the regular grid of broad streets, bounded by arcades on four sides, one of which is cut away to reveal the

Oaxaca's Zócalo was transformed in the late 19th century, like other Mexican plazas, from unpaved open space to formal French garden, with lacy cast-iron benches and central kiosk.

cathedral, set back and facing over its own half-block plaza, now known as the Alameda. The hinge that joins these two shady squares is a paved open space around two sides of the cathedral, which is used for concerts and public gatherings, for fireworks and fiestas. The Gobierno (state house) is severe, the Cathedral richly ornamented but squat, hunkered down against earthquakes. Though the population of Oaxaca has grown to a quarter of a million, it remains a low-rise city, and the encircling hills can be glimpsed at the end of each portico. The buildings of the plaza and historic core are unified by their use of *cantera verde*, a greenish local stone.

Throughout the colonial era, plazas were unpaved and unshaded, neutral ground for every practical need. Independence stirred civic pride, and the State Governor of Oaxaca paved this plaza in 1868, planting trees and installing lamps and fountains. Not until the stable, prosperous era of the dictator Porfirio Diaz (1876–1910) did Mexican plazas become gardens, with walkways radiating from a central kiosk: a plan borrowed from France, applied in the capital and quickly imitated. Oaxaca's Zócalo is infused with the spirit of the Belle Epoque, with its street lamps, parterres and promenades, and its lacy cast-iron benches. The flowers are as exotic as those in a Victorian hothouse: purple bougainvillea and the orange trumpets of cempozuchitl create luminous accents against the dark laurels.

The kiosk, built in 1882 to celebrate the city's 350th anniversary, is the star of the show. Its high arched domes suggest a balloon, and one can imagine it making a slow ascent, buoyed by the windpower of the municipal band playing – what else? – "Nearer my God to Thee." A few steps down in the base is a shopping arcade, with bar, newsstand and carry-out snacks. Serious music is performed by the State Band on Sunday afternoon, not in the kiosk, but under the trees. There is a printed program, listing Beethoven and Saint-Saens alongside those less familiar composers beloved of the brass. A clarinetist with a Mayan profile and the silver-haired distinction of Leonard Bernstein spends a half hour tuning the different sections of the band; the audience is rapt.

All the elements in the Zócalo are to be found in the northern cities of Morelia and Guadalajara, but the spirit of Oaxaca's is languid. Indians squat on the curb in the early morning, resting on their way to market. The cafés and balconied restaurants are full at lunchtime, but the pace slows through the afternoon, as people stretch out on the benches for siesta, or indulge in that most cherished of rituals, the shoeshine. This is no perfunctory polish, but a complete make-over, as the shoes are laved and buffed to mirror brightness. For a few hundred pesos, every man can imagine himself a king, perched on a high throne, immersed in a newspaper that is provided as part of the service. In the evening the Indians return, selling crafts and carrying trays of roses on their heads.

The Mexican plaza is a stage for everyday events and moments of high drama. In Taxco, the celebration of Holy Week culminates in a gruesome reenactment of Christ's Passion that recalls the fanaticism and cruelty of the Conquest. The Plaza Grande of Patzcuaro marks the Day of the Dead with a crafts fair in which the theme

On Sunday afternoon, the state band of Oaxaca performs in the Zócalo beneath a cempozuchitl tree, whose orange blooms light up the square.

of mortality is explored in candies and painted figures. In the week before Christmas, San Miguel de Allende presents traditional *posadas*, recreating Joseph and Mary's search for lodging, and these culminate with a parade in the plaza. Veracruz has its rumbunctious carnival.

The fiestas of Oaxaca reach a peak of activity in December. Carol Miller, a writer and sculptress in Mexico City, recalls her first visit there as a correspondent for *Life*. She and her photographer covered the three-day feast of the Virgin of La Soledad, then stayed for "a unique festival honoring the giant radishes that grow down in the valley. On the night of 23 December, they are carved, mounted or combined to form sculptures: some lewd, some ingenious, some completely outlandish. At the same time, the populace parades round the square, to a deafening symphony of band concerts, organ grinders, portable radios, and shrieking children who consume *buñuelos*, foot-wide bubbly pancakes drowned in cane syrup from green earthenware bowls, which are afterwards dashed to the ground. By midnight the plaza is knee-deep in fractured crockery." For Christmas, home-made crèches with figures inspired by the Indians who live in the surrounding hills are set out around the plaza.

The Plaza de Armas of Cuzco, Peru, was laid out by the Spanish on the site of an even larger square in the Inca capital.

The Plaza de Armas of Antigua Guatemala: a 19th-century engraving of the square as it appeared before the capital of Spanish Central America was devastated by the earthquakes of 1773.

The vitality of Mexico's plazas may reflect its prolonged stability, relative prosperity and the safety of its streets, in contrast to the turbulence and grinding poverty of so many other Latin American countries. Hardest hit in recent years has been Peru, whose city squares rival those of Mexico in scale and the magnificence of their architecture. The Plaza de Armas of Cuzco was laid out in 1533 on the site of the Incas' central plaza, which was twice as large. Three churches and the cathedral were built over the foundations of monuments that Pizarro destroyed, following the example of Cortés in Tenochtitlan. In Lima, most of the buildings around the Plaza de Armas have been reconstructed in this century. Far more impressive are the main squares of Peru's next largest cities: Trujillo, with its colonial mansions and white cathedral, and Arequipa, where the El Misti volcano rises behind the cathedral and two-storey porticoes.

Soon after the conquest of Mexico, Pedro de Alvarado subdued the Indians of Central America south to Panama, and became the first Captain-General of the Spanish Kingdom of Guatemala. Its capital, from 1541 to 1773, is today called Antigua Guatemala, to distinguish it from the chief city of the greatly reduced modern state of Guatemala. Before its destruction by the strongest in a succession of earthquakes, this was the third most important city of New Spain. Now it is a town of 15,000 people (down from 60,000), half ruined, half rebuilt and constantly at risk from fresh shocks, but irresistible in its ravaged beauty. At its center is the Parque Central, formerly the Plaza de Armas, a showpiece of colonial government.

The buildings around the square seem low in proportion to the expansive garden and are dwarfed by the three volcanoes to the south. All date from after the 1717 earthquake and have been repeatedly restored. The cathedral's façade has been pieced together, though its nave has been roofless for two centuries. The other three sides are bounded by stone or wood arcades, linking the *ayunimento* to the north, the Palace of the Captains General and Royal Mint to the south and the low commercial buildings between. Broad cobbled streets flank the garden; the occasional vehicle raises a cloud of dust in the clear upland air.

Antigua's plaza (left) now has a modern garden to set off its restored historic buildings; the volcano is a reminder that destructive tremors are a regular occurrence.

Worshippers and vendors use the steps of Santo Tomas in the plaza of Chichicastenango (right), a Guatemalan mountain village celebrated for its Indian market.

By day, the park is unworthy of its setting: municipal gardening of the 1930s, with a diminutive bust of a bearded revolutionary, and a clumsily reconstructed Baroque fountain. It is peopled by Indians attempting to sell rugs to tourists, and by flower children of the kind who summer in Katmandu. As darkness falls, the extras vanish and the scene changes. You can imagine yourself in an "atmospheric" movie palace of the kind that architect John Eberson built all over the United States on the eve of the Depression. The deco-scrolled benches resemble the sofas in theater lobbies of that era. The backlit arcades, tinkling fountain, shadowy volcanoes and starry canopy are too exotic to be real; this must be the painted decor for "A Night in Old Spain". All that is required to complete the illusion are uniformed ushers and the sound of a mighty Wurlitzer. Someone should have the imagination to rig up an outdoor screen.

The Spanish created separate towns, with market squares, for Indians. Patzcuaro in Mexico is one; Chichicastenango in Guatemala is another. Indians flock in from many miles around for the Thursday and Sunday markets. For most of history they walked for many hours, and even today many complete their journey on foot, carrying goods on their heads or in slings on their backs, and set them out for sale on the great plaza. Useful and decorative are mixed together; pots and toys, weavings and tools, soap and masks, with a separate arcaded courtyard for produce and live chickens.

Rough steps on each side of the plaza lead up to the whitewashed churches of Santo Tomas and El Calvario. The steps serve as altars for traditional Indian rituals. Clouds of incense waft over the pilgrims and the women who sell them flowers as offerings. The appeal of the market goes far beyond the need to shop or to seek the intervention of a saint. As in medieval Europe, it offers buyers and sellers a break in the routine of hard and repetitive work, the opportunity to catch up on news and exchange gossip.

Latin America once included much of what is now the south-west United States, but there was no gold or silver to lure adventurers, and few settlements were made in this vast territory. St Augustine, Florida, was a typical military outpost, established in 1565 to discourage the French and English from pushing south. Its waterfront parade ground survives, though much rebuilt and hideously commercialized.

The Plaza of Santa Fe, New Mexico, is only slightly more impressive, despite its colorful history. A provincial capital of New Spain, founded in 1610, Santa Fe remained an impoverished frontier town until recent times. On plan, the Plaza was ambitious: a rectangle 800 × 400 feet, surrounded by the Governor's Palace, military chapel, barracks, prison and *ayunimento*, with a log arcade all around. But the single-storey wood-and-adobe buildings were poorly constructed, required frequent repairs, and were out of scale with the dusty expanse of the Plaza. The Indian pueblo of Taos uses the same building techniques in a far more dramatic way to frame an open square that is the hub of the community's spiritual life.

A 19th-century visitor described Santa Fe as resembling "more a prairie-dog village than a capital." In the 1840s, under Mexican rule, the Plaza was used for bullfights, a corral, a market and for the departure of overland caravans, which took three years for the return trip to Mexico City — a measure of the town's remoteness. Anglo settlers began a long process of gentrification in 1866, planting cottonwood trees, and adding a picket fence and gingerbread bandstand.

The most impressive *plaza de armas* in the United States is in New Orleans. It was laid out by a French military engineer in 1721, as a waterfront parade ground facing the Mississippi, and as the focus of the 75-block city that is now known as the Vieux Carré or French Quarter. The territory passed from France to Spain in 1763, and later acquired two of its most distinctive features: the Cabildo and Presbytère (court house), flanking a rebuilt cathedral at the head of the square. New Orleans was acquired by the United States in 1803 as part of the Louisiana Purchase, and the Plaza was later renamed Jackson Square for the President and war hero Andrew Jackson. It was immediately fenced and planted, but the decisive improvements came in the decade of prosperity that preceded the Civil War.

In 1850, the square was given its present cast-iron railings and concentric walkways. At the center, on the site of the Spanish gallows, rose Clark Mills's spirited equestrian statue of Jackson — a replica of the one which rides through Lafayette Square in Washington, D.C. The cathedral was rebuilt in grander style, and on each side the three-storey red brick Pontalba Buildings completed the enclosure left open since the collapse of the Spanish barracks. These identical blocks of row houses were a speculative development by the Baroness Micaëla Pontalba, who has been described as "the closest the South ever came to a real Scarlett O'Hara." Inspired by Parisian squares, she pursued her vision with fierce determination, but her venture failed: society moved west and the houses became tenements. Renovated in the 1930s, and divided into apartments owned by the city and the state, they are now eagerly sought after.

The Pontalba Buildings' fortunes have mirrored the ups and downs of the square. An engraving of 1858 shows them as an oasis of gentility amid the raucous trade from the ships that docked along the levee. During its social eclipse, railroad sheds divided the square from the river. In 1929 they were removed, and during the next decade the square was restored by convict labor, ridding it of what an editorial of the time called "moochers, dope peddlers, muggle smokers, street walkers and others of the same character". In the 1960s, the twin threats of an elevated riverfront expressway and a sound-and-light show in the square were averted. It became a spicy stew of hippies and artists, a place for neighbors to shop in the Italian food stores and find out what was going on. George Gureau, an artist who has lived in the Quarter for thirty years, recalls it as a village in those years. But another generation of moralists objected to the return of the moochers and dope peddlers, and the square was locked for the first time during Mardi Gras to protect it from the crowds.

Today, it is an impeccably maintained enclave. Traffic is banned from the square, except along the waterfront. The terraces of Washington Artillery Park mask the concrete flood wall and create a rival pole of attraction for crowds and entertainers, who also throng the pedestrian walk on three sides of the square. Residents are far outnumbered by tourists, here and throughout the Vieux Carré; the neighborhood food shops have gone, though there is a new French bakery. Everything else is geared to visitors and the jazz musicians, guitar players and mimes who entertain them. Few serious artists hang their work on the railings.

The square still has its moments of glory. It is the city's official front door; President de Gaulle and the Pope were among the celebrated visitors welcomed here and invited to mass in the cathedral. And it is a peaceful retreat from the bustle, for a walk in the shade of the cottonwoods and crape myrtles, or a coffee and doughnut on a bench. But, be warned, feeding the pigeons can bring you a $25 fine! At night, the locked enclosure is full of mystery, another of the city's impenetrable courtyards.

Its French and Spanish heritage, brief but formative, has set New Orleans apart from other American cities, and it has exploited its reputation as the Big Easy, even as its business community becomes increasingly mainstream. Jackson Square was shaped and energized by a ferment of cultures; only in recent years has it lost its raffish community flavor and become a tidy, well-regulated tourist site. Other American cities never had such a square, and part of the explanation lies in the radically different patterns of urban development in North and Latin America.

The Spanish began a century earlier than the British or French, and within fifty years of discovering Central and south America they had subdued huge tracts of land. Theirs was a sacred crusade: to win souls for the church, treasure and territory for the king, fame and fortune for themselves. The soldiers were swift and ruthless, the friars unflinching. They were sons of the greatest European power of the day and of the Renaissance; cities were a tool for conversion and secular domination, a method of organizing and exploiting a vast domain.

In contrast, the French crown encouraged but gave little support to the individuals and companies that established trading posts along the St Lawrence River from 1608 on. Urban design was left to the settlers and thus, as J.W. Reps has noted, Cadillac laid out Detroit in 1701 in the image of the *bastides* he knew from his native Gascony. Similar grid plans, centered on a waterfront Place des Armes, were adopted for Mobile (1711), New Orleans, and St Louis (1764). Pragmatism and individual effort guided the colonization, not centralized planning or state direction.

The first British colonies were equally scattered and improvised. The farmers

Jackson Square, New Orleans, in 1858: an oasis of gentility amid the raucous Mississippi River trade, soon after its final transformation from Spanish parade ground to American park.

Below left: looking across Jackson Square to the cathedral and court house from a balcony of the Pontalba Buildings, identical blocks of brick row houses developed as a speculation in 1849–50.

Below right: in the pedestrian zone around the square, visitors can hear jazz, shop and absorb the spirit of a city that calls itself the "Big Easy".

and traders who settled the south, beginning in 1607 at Jamestown, Virginia, did so in the name of the king, but they had no idea of building an empire. The rich planters among them shared Jefferson's conviction that "cities are sores on the body politic." For nearly a century, they impeded the development of urban centers as harmful to their interests. The Puritans who landed at Plymouth in 1620, and later established Massachusetts, Connecticut and Rhode Island, were fleeing religious persecution and social injustice. Their greatest wish was to be allowed to live and worship in their own fashion, independent of church and crown. They recognized the need to establish villages for mutual assistance in a harsh and hostile wasteland, but as soon as these settlements grew beyond their original bounds, new ones were established for the surplus population. Philadelphia, New York and Boston were the only substantial colonial towns.

This pastoral bias found expression in the New England village greens. At first they were called commons, drawing upon the ancient tradition of land set aside for community use. In England that tradition was ending as landowners enclosed these spaces for their own profit, and the Puritans made sure this would not happen in the New World by assigning ownership of the commons to the original settlers in a community, the proprietors. Each proprietor was given a building plot beside or near the common, but the land was accessible to all — as a pound for cattle being moved from private plots to the fields outside the town, as pasture for horses, and as a drill ground for the militia. The Meeting House was church, town hall and community center, and it stood on the common, beside the burying ground.

The common came in every size and shape, determined more by topography than a plan, and soon became the center of community life, as versatile as a Greek agora or Venetian campo. A nooning house was added to shelter residents who lived too far away to return home for lunch between the two obligatory Sunday services, and this was later supplanted by taverns offering board and lodging to all. Later additions included a courthouse, school, market hall, blacksmith, powder magazine (for the militia), and such amenities as a public scale, stocks and bulletin board. The land remained in its natural state, rutted and strewn with rocks, throughout the colonial era.

The transformation of useful, but unsightly, common into decorative green began in the early 19th century and is still continuing. The United States established a standing army in the war of 1812; local militias were disbanded, and with them went the need for a community training ground. The Puritan monopoly was broken and the churches of other sects were built alongside. Often the original meeting house and its burial ground were relocated. The common was cleared, fenced and bordered with elms or poplars. By 1870, notes urban designer Ronald Lee Fleming, there were two hundred village improvement societies in New England, working to plant trees and remove eyesores. As American cities became huge and polluted, the nostalgic appeal of a romanticized past took hold.

New England's greens are country cousins to the city square. Now that many have been overrun by traffic, and others have been transformed into idealized landscapes, it requires imagination to see them as embryo urban spaces. Massachusetts offers a wide choice. The greens of Harvard and Cohasset are

Harvard Green, Massachusetts: a common that has lost most of its useful functions to become an idealized landscape.

elongated rectangles, flanked by churches, civic buildings and houses, which gracefully accommodate the natural contours of the land. Salem's common, a large trapezoid dating from 1626, was renamed Washington Square to honor a visit by the first President; as part of the most recent restoration its name has been changed to The Green. Lexington's triangular Green is venerated as a birthplace of the American Revolution, a photo opportunity for tourists and a civics lesson for kids, with markers to plot the route the Minutemen followed in their retreat from the Buckhead Tavern towards Boston. In shape, function and proportions, all four have the character of parks.

Smaller, regular greens have a more urban feel, illusory though this may be. The Moravian Church Square in Lititz, Pennsylvania, is tidily framed by school, clapboard church and houses on three sides, and by the shopping street that runs down the fourth. The Green in New Castle, first capital of Delaware, was laid out in 1651 by Peter Stuyvesant, who came as a settler from New Amsterdam. It comprises a two-block grassy rectangle that extends from the Immanuel Church, with its walled graveyard, and Academy (now the parish house) at one end, to the Old Court House and Old Town Hall at the other, with an inn between them. These white clapboard and brick public buildings anchor the space, which is nicely enclosed by unbroken rows of 18th- and 19th-century houses down the long sides.

A resident, sweeping leaves, conceded that "Not too many people use it now, just the old timers who sit here. Of course, there's the Easter Parade, weddings and an art fair in the summer. It's not been the same since they took down the fence that kept the cattle in." "When was that?" "Oh, about 150 years ago."

In Puritan New England, the meeting house and later the churches were the prime focus. In Quaker Pennsylvania, the South, and later the Midwest, the courthouse often took center stage. According to Edward T. Price, new settlements often set aside space for a courthouse in the hope of becoming county seats. If they failed in their bid, the space was usually built over or abandoned; if they succeeded, the courthouse was built at the center of the vacant block, like the town hall in medieval Poland. The square became a container, framing the town's most significant building, which housed the town clerk, record office and jail, as well as judges and juries. Everyone had some business here: lawyers hung out their shingles, farmers gathered to discuss prices or buy horses, a hotel opened for out-of-towners. Other businesses followed, and there might be a weekly market. Through its 19th-century heyday it was more than an economic hub. As Spiro Kostof remarks in *America by Design*, the square was "political territory. Within its confines, people knew their place and found strength in their local tradition."

The emphasis was on the building; the space around was treated as a service area; the commercial structures were strictly utilitarian. Public space had to be useful to survive in American cities, even during the colonial era. Philadelphia soon fell from grace: one of William Penn's four recreational squares was used as a burial ground, another as a brickyard, though the city restored them to their original purpose in the early 19th century. Charleston, South Carolina, built over its one and only square in 1788. Savannah, Georgia, was unique in realizing and extending its

New Castle's Green is a rectangle that links church, inn, town hall and courthouse, with brick and clapboard houses along the sides.

Salem Common on Training Day, 1808, *a painting by George Ropes that shows the New England green in its original role as a training ground for the militia and a gathering place for the community — a country cousin of the city square.*

Thomas Hart Benton's 1973 lithograph, County Politics, *which depicts the Dallas County courthouse, Buffalo, Missouri. The courthouse and its surrounding square became the social and commercial hub of the Southern and Midwestern county seats.*

119

founder's vision of a multicellular city that combines a grid plan with a network of neighborhood squares. It was the first settlement in Georgia, last of the thirteen original colonies. The visionary was James Oglethorpe, a general and philanthropist, who founded Savannah in 1733 to provide a new start for debtors and other unfortunates. What inspired the distinctive plan? Historians such as J.W. Reps have cited sources as varied as Palmanova, English colonial towns in northern Ireland, and Sir Robert Montgomery's unrealized project of 1717 for the Margravate of Azilia — which was to have been located in what became Georgia. All have patterns of small squares, but none matches what Edmund Bacon has called "one of the finest diagrams for city organization and growth in existence."

The original plan comprised four wards, each laid out around a square, 315 × 270 feet, which served as a marketplace and as a haven for people and animals in the event of attack by Indians or by the Spanish from Florida. Four trust lots on the east and west sides were reserved for public buildings. Construction began as soon as the forest had been cleared, though the first buildings were crudely built wooden houses that were destroyed by fire in 1796. The peace of 1815 brought prosperity and improved construction. Squares were fenced and planted with Bermuda grass. Merchant princes built houses of brick and stone; the trust lots filled out with churches and banks, academies and civic buildings. By 1856, the original four squares had grown to twenty-four. Then came the Civil War. Sherman's troops camped in the squares and spared the town; the cotton trade revived, but the town never recovered its momentum.

Post-war expansion ignored the old plan, and the squares grew shabby from neglect. Unsightly buildings were added, gardens vanished and classic houses were pillaged for their gray bricks. The Historic Savannah Foundation was founded in

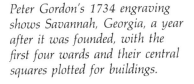

Peter Gordon's 1734 engraving shows Savannah, Georgia, a year after it was founded, with the first four wards and their central squares plotted for buildings.

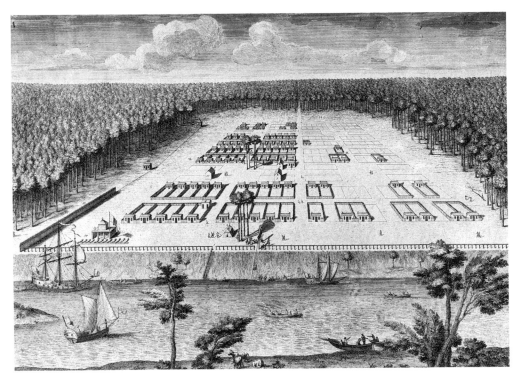

1954 and has served as a catalyst in the restoration of buildings and squares throughout the old town. With the support of the Lane Foundation and concerned citizens, it has won over the business community and civic authorities, and has mastered an even greater challenge: to restore and upgrade without creating a ghetto of affluence.

As Charles Mackay observed in 1857: "If four-and-twenty villages had resolved to hold a meeting and had assembled at this place, each with its pump, its country church, its common and its avenue of trees, the result would have been a facsimile of Savannah." Twenty of the squares survive; shady, sun-dappled oases planted with wisteria, azalea and dogwood, magnolia and Pride of India trees. Spanish moss cascades from live oaks. The foliage blocks out such eyesores as the De Soto Hilton, but allows glimpses of brick and wood siding, tawny stucco and fretted iron, spires and colonnades.

Savannah's architecture is homely compared with the 18th-century splendors of Charleston, up the coast, but it has a pleasing diversity. The grandest prospect is from the State House, high above the Savannah River, looking south down Bull Street, which bisects the five most important squares. The brick paths within the squares are aligned with the sidewalks of the axial streets, allowing you to walk across town, north-south and east-west in an undeviating line. In doing so, you have

J.W. Hill's bird's-eye view of Savannah in 1855, looking north from Monterey Square up Bull Street to the State House.

121

the illusion that each street terminates in a green wall, for the planting is so dense that it is hard to see beyond.

Each of the five squares has its distinctive flavor. Public gatherings were held in Johnson Square, the first to be completed; in 1776, the Declaration of Liberty was read aloud there to an ecstatic crowd. Now it is a sober enclave of banks. Wright, the next square down Bull Street, has the County and State Court Houses, the Post Office, a church and a granite memorial to the Indian Chief, Tomo-chi-chi. Chippewa, named for a victory over the British, is perhaps the finest. Huge live oaks canopy Daniel Chester French's monument to Oglethorpe. The needle spire of the Unitarian Church, a half block away, complements the First Baptist Church and pedimented Chatham Academy, and several grand houses. Madison Square links a Gothic Revival church and mansion with a huge Romanesque armory, now an art school. Last and most rustic of the five is Monterey, named for a victory over the Mexicans, with its obelisk that celebrates a Polish hero of the Revolutionary War, Casimir Pulaski. Beyond is Forsyth Park; on each side of this central axis are the other squares, trim or untidy, modest or imposing.

Savannah was too remote to influence other American cities; Washington D.C. was too special. The capital of Georgia was shaped by an Englishman's vision of the ideal city, the nation's capital by a French military engineer, Pierre l'Enfant, who drew on the Baroque plan of Versailles, where he had grown up. His diagonal axes, broad vistas and traffic circles were anticipated in the plans for Annapolis, the capital of Maryland, and Williamsburg, the early capital of Virginia, both developed in the 1690s by their English Governor, Francis Nicholson. St Mary's City, Maryland's short-lived first capital, had been laid out on Baroque lines in the 1660s.

But these were provincial in scale: L'Enfant's plan of 1791 for the fledgling democracy was so grand that it would not be fleshed out for another century. According to J.W. Reps, L'Enfant intended that there should be fifteen squares, each to be built and adorned by a different state. As built, the squares and circles are overwhelmed by the thrust of the great avenues, so that Washington is a city of prospects, not enclosures. Lafayette Square, the parklike forecourt to the White House, is the one notable exception.

The older Eastern cities were inspired by more traditional models. In Boston, Louisburg Square is as tightly enclosed and as restrained as any Georgian enclave in London. Built in 1834–48, it is the epitome of the Beacon Hill neighborhood above the Common — dignified and varied brick row houses, enclosing a private railed garden with statues of Columbus and Aristides at each end. The streets are cobbled, the brick sidewalks have high granite curbs, and the original gas lamps have been retained. The houses are higher to the west; some have curved bays, others are flat, but they form a single harmonious composition. The garden is more a symbol of privacy than an amenity for residents; it is too narrow and exposed to offer the sanctum of Bedford Square, but the residents have fiercely defended their property rights since they formed America's first homeowners' association around 1850. Another tradition, which everyone can enjoy, is the caroling and bell-ringing on Christmas Eve.

In Baltimore, the Washington Monument (1812–42) marks the intersection of

Unitarian Church and Chatham Academy on Chippewa Square, Savannah. In each of the 24 squares that were laid out before 1856, the lots on the short east and west sides were originally reserved for public buildings.

Louisburg Square, Boston. Christmas Eve is celebrated with caroling and bell-ringing.

The square's sober brick row houses and private railed garden epitomize the dignity of Boston's Beacon Hill neighborhood.

123

Washington Place and Monument, Baltimore: a lithograph of 1850. Two elongated squares intersect at the hill-top column.

two elongated squares. Mount Vernon is a quiet preserve of mid-19th-century houses, running along the ridge of a hill above the harbor. Washington Place runs up and down the hill along the cross axis of Charles Street, and is framed by the Peabody Institute and adjoining School of Music, and the Walters Art Gallery, as well as an aggressively neo-Gothic, green stone Methodist church. Washington looks down from his marble column on a wonderfully inventive urban ensemble, whose dignity survives the assault of through traffic.

Only the toughest survive in New York, and its downtown squares have endured a battering that few urban spaces could withstand. Squeezing the last buck from a restricted site has been the guiding principle since the first Dutch settlers ditched the plan they had been sent from Holland, and improvised their own chaotic but profitable New Amsterdam. After the British took over and the city expanded beyond its wall, each generation of society moved higher up the island of Manhattan to stay ahead of the rot. Their path and that of the builders was made more predictable by the Commissioners' Plan of 1811, which imposed an unvarying geometrical grid of streets on a still green and hilly island. Only Broadway escaped the Commissioners' straitjacket to meander on its ancient path. Most of the city's squares north of 14th Street — the true, and impostors like Herald and Times Squares — are strung along its course.

All date from the first half of the 19th century. Washington Square was laid out in the 1820s on the site of a potter's field and gallows as a public park and parade ground. Handsome row houses of the 1830s survive along the north side (Henry James wrote *Washington Square* while living at No. 1). New York University was established in the same decade and has since vandalized the remaining sides with ugly, overscaled buildings. The square is the agora of Greenwich Village, a mirror of its cultural and ethnic diversity, and a microcosm of New York. Staggering under the intensity and violence of its use, it provides an unsightly but essential civic amenity — a place to celebrate and protest, skate and exercise your dog, listen to music in the central amphitheater or sprawl on the grass, jog and exchange gossip. All these activities — and many that are less socially acceptable — can be observed all at once on any fine Sunday afternoon. And the human vitality is matched by one of New York's most stirring vistas: the view through the 1892 Memorial Arch up Fifth Avenue. Arrow-straight it runs, seven miles north to the Harlem River, bisecting another neighborhood square, Marcus Garvey Park, at 120th Street.

Off Lexington Avenue, at 17th Street, is Gramercy Park, roughly contemporary with Washington Square, which has kept its exclusivity and its locked private garden. Union Square, at 14th and Broadway, appears equally genteel in a lithograph of 1849. There is a fenced garden with lawns and a fountain, private carriages, a church and solidly built houses. Twenty years before, it had been a crossing of muddy tracks; twenty years later it would be invaded by crowds and commerce. A print of 1882 depicts a "Grand Demonstration of Workingmen", and from then on it would be a symbol of radical politics, home to the *Daily Worker* and activists of every kind; the scene of May Day rallies, protests against the execution of Sacco and Vanzetti, and Depression-era confrontations. Only the name stayed the same: Union referred to a road junction, not organized labor. As its character changed, from refined to raffish, the buildings kept pace. By 1882, its houses had all been replaced, by a theater, a hotel, and restaurants; the German Savings Bank and *New York Mirror*; a theatrical costumier and a plumber. The sidewalks were jammed, the road full of brewers' drays and omnibuses. By 1919, it had become what Herald and Times Squares have always been: a glorified traffic intersection, lacking any coherence or sense of enclosure, a jumble of unrelated buildings and straggly turf.

In his *Travels in New York and New England* of 1821, Timothy Dwight, the President of Yale, complained: "It is remarkable that the scheme of forming public squares, so beautiful, and in great towns so conducive to health, should have been almost universally forgotten. Nothing is so cheerful, so delightful or so susceptible of the combined elegance of nature and art." And the landscape historian J.B. Jackson has observed that, in the 19th century, communal activity was in decline and the square was losing much of its prestige. Increasingly, as city plans were stripped of all frills and became uninterrupted grids, the public demanded not squares but parks, an escape from the urban jungle.

Lower Manhattan from Union Square, a lithograph drawn by C. Bachmann, c. 1849. As New Yorkers began to move north, the square became a bustling commercial center and a forum for radical demonstrations.

Romantically landscaped cemeteries and, later, the great civic parks of New York, Chicago and San Francisco, were popular for their informality; as Jackson notes, you didn't have to dress up or put on airs to go: "It was public space of a novel kind . . . and represented the rejection of structure, the rejection of classical urbanism with its historical allusions, and the rejection of architectural public space." The American people in the 19th century associated beauty with morality, and Frederick Law Olmsted, the greatest and most influential landscape architect of his day, advocated scenic recreations of nature for "their harmonizing and refining influence upon the most unfortunate and lawless classes of the city — an influence favorable to courtesy, self-control and temperance." And Jackson points out that city squares were increasingly treated as parks, "with little or no relationship to their urban surroundings." It is no wonder that the city square, squeezed between the grid and the park, private greed and public need, became an endangered species in the United States.

Union Square from the south in 1919. Most American big city squares lost their original European character through unco-ordinated and overscaled development.

With Rome as their model, early
17th-century rulers of Salzburg,
Austria, laid out three expansive
squares to flank a new cathedral
and Residence, shouldering aside
the old burgher town.

128

Urban Theater

SALZBURG, best-known today as the city of Mozart and *The Sound of Music*, once aspired to be the Rome of the North, and the three squares that frame the cathedral have a touch of papal grandeur. The city had been ruled since its foundation in 682 by prince-archbishops, whose temporal power extended to Italy in the Middle Ages. Salt mines brought them wealth; the Hohensalzburg fortress gave them security. Between castle and river lay the tight-packed medieval town. Three rulers transformed it into a Renaissance showcase.

The vision came from Wolf Dietrich von Raitenau (1587–1612), a true Renaissance man. Raised in Rome, he had twelve children by a Jewess of great beauty for whom he built Schloss Mirabell. He spent his last years imprisoned in the family fortress, under sentence from the Court of Rome. Despite (or, perhaps, because of) his worldly appetites, he commissioned Scamozzi to replace the fire-ravaged cathedral with one that would outshine St Peter's, and on an adjoining site he began to build a new Residence.

Marcus Sitticus, his successor, began construction of a scaled-down cathedral; Paris Lodron (1619–53) completed cathedral and Residence, and laid out the squares to focus attention on these symbols of ecclesiastical and secular power. A hundred burgher houses were demolished to enlarge the site, and, as seen from the air, the expansive squares contrast sharply with the congestion of the old town. A similar pattern developed all over Europe as the influence of papal Rome and, later, Versailles, spread like the ripples from stones thrown into a pond.

Each of Salzburg's squares sets off the boldly modeled Baroque cathedral and leads the eye to the spaces beyond. Conceived as a unified composition of solid and void, in three dimensions, it brings into harmonious balance the fortress on its crag, the green hills across the river, and a succession of subordinate squares. Plain gray-stuccoed church offices seal off the Domplatz and serve as foil to the soaring west front of the cathedral, with its statues of saints, and the Rococo Virgin column. During the summer festival, Hugo von Hofmannsthal's *Everyman* is performed on an open stage, a tradition that begins with Max Reinhardt's productions in the 1920s. Corner loggias link the space with the flanking squares.

The Kapitelplatz is a loose, open square to the south of the cathedral, dominated by the Hohensalzburg, 400 feet above. Carriages still roll past the Neptune fountain,

129

formerly a horse trough. Most expansive and lighthearted of the three is the Residenzplatz (once a cemetery), which sets off the cathedral, the Residence, the toy pink church of St Michael's and the New Building with its glockenspiel. Carriages wait for hire beside the fountain, a wedding cake of sculptured rocks, prancing horses, and writhing titans, crowned by a Triton blowing a shell. Leading off to one side is the Mozartplatz, with its statue of the composer, benches and cafés; on the other, a street leads into the narrow, medieval Alter Markt, with its froth of pink-and-green Rococo façades. Thus, in a few steps, the visitor moves through nine hundred years of history, and a beguiling sequence of urban spaces.

Salzburg's squares, for all their splendor, represent a modestly scaled transition from the quiet balance and enclosure of the Renaissance to the kinetic energy and spatial flow of the Baroque. Rome was the fountainhead of large-scale urban planning and the dynamic squares it embraced. Popes took the bold steps that were needed to revive a ruined city. The Counter Reformation of the 16th century borrowed from the theater, creating elaborate stage sets in its temples and public places, to dazzle believers and win over sceptics. Scale, sumptuous ornament and illusion were combined to make a direct appeal to the emotions. Religious ecstasy and worldly pomp infused the work of architects, painters and sculptors.

Michelangelo was all three, and a deeply religious man, but the Piazza del Campidoglio appeals to the intellect more than to the emotions, and its inspiration was political rather than religious. The project took over a hundred years to complete. It began in 1536, with a commission from Paul III to create a worthy setting for the Emperor Charles V, who had resolved to crown his victory over the Turks in Tunisia with a Roman triumph. The city was still recovering from the assault of Imperial troops ten years before, and time permitted only cosmetic improvements.

The Hohensalzburg, a fortress begun in 1077, dominates the Kapitelplatz to the south of the cathedral.

Looking across Salzburg's Residenzplatz, past St Michael's, the fountain and glockenspiel, to the Mozartplatz.

Beyond the temporary decor lay a muddy hill and two crumbling medieval buildings occupying the site of the first fortress of ancient Rome, and the sanctuary where victorious generals made their offerings to the gods. In 1143, Romans met here to revive the Senate and to protest the misgovernment of the Pope; in 1341 Petrarch was crowned poet laureate; Cola di Rienzi was killed on the slope in 1354 after failing in his bid to revive the Roman Empire. Michelangelo's plan, modified and completed by Giacomo della Porta and Girolamo Rainaldi in 1640, manipulated the topography and existing buildings to create a wholly original work of art, a stage for ceremony and a symbolic link to the ruins of the Forum below.

First he installed, as a pivot for the whole composition, the equestrian bronze of Marcus Aurelius, one of the greatest statues of antiquity, once thought to represent the Christian Emperor Constantine and thus spared from destruction by zealots. The Senate was reconstructed with a tower, steps and a fountain; the Palazzo Nuovo was built to screen the medieval church of Santa Maria d'Aracoeli and balance the refaced Palazzo dei Conservatori. By following the lines of the existing buildings, Michelangelo created a trapezoid piazza, similar in plan to that of Pienza. But the effect is entirely different. Pienza's square is tiny, static and contained; it can be understood from a single vantage point. The Campidoglio reveals itself only as you move through and around it.

Two contrasting staircases lead up from the street below. That of the Aracoeli was built in 1348 to mark deliverance from the plague; its steep treads recall "the medieval concept of life as a weary pilgrimage, leading ultimately to heaven", in Georgina Masson's phrase. The *cordonata*, Michelangelo's stair to the piazza, is broad and shallow, a ceremonial ascent for a mounted Emperor to greet his ancient

Bernardo Bellotto's painting of the Campidoglio in the 18th century dramatizes the contrast between the steep medieval steps of the Aracoeli and the broad, shallow Cordonata, leading up to the statue of Marcus Aurelius and the Roman Senate.

131

The pivot of the Campidoglio was the statue of Marcus Aurelius, one of the greatest to have survived from classical antiquity, which was removed in 1980 because of polluted air.

The multiple perspective sketch by J.H. Aronson shows the new palace which was designed by Michelangelo to fill the left side of the open space, thereby screening the medieval Aracoeli church and creating a trapezoid piazza.

Looking into the Campidoglio from the ramp that leads down, past the Senate, to the ruins of the Roman Forum.

counterpart. The steps and tower of the Senate lead the eye on and up, and abruptly terminate the vista. The piazza is a battleground of contesting forces. Within the trapezoid is an oval pavement inlaid with a twelve-pointed star of black and white marble (reinstalled as recently as 1940), a kaleidoscopic image that fragments and reunites the separate elements. The pavement is domed to suggest the crest of the hill, and the travertine steps are sharply cut away (you might say, carved) to each side of the Senate. Everything seems to be in motion. This is the smallest of Rome's principal squares (237 feet deep, 126–180 feet wide), but the most energized.

At the time of writing, Marcus Aurelius is in protective custody, a victim of polluted air. Forty years of progress have done greater damage than the wars and neglect of nineteen centuries. But that is the only flaw. Uncluttered by cars (stout chains keep even senators at bay), mercifully free of the punks and graffiti that have invaded other Roman squares, the piazza is a breathtaking spectacle, despite its empty pedestal. Every form and space, shift of level or direction speaks of genius. Above the Palazzo Nuovo (a museum like its twin) rear the bronze chariots of the Victor Emmanuel Monument, to remind us of the visual chaos beyond and the traffic snarls of the Piazza Venezia, which demonstrate the bankruptcy of urban planning over the past hundred years.

But it is easy to shut it out and relive the past. At Christmas, shepherds come down from the hills to play their bagpipes on the steps of the Aracoeli before midnight mass. On any night in summer, you can walk a few steps beyond the Senate and look out over the floodlit ruins of the Forum, a prospect that stirred the humanists of the Renaissance. Georgina Masson evokes "the blood-soaked memories of medieval Rome, when the present piazza was used as a market and a place of execution. On a winter night, when a freezing *tramontana* whistles through its colonnades, it is somehow easier to imagine the hill as it then was, with the fortress of the Corsi huddled among the ancient ruins, and wolves fighting in the streets below . . ."

No Pope so decisively improved Rome as Sixtus V (1585–90), who employed ancient obelisks to define axial vistas and piazzas that would be completed long after his death. The obelisk he ordered to be erected in the irregular space before the unfinished basilica of St Peter's had been brought to Rome by Caligula. In the Middle Ages it was believed that it marked the center of Nero's Circus and that it had supported a golden urn containing the ashes of Julius Caesar. It took four months, 900 men and 140 horses to move the monolith, and as it was being winched upright the ropes began to sag. A sailor from Bordighera defied the papal edict of silence to shout, "put water on the ropes", knowing this would cause them to tauten and avert disaster. The marker was in place, but the site was still a building yard.

It took 120 years to rebuild St Peter's over the foundations of Constantine's 4th-century basilica. Bramante had begun the job in 1506, intending a symmetrical Greek-cross plan with a shallow dome, framed by a colonnaded piazza, a centralized Renaissance concept he tried out in miniature in the circular Tempietto, which marks the spot on the Janiculum where St Peter is supposed to have been crucified. Over the next century, the program changed to a high-domed, long-naved church, designed by Michelangelo and Carlo Maderno.

By contrast, the Piazza di San Pietro was built in three years by one man: Gianlorenzo Bernini, the most acclaimed architect and sculptor of 17th-century Rome. One of his first commissions was the great baldacchino beneath the dome of St Peter's. In 1655, Alexander VII asked him to transform the irregular space before the basilica into an appropriate setting for the crowds of pilgrims attending papal blessings, and to unify the church and the uncoordinated buildings of the Vatican. Bernini designed columned loggias (as severe as the baldacchino was flamboyant) to enclose a stepped trapezoid as an entrance forecourt to St Peter's, and branch out in two great hemicycles. To complete the enclosure, he planned a columned, semicircular vestibule that would have screened the piazza from the approach road. Tragically, this was never built, and the narrow medieval streets, which achieved a similar effect of enclosure, were demolished in 1940 to create the Via della Conciliazione. So the container gapes open, and the element of surprise is lost.

In every other way, Bernini realized his vision, two hundred years after Pope Nicholas V had sought to strengthen the authority of the church "with the confirmation of grandiose buildings." The piazza inspires awe, but it also reaches out, in an embrace as wide as that of mother church. With masterly skill, the architect has created an amphitheater in which the pavement slopes down towards the center, allowing everyone a clear view over the heads of the crowd as the pope circulates to give his blessing. Reason and emotion are united in the plan. Two round slabs mark the centers of the two interlocking circles of the piazza; from these points the quadruple ranks of columns in the loggias are perfectly aligned. This is a moment of arrest, on the cross axis of obelisk and fountains, where you can best appreciate the amplitude of the space, 588 feet wide and 426 feet deep. Its grandeur has been much imitated — the neo-classical Piazza Plebiscito in Naples borrows one of its semicircular colonnades — but never matched.

Between 1655 and 1657, Bernini created twin loggias to frame St Peter's and embrace the crowds of pilgrims (opposite). He also planned a vestibule to complete the enclosure, but this was never built.

The four ranks of columns that surround the Piazza di San Pietro are scaled to the façade of St Peter's; the grandeur of this colonnade has been much imitated, but never matched.

The Piazza di San Pietro as it appeared (right) in a late 16th-century fresco in the Vatican. The obelisk, set up in 1586, dominates an unimproved space and a half-built basilica.

Bernini had earlier contributed to the improvement of Rome's oldest enclosed space, the Piazza Navona, which derives its name and elongated form from the Circus Agonalis, a stadium built by Domitian in AD 81–96. The galleries were walled up with houses (as in the amphitheater of Lucca), but the populace watched jousts from the ancient benches as late as 1450. After that, the city market was moved here from the foot of the Capitoline Hill and the surface was paved to create a public square. Inns and eating houses were built over the surviving seats. The Pamphilj family built their palace in the piazza and in 1645 a descendant, Pope Innocent X, began its transformation. Within twenty years it had become the most picturesque square in Rome, a fashionable place to live and promenade.

The renovation of central Rome was made possible by the restoration of ancient aqueducts. Innocent brought water to the Piazza Navona, and Bernini channeled it through the Fountain of the Four Rivers (1648–51). Reputedly he stole the commission from his rival, Francesco Borromini, by bribing the pope's sister with a solid silver model of his design. Construction was financed by a tax on bread, which produced a public outcry. But the end justified the means. A broken obelisk, brought from the Appian Way, defines the center of the elongated square; Bernini's sculptured rocks and allegorical figures – of the Nile (Africa), Ganges (Asia), Danube (Europe) and Plate (America) – animate the entire space. The architect added the figure of a Moor (supposedly based on his sketch of an ambassador from the Congo) to the existing fountain at the south end. The Neptune fountain at the north end was added in 1878.

Anonymous print of the Piazza Navona, c. 1630. It occupies the site of an ancient Roman stadium, which was built up in the late 15th century and used as a market.

Balancing the central fountain is the church of Sant'Agnese in Agone, built over the site of her martyrdom in a Roman brothel. Borromini had to share the credits with lesser architects, but he put his stamp on the façade, a marvelously sophisticated interplay of dome and open lanterns above a concave central bay, sharply chiseled moldings, cartouches and swags. Borromini also designed the interior of Carlo Rainaldi's new Pamphilj Palace, which is now the Brazilian Embassy.

The piazza became a set for the pageantry of Baroque Rome. In August, it was flooded to a depth of two feet, and carriages drove around to the sound of music on the very site of the mock sea battles fought in the ancient circus. The square was elaborately decorated for fiestas and special celebrations. A modest survival of these customs is the Christmas fair, with its stalls selling toys, nativity figures and sandwiches of roast pork. Those who complain that it has become seedy and overrun with riffraff should remember that Rome was never as well-groomed as it appears in historic prints. Tobias Smollett declared, in his *Travels through France and Italy* (1765): "The noble Piazza Navona is adorned with three or four fountains, one of which is perhaps the most magnificent in Europe [but] the piazza is almost as dirty as West Smithfield, where the cattle are sold in London."

Early morning is a good time for a visit. The sun brings the fountains to life, one after the other, and imparts a glow to the faded ochre façades. Their flat painterly surfaces suggest old frescoes; the rich colors set off the gleaming travertine and sculptural fireworks of church and fountains. So dramatic is the dialogue between Bernini and Borromini (who never spoke to each other in life) that everyone is drawn to the center and hardly notices that the piazza is an extended corridor which defies conventional rules of proportion. From each end the space seems foreshortened and comfortably balanced. Whenever it's time for a pause, there is a café or a stone bench. Nine narrow streets draw in life from the neighborhood without disturbing the sense of enclosure. Cars have long been officially excluded.

Nine narrow streets feed into the Piazza Navona without disturbing the sense of enclosure: detail from Giambattista Nolli's plan of Rome, 1748.

Piazza Navona, Flooded, Giovanni-Paolo Pannini, 1756. As late as the 19th century, the piazza was transformed into a shallow lake on summer weekends for carriage parades and water jousts.

The elongated Piazza Navona (above) is given a central focus by Bernini's Fountain of the Four Rivers.

Cars park where actors should strut in the Piazza di San Ignazio (right), Rome's most appealing small square.

Barcaccia fountain and the Spanish Steps from the Via Condotti: one of Rome's most theatrical vistas.

Surprise is the Trevi Fountain's greatest asset: you hear the gushing of water and glimpse the rocks (below left) before it bursts upon you, filling its tiny piazza (below right) with an exuberance of sound and sculptural form.

139

Piranesi's engraving of the Piazza di Spagna in the mid-18th century. The steps have been described as "a petrification of the dancing rhythm of a period of gallantry".

The same sense of theater infuses the Piazza di Spagna and the steps that lead up to the church of Trinità dei Monti. To emerge into the piazza from the Via Condotti on a fine Sunday afternoon is as overwhelming an experience as straying onto the stage of La Scala halfway through a Verdi opera. You don't have to perform, and you may not be applauded, but the light is as dazzling, the tiers as jammed. In the foreground is the Barcaccia fountain, a marble barge designed in 1629 to make effective use of the low water pressure. It may have been inspired by the discovery of a Roman boat fountain, or by the memory of a ship that was beached here in 1598 during a flood of the Tiber. Beyond are flower stalls and the Spanish Steps, which dance up the hill in three great leaps to the church and its obelisk. To the left, leading out of the wedge-shaped piazza, the Via del Babuino runs arrow-straight to another obelisk, at the center of the Piazza del Popolo. It's hard not to burst into song.

Until the early 18th century, only a rustic path led up the hill. Spain had its embassy here, but the church was founded (in 1495) by Charles VIII of France, and it was a French Ambassador who paid for the steps. Francesco de Sanctis's plan met four conditions: the stairs could be seen as a unity, their tripartite division alluded to the Trinity, they were suitable for strolling and festive events; last, they provided efficient drainage. Michelangelo's *cordonata* was merely an overture to his piazza; the Spanish Steps (officially, the Scalinata della Trinità dei Monti) are the main event, a concourse in three dimensions.

They were built 1723–26, and quickly became a draw for tourists and expatriates. Visitors included Stendhal, Balzac and Wagner, romantic poets and milords on the Grand Tour. In the 18th century the area around was known as the "English ghetto", and the Via delle Carrozze was named for the travelling coaches that were brought there for repairs. It was Rome's chief hotel district before the Via Veneto was opened up in 1870. Relics of that era include the Caffè Greco and Babington's Tea Room; the house where John Keats died at the age of 25 is now the Keats-Shelley Memorial.

Long vanished are the artists' models in colorful country attire whom Charles Dickens observed, seeking work from artists whose studios were close by in the Via Margutta. Poets and painters have been priced out of the neighborhood, but it remains a great pick-up place for the young. In *Experiencing Architecture*, Steen Eiler Rasmussen describes the Scalinata as the embodiment of the 1720s, "a petrification of the dancing rhythm of a period of gallantry." He imagines ladies in farthingales and men in silk breeches doing a Polonaise up the steps: advancing, separating, meeting again on a landing to bow and curtsey, and continuing until they could turn and look back over the city from the topmost terrace.

If the Spanish Steps make you feel like dancing, the Piazza di San Ignazio is a place to watch 18th-century opera — Mozart's *Così fan tutte* would be ideal. Filippo Raguzzini, one of the most spirited and inventive of Rococo architects, designed this miniature masterpiece in 1727, across from the outwardly severe, inwardly opulent 17th-century Jesuit church of San Ignazio de Loyola. In a witty gesture that can best be appreciated in Nolli's classic map of Rome, the architect echoed the plan of the church apse in his piazza, thus extending the interior into the street. And he aligned his four-storey blocks with the cornice of the church.

A detail of Nolli's plan of Rome shows how the Piazza di San Ignazio mirrors the plan of the church it fronts.

In spirit, they could not be more dissimilar: sacred faces secular, a solemn monument confronts shifting perspectives and a delicious interplay of light and space. The shuttered façades of faded stucco are set off by scallop-shell moldings. You half expect to see performers making their entry through the wings on each side, but, alas, only cars thread in, vainly seeking a parking place. Lovers might serenade a beauty at her balcony, except that the building houses the carabinieri. Even the corner trattoria is a let-down. Rome is steadily reclaiming its heritage from the scourge of traffic; this enchanting piazza must surely be rescued soon.

The Trevi Fountain never disappoints. If San Ignazio suggests Mozart, this is Puccini: larger than life, unrelentingly dramatic, with tunes everyone can hum. Who has not tossed a coin in the hope of returning? And who does not remember the classic scene from Fellini's *La Dolce Vita*, in which Marcello Mastroianni and Anita Ekberg wade in just before the fountain is turned off for the night?

Alberti designed the first simple fountain, drawing on the water from an ancient aqueduct, restored by Pope Martin V in 1447. Its bowl was used for washing wool, but the water was considered the sweetest in the city, and in later years English residents bottled it for making tea. The Piazza di Trevi acquired its name from the meeting of three streets, *tre vie*. Not until 1732 was Nicolò Salvi selected to design the present fountain, and he died before it was completed in 1762. His design drew on a sketch by Bernini of Neptune drawn by seahorses, but he went much further in creating what James Lees-Milne has called, in *Roman Mornings*, "a palace dissolving into a fountain." It is liquid architecture. Water is used, as mirrors were in Rococo interiors, to create shifting patterns, to transform solids into shimmering illusions.

Surprise is the Trevi's greatest asset. Walking along a narrow street, you hear the gushing of water, glimpse rocks spilling down onto the sidewalk, and suddenly you are in the tiny plaza and the fountain overwhelms you with its exuberance of shape and sound. Steps wrap like bleachers around the basin; brown and yellow façades wall the space; set back in a corner is the tightly compressed Baroque façade of SS Vicenzo e Anastasia. A misguided early-19th-century plan by Giuseppe Valadier to double the size of the piazza was mercifully abandoned.

Throughout the 18th century, European cities competed to build squares as they had once vied in the construction of medieval cathedrals. The Rococo piazze of Rome were too playful to inspire imitators; a preferred model was the French *place royale* — for its adaptibility and its prestigious associations with the supreme monarch of Europe. The most inventive adaptation of the form was achieved by a Polish king in Nancy, the capital of Lorraine.

Stanislas Leszczynski (1677–1766) fought three times to regain his Polish crown, but had to settle for the lesser title of Duke of Lorraine, which he acquired from France in 1737 after his daughter had married Louis XV. As Wolfgang Braunfels has pointed out, Nancy became the physical expression of Stanislas's ambitions, the counterpart of Dresden, which was enriched by his rival, Augustus the Strong. He was propelled to make a mark by the fact that he was only a leaseholder; Lorraine would revert to France on his death. To assert his independence of Paris, Stanislas employed a local architect, Emmanuel Héré de Corny, to create new monuments within the medieval and Renaissance walled towns that comprised his capital. Not until 1753 did Héré begin his masterpiece, the sequence of three spaces that link the old and new towns. Closely supervised by the aging Duke, he completed the project by 1760.

Héré skilfully exploited existing features. The Place Royale, honoring Louis XV, was located on open space at the edge of the new town. A new Hôtel de Ville occupied its south side; on each side were matching blocks containing the customs house (now a hotel), an academy of music (now a theater), and two mansions, which today house a museum and offices. Along the north side he built a low range which still comprises cafés and shops.

Axial streets feed into the grid, linking square and city. The principal axis runs north, bridging the former moat, passing under an arch that marks the original line of fortification, and into the elongated rectangle of the Carrière. This was a broad medieval *place*, formerly used for tournaments, which now became a fashionable parade, flanked by law courts and the stock exchange. Edmund Bacon has noted that its newest house, the Hôtel de Beauvau-Craon of 1715, provided the architectural model for the Place Royale; Héré simply enlarged the scale and added a rooftop balustrade with urns and sculptures.

Gilded wrought-iron arches frame the corners of the Place Stanislas in the north-eastern French city of Nancy. The square was commissioned by Stanislas Leszczynski, who was Duke of Lorraine before that territory was annexed by France.

A plan showing the sequence of three spaces — the Place Stanislas (1), the Carrière promenade (2) and what is now the Place Général de Gaulle (3) — which were laid out in the 1750s to link the old and new towns of Nancy.

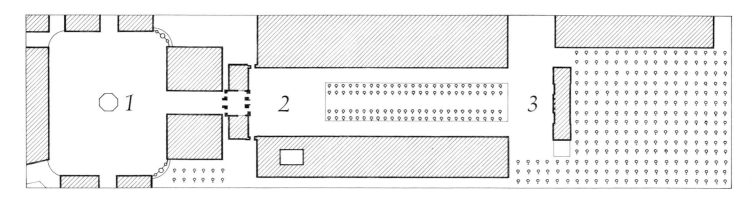

The vista is terminated by colonnaded hemicycles, now the Place Général de Gaulle, which screen out the irregular old town and a park. It frames the Palace of Government, built for Louis's representative on the site of the old ducal palace. Thus, at each end of the sequence are symbols of royal and civic authority, while everything between pays tribute to the generosity and enlightenment of "Stanislas the Benefactor" as he is now celebrated on the statue that replaced the effigy of the king, at the center of the square which has been renamed for him.

The irreverent British cleric Sydney Smith cited a friend's definition of heaven as "eating *pâtés de foie gras* to the sound of trumpets." Evidently he had never seen the Place Stanislas lit up on a summer's night. The buildings alone would be reason enough to come, but the gilded ironwork of Jean Lamour is a greater marvel. Gates and lanterns frame the streets on both sides of the Hôtel de Ville; at the far corners, golden screens arch over allegorical fountains. The square is a stage with wrap-around decor, as fanciful and delicate as the setting for a royal masque. All the elements, light and grave, combine to achieve a dizzying splendor: the crown-

The theatrical aspect of the Place Stanislas.

capped lamp standards, wrapped in spirals of gold leaves; the elegant wall brackets and balconies; the posturing water deities; and the uniform façades crowned with putti and trophies. Lamour's Rococo flourishes lift Héré's sober classicism into the realm of fantasy.

Morning light underscores the harmony of proportion and delicacy of ornament. The froth of gold seems as improbable as fairy treasure. A white stone grid frames the expanse of cobbles. The rooftop statues are jaggedly silhouetted against the rising sun. Victor Hugo called the Place Stanislas "the gayest, prettiest and most complete of any Rococo square I have ever seen . . . a marquise of a square." The spectacle of night becomes, by day, a spatial adventure. To walk out of the square and through the triumphal arch, to glimpse the graveled promenade of the Carrière beyond Lamour's iron tracery, and to emerge into the sweeping colonnade of the hemicycles, is to experience again the suspended animation and dramatic revelations of Roman Baroque.

Contemporary French squares were sober by comparison. Bordeaux's Place Royale (now the Place de la Bourse) was designed by Jacques Gabriel in 1729, and completed in 1754 by his son Jacques-Ange in elegant but severe classical style. It is a waterfront square: a shallow rectangle with champfered corners, facing out over the Garonne. An equestrian statue of Louis XV was the focus of the streets that converged from the rear, on both sides of a detached pavilion — a riverfront balustrade defined the fourth side.

Engraving of the Praça do Commércio, the waterfront square in Lisbon, as it was originally designed following the earthquake of 1755.

The buildings survive; the square has been emasculated. Cars compete for space with municipal shrubberies, a hideous fountain has replaced the statue, a broad highway has obliterated the waterfront enclosure. The intended spirit of Bordeaux's forecourt survives better in the square it inspired: Lisbon's Praça do Commércio.

The Portuguese capital was devastated by earthquake and tidal wave on November 1st, 1755. There was an urgent need to restore the city that was still the hub of an empire extending from Brazil to Macao. The king gave his chief minister, the Marquis de Pombal, absolute authority over the rebuilding, and he commissioned a grid plan to replace a tangle of medieval lanes in the city center. As a flourishing port, Lisbon had already opened up its waterfront, and the new square was located on what had been the forecourt of the royal palace, the Terreiro do Paço, a name that is still used. Commerce usurped royalty: customs house, post office and city hall occupied the three porticoed blocks and the handsome waterfront pavilions. Today, much of the space has been taken over by government ministries.

The equestrian bronze of José I in the Praça do Commércio.

A 17th-century painting by Dirk Stoop shows that the principal architect, Santos de Carvalho, took his cue from the royal palace as it appeared before the earthquake, much as Héré cloned a house to create a square in Nancy. A contemporary painting shows that he planned to add faceted domes to the corner pavilions, trophies along the parapet, and a graceful arch over the Rua Augusta—the main street entrance. All these refinements were dropped, probably for reasons of economy, and the present triumphal arch was not built until 1873.

The focus of the square is Machado de Castro's equestrian bronze of José I, the king who oversaw the restoration of Lisbon. Erected in 1775, it is set high and well forward to dominate the view from the Tagus. Sacheverell Sitwell acclaimed it as the most beautiful equestrian statue of its time, a "Roman Emperor of the Riding School", recalling José's links with the Habsburgs, his love of Italian masques, and the golden coaches that were the glory of his court. The English used to call the Praça "Black Horse Square"; now the statue and its railing have weathered to green.

The square, originally unpaved, is bordered by a tesselated sidewalk; for a time it was planted with trees, but these have been removed to create a car park. The broad stone steps down to the river survive, though the ferries now tie up to jetties away from this central landing. The cars can and must be eliminated, but the space is too grand to be spoilt by such temporary annoyances.

On a stormy day—and Lisbon has more than its share—when the clouds billow in from the Atlantic, when sun alternates with showers and a silvery light is reflected off the Tagus, the square comes alive. If one approaches down the Rua Augusta, the arch frames the statue. From the shadow-barred arcades, beyond the toy trams, the white stone seems like crystallized foam, and as you walk towards the quay and glance up, Dom José seems to be riding along with the scudding clouds.

Only fragments survive from the second of Pombal's squares, the Praça de Dom Pedro IV, popularly known as the Rossio. A late-19th-century print shows a tree-bordered expanse of wave-patterned mosaic paving. Fountains flank a central column, and the long rectangle is surrounded by uniform houses leading up to the National Theater. All but the theater have been replaced by shabby commercial structures; the pavement was carved up in 1950 to improve traffic circulation.

Plan of Amalienborg Square and its surroundings.

Opposite: statue of Frederik V and one of four identical houses in Amalienborg Square, Copenhagen, which have served as royal palaces for 200 years. The square was designed for the king by Niels Eigtved in the 1750s. The patterned pavement and the guard boxes are Rococo flourishes.

The best-kept Rococo square in Europe is the Amalienborg Plads in Copenhagen. Commissioned by Frederik V in 1749 as the centerpiece of a new quarter, Frederiksstad, it doubles as the forecourt to the royal palaces. The king presented building plots to four noble families on condition that they build identical palaces to the design of his chosen architect, Niels Eigtved. A similar uniformity was achieved in the surrounding streets. The square has an octagonal plan, similar to that of the Place Vendôme in Paris, or the Place Hoche in Versailles. Eigtved may have been inspired by French models, but the execution is distinctively different. The Place Vendôme was built as a grand façade; the Amalienborg square comprises four symmetrical pavilions, with low side wings set at an angle.

A second storey was added to Eigtved's original wings when Christianborg Palace was destroyed by fire, and the king bought all four palaces for himself and his family. Two still serve that purpose; a third is now a museum. The architect's design for the Marble Church which closes the main axis out of the square proved too expensive; a less audacious design was completed in 1894. On the line of this axis, which leads up from the inner harbor, is the bronze equestrian statue of Frederik, as green as if it had been dredged from the ocean floor.

Life has ebbed from the square. A hundred years ago it was thronged with peddlers and with townspeople watching the changing of the guard. A block away was a busy quayside; ten years ago that was replaced with a linear park and pedestrian promenade. Etched bronze columns frame the great dome of the Marble Church. But for the odd car and cyclist bouncing over the cobbles, the Amalienborg looks today as the *places royales* do in 18th-century engravings. Guards in period uniform stand or pace slowly past the palaces, hissing like geese at loiterers. Their red boxes, as narrow as coffins, contain capes for chilly weather.

But the coolness is tempered by the human scale and characteristically Danish grace notes. Rococo ornament enlivens the sober façades; the guard boxes have heart-shaped spy holes. The cobbled pavement is a warm brown and slightly domed; sidewalks are patterned with an exuberant mosaic of flowers. The ornamental soldiers, changing guard with clockwork precision, the cyclists swinging around the statue, the rooftop statues and urns, all suggest a hilarious and subversive notion: that this royal courtyard is a petrified carousel that will again revolve, as cheerfully as a ride in the Tivoli Gardens, with the statue of Frederik spinning at its hub.

The real world is just around the corner. As you are admiring the three-masted clipper that is moored on the far side of the harbor and a sprightly ketch newly arrived from Boston, the Norwegian car ferry slides into its berth, like a painted flat moving across stage for a change of scene.

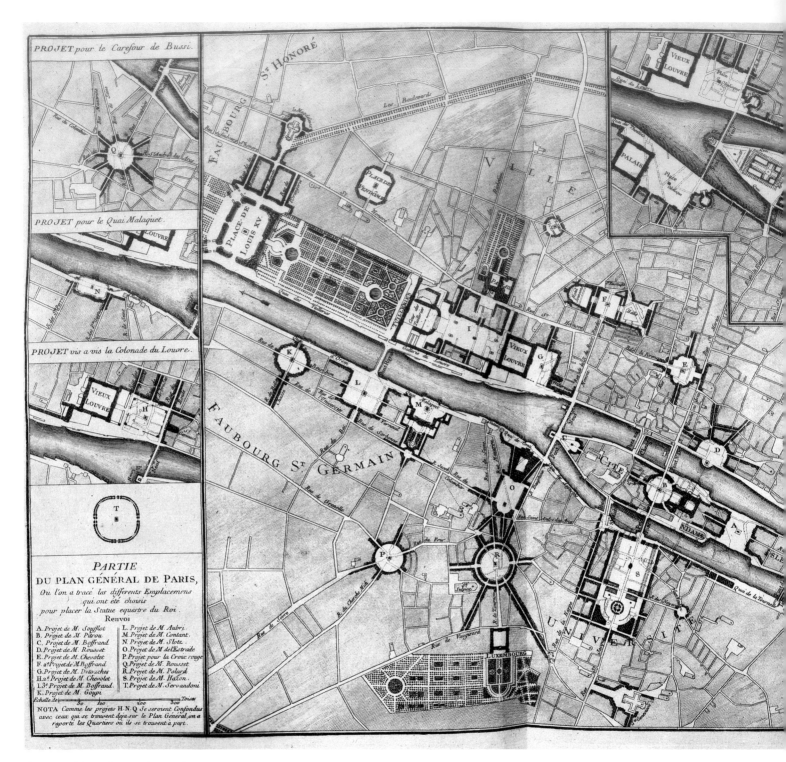

A competition of 1748 to create a monument to honor Louis XV yielded a hundred proposals for new Parisian squares, some of which were outlined on this plan of 1763 by Pierre Patté.

148

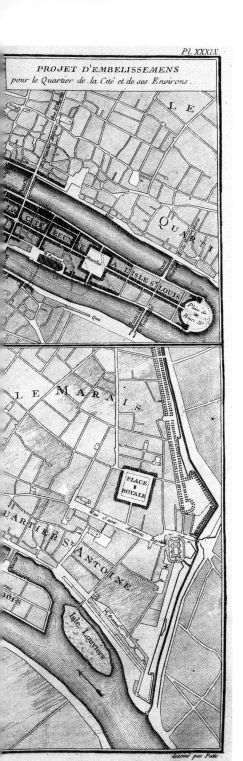

Enlarging the Bounds

"A THEATER for dramatic and glorious events . . . the last, largest and most beautiful of royal squares", is how Jacques Chirac, Mayor of Paris and a former Premier of France, described the Place de la Concorde. For once, a politician's rhetoric was precisely on target. It is all those things, and more. The largest square in Europe — 1,000 feet across — it is defined by perspectives and the whirlpool of traffic, more than by physical boundaries. It is the symbol and heart of Paris. The vision of its architect, Jacques-Ange Gabriel, has survived two centuries of change he could not have foreseen.

It began with a competition. The merchants of Paris desired to honor Louis XV by erecting a statue; the King granted their request, and in June 1748 his Superintendent of Buildings invited architects to submit designs for a square to frame the effigy. A hundred proposals were received, and nineteen of them were described by Pierre Patté in his celebratory volume of 1763, *Monumens Erigé en France à la Gloire de Louis XV*. Patté was an avid royalist, and his text captures the spirit in which royal squares were conceived all over France. He begins: "J'éprouve une satisfaction délicieuse . . . de célébrer un bon Prince, un vrai héro de l'humanité . . ."

What these plans reveal is far more interesting than Patté's idol-worship: a bold attempt to bring order to the streets of Paris by creating useful squares and traffic circles. The projects include a marketplace, joining the Ile de la Cité to the Ile St Louis, and an agora flanked by arcaded market halls on the site of Les Halles. A circle on the left bank anticipates the Etoile with its axial avenues; another defines a river crossing at the heart of the old city.

None of these concepts was realized; the king wanted to avoid the trouble and expense of clearing private property, and it was not until a century later, when Napoleon III gave Baron Haussmann sweeping authority, that the medieval tangle was unraveled. Instead, Louis XV decided that the square should be laid out on crown land between the Tuileries Gardens and the Champs-Elysées. It was an apt choice, for it strengthened the royal axis that extended from the Louvre, and it stimulated the westward expansion of Paris, as had the Place Vendôme a half-century before. A second, limited competition was held for the site: all nineteen entries were rejected, and the king's architect, Jacques-Ange Gabriel, was asked to create a synthesis of their best features.

Drawing on his experience in Bordeaux, Gabriel created a new kind of royal

Above left: Jacques-Ange Gabriel was commissioned to design what became the Place de la Concorde on open land between the Tuileries Gardens and the Champs-Elysées. Painting by Jean Baptiste Leprince, 1775.

Above right: the twin fountains of the Place de la Concorde were modeled on those flanking the obelisk in the Piazza of St Peter's in Rome. In the background are the horses of Marly, brought from a royal château in 1795 to frame the Champs-Elysées.

square for the capital: as open to nature and traffic as the Place Royale and the Place Vendôme were closed and secluded. It heralded the Age of Reason and the decline of absolutism; the royal statue at its center became, not an end, but a means — for enlarging the city and creating an arena for popular spectacles. To define the square Gabriel walled in the Tuileries Gardens behind a high terrace, and enclosed the north side with two imposing buildings, inspired by the east front of the Louvre. To unify the space and reduce it to manageable size, he dug a trench, 60 feet wide, 15 feet deep, and protected by balustrades, to serve as a decorative moat, bridged by the cross axes and the promenades that ran obliquely through the Champs-Elysées.

Edmé Bouchardon's equestrian bronze of Louis XV was inaugurated in 1763; the square had its grand debut in 1770, when the marriage of the future Louis XVI and Marie Antoinette was celebrated with a fête and fireworks. The crowd panicked and a hundred were killed, many by falling into the trench. It was an augury. The Revolution began with the seizure of arms from the royal furniture store in one of the newly completed north buildings. A Fête of Liberty was held in April 1792; in August of that year, the King's statue was toppled and a guillotine was set up on the west side.

The symbol of Reason and the *ancien régime* became a killing field, echoing to the roll of drums, the crunch of the blade and the cries of the mob. The king, queen and two thousand nobles and revolutionary leaders were executed here. The earth reeked so strongly of blood that cattle refused to cross it. At the end of the Terror, the square (now named Concorde) became a setting for revolutionary celebrations, many designed by its official artist, Jacques-Louis David. For a fête in November 1801, temples of peace, the arts and industry were constructed on the west side, and the crowd enjoyed a ballet, fireworks and all-night dancing — as extravagant an entertainment as any royal gala.

During this era, the Pont de la Concorde across the Seine was completed, incorporating stones from the Bastille. Napoleon gave the Palais Bourbon an impressive columned façade to emphasize its importance as the National Assembly and to close the south axis of the square. The west axis was framed by the horses of Marly, sculpted by Guillaume Coustou fifty years before. To the north, the raised temple of La Madeleine has the effect of foreshortening the vista up the Rue Royale. Its importance as a monument was clear, but it was proposed for use as a bank, theater, railway station and memorial to Napoleon's army, before it was consecrated as a church in 1842.

In the 1820s, the square still had a rural look; the Abbé Laugier described it as "an ornamental esplanade in the midst of a smiling countryside." In 1834, Jakob Ignaz Hittorf was selected (in another competition) to reshape the space. He proposed an obelisk for the site of the statue, since its form was politically neutral and the inscriptions of Ramses II were too obscure to offend any faction. It was brought from Luxor, the gift of Mohammed Ali to Louis-Philippe, and erected in 1836. Twin fountains, inspired by those in the piazza of St Peter's, were added, and, around the perimeter, eight monumental figures symbolizing French cities. The stone pavilions that support them were rented as two-room cottages. In 1854, at Baron

The Place de la Concorde became a stage for the French Revolution and every successive uprising. Jean-Jacques Champin's Fête de la Liberté *of 1848 shows the Egyptian obelisk that replaced the equestrian statue of Louis XV.*

151

Haussmann's insistence, the trenches were filled in, leaving only the inner balustrade. This created a broad roadway for traffic, and critics opposed the change on the grounds that speeding carriages would endanger pedestrians — a complaint that has gathered weight over the years.

The revolutions of 1830 and 1848 were partly fought here, the Commune of 1871 raised its barricades and was crushed; in 1934, protestors tried to storm the National Assembly and were violently repulsed. Partisans battled Nazis during the Liberation, attacking the Crillon Hotel, headquarters of the German Governor of Paris. A huge demonstration was held here in 1968 in support of the beleaguered President de Gaulle; Pope John-Paul II addressed an even larger crowd two years later. Every year, the square is packed for the celebration of Bastille Day and the start of the Paris-Dakar motor race.

Like Paris, the Place has many moods. It looks its best on a fine spring morning, when the trees are sprouting, the fountains sparkling, and the white stone horses leap into an azure sky — a place to pause for breath on the promenade from the Louvre to the Arc de Triomphe, or to strike off for an exhibition at the Grand Palais,

The Place de la Concorde is the symbol and heart of Paris, "a theater for dramatic and glorious events."

or coffee and patisserie at Fauchon's. At night you can be caught up in the great carousel of light, as the traffic spins around the fountains, and half the monuments of Paris emerge, floodlit, from the darkness. Or you can come at dawn on Sundays, when the square is still, the fountains have been turned off, and Gabriel's façades are mirrored in their basins.

Perhaps the most magical of visions was conjured up by director Vincente Minnelli in *An American in Paris*. At the end of the film, the Place materializes as in a dream from a pencil sketch; Gene Kelly and Leslie Caron emerge from the *corps de ballet* to dance a love duet to the music of Gershwin in a replica of the Concorde fountains, created on stage at M-G-M's Culver City studios from wood and jets of smoke. It is a mirage of the square, with a painted backdrop in the style of Dufy, that captures its inimitable style and *joie de vivre*.

The Place de la Concorde evolved from a single plan over the next hundred years; the Piazza del Popolo in Rome was shaped by many hands over at least three centuries. From ancient times until the present century it was the main entrance to Rome from the north, along the Via Flaminia through a gate in the 3rd-century wall, and down what is now the Corso to the heart of the city. The space inside the gate served as a market and gathering place for travelers long before it was shaped as a piazza.

Change came slowly. A chapel, built in 1099 over the reputed site of Nero's tomb, was rebuilt as the Church of Santa Maria del Popolo in 1227 and again in

Rome's Piazza del Popolo in the 17th century when it was a stopping place for travelers' carriages and a fashionable rendezvous for residents.

1477. In the 16th century, the crumbling medieval gate was replaced and Sixtus V erected his obelisk, but the space remained rustic in character. The decisive shift came in the 1660s. Alexander VII commissioned Rainaldi to create a symbolic portal to the city by designing twin churches at the junction of the three axial streets that lead out of the piazza. Their façades frame the Corso and are angled inwards to draw the traveler down this main avenue. Rainaldi cleverly compensated for the different width of the sites: the dome of Santa Maria dei Miracoli is round; that of its twin, Santa Maria di Monte Santo, is oval.

In 1665, the pope commanded Bernini to redecorate the gate and put out a welcome mat in the form of an inscription, "For a Happy and Blessed Entry". The occasion was the arrival of Queen Christina of Sweden, who had abdicated her throne, turned Roman Catholic and come to settle in Rome. The pope was as delighted as an American President would be today if Fidel Castro were to renounce Marxism and seek asylum in Washington.

Soon after, an Italian traveler found the prospect "so majestic as to promise well from this beginning how many marvels must lie within so famous a city." The piazza

Public proclamation in the Piazza del Popolo that the pope had ceded temporal authority to the Roman Republic of 1848–49; painting by Macchioli, 1849.

View from the Pincio Gardens over the Piazza del Popolo to the dome of St Peter's.

Detail from Nolli's plan of 1748, showing the Piazza del Popolo, the main entrance to Rome from the north.

Right: in 1816–24, Giuseppe Valadier opened up the Piazza del Popolo, building low semicircular walls on each side, and developing the monastery garden to the east as a public park, with a ramp leading up to a belvedere in the Pincio Gardens.

became not only a stopping place for traveling coaches, but a fashionable rendezvous for evening carriage drives. Distinguished visitors made grand entrances: Bernardo Bellotto painted the arrival of the Polish Ambassador – with artistic license – as an SRO spectacle, in which every roof is crammed with eager spectators.

The crowds obscured the piazza's lack of distinction. Between the churches and the gate was an unpaved wedge of space, flanked by low buildings and garden walls. In 1794, Giuseppe Valadier proposed that the piazza be transformed into an expansive oval, framed by buildings and vistas of nature in the manner of the Place de la Concorde. His semicircular enclosures resembled those of St Peter's on plan, but took the form of low walls – to reveal, not conceal what lay beyond. The monastery garden to the east was developed as a public park, with a ramp leading up the steep slope to a belvedere in the Pincio Gardens: a vantage point from which to survey the piazza and the city. To the west, a new street led to the Tiber. To balance the twin churches, he designed rusticated pavilions with cupolas on each side of the gate.

Nothing else in Valadier's long career as an architect and planner rivaled the brilliance of this plan, which fused city and country in a three-dimensional composition. Napoleon's invasion and his imprisonment of the pope delayed the start of construction until 1816, but the project was carried out, according to plan, by 1824. At last, Rome's ceremonial gateway was complete. So great is the expanse that all its varied roles can be reconciled: there is space for outdoor cafés, plentiful traffic, tourists and demonstrations, all at once. Cars have recently been barred from much of the piazza, giving the pedestrian the unfamiliar pleasure of strolling from the gate to the obelisk to contemplate the vistas, or up to the belvedere to admire the sunset behind the dome of St Peter's.

Popes built on the legacy of Imperial Rome. Elsewhere in Europe, from 1700 on, absolute rulers were seduced by the image of Versailles, where town, palace, and gardens were conceived as a unity and as an ideogram of power: vast, hierarchical, and abstract. What prince could resist a plan in which all roads converged on his palace, or radiated from it like the beams of the sun? The concept had been explored before; the scale and authority of its execution were new.

Ambitious schemes were proposed, but, as during the Renaissance, few were realized. For Karlsruhe, the Margrave Karl Wilhelm commissioned a circular plan (1715–19) in which thirty-two alleys would radiate from his castle like the spokes of a wheel – as streets through his new town and as paths through the forest. Little of this was built. Berlin acquired three schematically designed squares: the octagonal Leipziger Platz, the circular Belle-Alliance Platz and the square Pariser Platz, all dating from 1734–37 and serving as the focus for axial streets. Devastated in the Second World War, they were obliterated by the Wall and by rebuilding. Bordeaux proposed a Place Louis XVI: a colonnaded semicircle facing over the river, with thirteen axial streets converging on a statue of the king. The site is now the Esplanade des Quinconces, and five streets line up on the monument to the Girondins.

Ironically, the most successful reincarnation of Versailles was Washington, D.C. The next best was St Petersburg, created by a succession of rulers who were even

more ruthless than Louis XIV. But there is an essential difference between the model and its counterfeit: in Versailles (as in Washington) the emphasis is relentlessly linear and the squares are subordinate. In St Petersburg, French, Italian and Russian architects achieved a balance between street and square, movement and stasis.

Peter the Great founded the city that is now Leningrad in 1703, to secure territory he had captured from the Swedes on the Gulf of Finland, and to open up Russia to the West. His model was Amsterdam: well-planned streets and canals lined by trim brick houses. A French architect prepared an elaborate geometric plan that proved far too costly — merely surviving in the early years was a struggle against climate and disease — but bequeathed a key feature: the three great avenues that radiate from the Admiralty, in the manner of Versailles and Rome. The capital was moved from Moscow in 1712, and Peter's successors realized his dream of creating "squares, surrounded by fine buildings, to beautify the city, and to contain monuments commemorating great Russian deeds."

In the first decades of the 19th century, a sequence of three major and two minor squares was created from loosely defined spaces at the heart of the city. They served as the setting for political, religious and military ceremonies: a parade ground over half a mile long, scaled to the immensity of the state it symbolized. At its center was the Admiralty, begun by Peter as a fortified shipyard, and now transformed into a

St Petersburg, for two centuries the Russian capital, was replanned in the early 19th century to create a parade ground over half a mile long, extending from Palace Square, past the Admiralty (distant right) to the Senate.

157

Palace Square, Leningrad, and a view into it through Red Army Arch to the Alexander Column and Winter Palace.

vast stuccoed range facing over the Neva River, its gilded spire the focus of the three axial avenues. To the west was Senate (now Decembrists) Square, framed on two sides by the Senate buildings and the high-domed St Isaac's Cathedral. Facing out over the river was Falconet's statue of Peter the Great, immortalized by Pushkin in his poem, ''The Bronze Horseman''.

Admiralty Square (now Gardens) linked Senate with Palace Square to the east. A cluster of squares around the Admiralty was first proposed in 1764, to set off Bartolommeo Rastrelli's newly completed Winter Palace, which overlooked an irregular sheep pasture, and later the backyards of new buildings along Nevsky Prospekt. In 1819, Carlo Rossi developed an earlier proposal by Rastrelli to enclose Palace Square with a semicircular colonnade, by designing the General Staff Building, with its concave central section, pierced by a triumphal arch. A point of focus was added in 1834, when the red granite Alexander Column rose from its sculptured base of captured French cannon.

The squares, planned as the physical expression of the Tsar's authority, soon became the cradle of revolution. In 1825, rebel officers and men were shot down beneath the bronze horseman, in the square that was later renamed Decembrists in

Decembrists (formerly Senate) Square in Leningrad is dominated by the memorial to Peter the Great and St Isaac's Cathedral. Painting by Vasilii Ivanovich Surikov, 1870.

their memory. In 1905, troops massacred peaceful demonstrators advancing on Palace Square; "Bloody Sunday" provoked nationwide strikes and protests that led inexorably to revolution. When it came, in 1917, Bolsheviks seized the Winter Palace from Kerensky's provisional government, marching past demoralized defenders without firing a shot. Ten years later, history was rewritten. Eisenstein's commemorative film, *October*, shows heroic Bolsheviks charging across the square and defying the enemy's guns to wrench the gates from their hinges.

"These squares are always silent and sad because of their grandeur, and particularly because of their imperturbable regularity," wrote the Marquis de Custine in 1839. They still are. Countless thousands died to build the city and then to save it during the Nazis' three-year siege; millions were spent to rebuild it as though these horrors had never occurred. The serenity of the monumental core, coldly beautiful in the clear northern light, is almost surreal. Russians lay bunches of carnations and lilies at the base of the bronze horseman, and watch their children play around the fountain in the Admiralty Gardens. The Winter Palace is now a museum, and the arch it faces has been renamed for the Red Army. But the column still carries the statue of an angel with a cross, and there are no visible monuments to the events that changed history.

It is easy to forget that they occurred within living memory, so encrusted have they become with myth. In *Valse des Fleurs*, Sacheverell Sitwell gives an imaginary account of a day in 1868, on which the Tsar rode out from the Winter Palace to review 40,000 officers and men of the Imperial Guard — a marvelously colorful spectacle that culminated in a Cossack charge across the square. As a young cavalry officer in the First World War, Sitwell was old enough to have witnessed such an event.

Now the architecture supplies most of the color: mustard yellow on the General Staff Building, pistachio and vanilla on the Palace, lemon on the Admiralty. Azure and crimson lurk close by. Mothers wear flowery prints and dress up their daughters in party frocks and hair bows for a Sunday stroll during the few precious months of summer. Families from the country, here to see the sights, walk arm-in-arm at the unhurried pace of a quieter age, posing stiffly for the professional photographers who conduct their business around the column. They seem lost amid the immense splendors of the place — but even an army would be dwarfed.

Without warning, a storm blows in from the Gulf. The sky becomes black, and the low sun turns the Palace a phosphorescent green like a merman's castle. Lightning flashes, a few heavy raindrops wet the cobbles. Strollers unfurl the umbrellas they had earlier used as parasols. There is a sense of impending drama; the light is so theatrical that you half expect to see Cossacks charge through the arch, sabres drawn, or to experience a natural catastrophe. Then the storm passes, as quickly as it came, leaving the soft glow of a summer evening which modulates, imperceptibly, into one of Leningrad's famous white nights.

As the squares of St Petersburg were taking shape, Munich was bursting out of its medieval straitjacket. The first Bavarian king, Max I Josef, commissioned his court architect Leo von Klenze to create a royal square, the Königsplatz, on open ground north-west of the old city. Klenze shared his contemporaries' fascination with ancient Greece and, as the plan evolved from 1812 to 1821, the square became a modern agora, flanked by two porticoed temples. First came the Glyptothek (1831), a museum of classical sculpture. Its twin was to have been a church; instead, an exhibition building, now the State Collection of Antiquities, was built on the site in 1838.

Meanwhile, Klenze had fallen out of favor with the king, and he embarked on a new project. Greece had won its independence from the Turks, with the help of Byron and other philhellenes, and Otto, son of Bavaria's Ludwig I, became its first King. But the real Greece was a sad disappointment to its foreign admirers. Klenze decided to help improve it. In 1834, as Otto sat enthroned in the ruins of the Parthenon, garlanded with laurels, the architect declared: "All the vestiges of barbarism must be eradicated from the Acropolis and from all of Greece." Others continued what he began, removing the accretions of two millennia to enhance the pure white ruins that have shaped our vision of the ancient world.

Back in Munich, Klenze designed a Propylaeum, inspired by the ruin on the Acropolis, as a gateway to the Königsplatz. In 1862, it was dedicated to the memory of King Otto. Trees filled in the fourth side. A plan of 1883 would have replaced them with colonnaded galleries; another, of 1924, proposed that the square become a memorial to the war dead. Nothing was done until 1933, when Hitler's architect, Ludwig Troost, redesigned the square as a Nazi parade ground. The grass was paved over, and the houses and trees along the fourth side were replaced by two stripped classical blocks: the Fuehrer Building and the Party headquarters. Between, on each side of the axial avenue, Troost designed two "Temples of Honor", open-roofed pavilions that celebrated the National Socialist ideology and its "martyrs".

In 1943, the square was painted with *trompe l'oeil* houses and trees to camouflage the location against Allied air raids. Ironically, the bombs that devastated Klenze's buildings and most of the city's historic core spared the Nazi additions. After the war, local authorities began to do to the square what Klenze had done on the Acropolis: *Verlegenheitslösung*, German for sweeping away unpleasant things. In 1947, the temples were dynamited, and Troost's other work would have gone the same way, but habitable buildings were in short supply that year. Music students now practice where Hitler signed the infamous Munich Agreement; the party offices house the State Collection of Graphic Art.

The square became a parking lot, and another forty years passed before the original lawns were replanted. The square has regained the idyllic character Klenze intended. Trees have sprouted from the bases of the temples, and again screen the fourth side. The museums and gateway have been fully restored. There's a steady flow of cars along the Briennerstrasse, but they keep moving. Cyclists and pedestrians have returned, like fish to a once-polluted stream. Music students carry their instruments or rehearse an aria as they skirt the lawns – nobody walks on the grass in Germany. Museum-goers rest on the steps before storming another citadel of culture. Photographers discover the architectural delights of the space and exploit them as a backdrop for fashion shoots. The Königsplatz has shed its worldly pretensions to become, once again, a shrine of and to the arts.

The Königsplatz in Munich has regained the idyllic character its architect intended. Here the Glyptothek serves as a backdrop for a fashion shoot.

Parade through the Königsplatz to celebrate the "Day of German Art" in July 1937. The Nazis paved the square and erected the Führer Building, twin "Temples of Honor" and the Party headquarters along the fourth side.

The Königsplatz was designed in the early 19th century with a ceremonial gateway and museums of classical art as a tribute to ancient Greece. Its original lawns have recently been restored.

In 1943, the Königsplatz was painted with illusory houses and trees to camouflage it from Allied air attacks.

It was one of the last important squares to be laid out on open ground. From the mid 19th century on, railroads stimulated the growth of commuter suburbs, most of which were speculative developments that lacked all but the most basic urban amenities. Continental cities followed Britain's lead in developing residential squares that were segregated from through traffic. Within a screen of trees was a neighborhood park, a surrogate for the fast-receding countryside. In Berlin, a sequence of these squares marks the course of residential development. Miraculously, they survived wartime devastation and are cherished by residents as links to the past. In the tranquil gardens of the Rudesheimerplatz, Ludwigskircheplatz and Platz Viktoria Luise, in the years of the Cold War, you could forget you were on a battered raft in a hostile sea.

Within the city centers, old squares were replanned to accommodate the crowds that flocked in every day from the suburbs and to improve traffic flow. As the nation-states of the modern world grew in size, wealth, and power, the square became a symbol of these attributes, as it had been for medieval merchants and Renaissance princes. But its prime role was no longer as a stage for communal activity or civic ceremony, as a market or parade ground. Instead, it was an impersonal place of assembly and circulation; a place to walk around and admire, or to traverse briskly

Trafalgar Square was laid out in the mid-19th century as London's grand civic space. T.H. Shepherd's view of 1840 shows its three strongest features — the new National Gallery, Nelson's Column and the church of St Martin's in the Fields.

on the way to somewhere else. Open to all, exclusive to none, the square became a forum to impress strangers and simulate a sense of community.

An idealized view by moonlight of the south side of Trafalgar Square, painted by Henry Pether, c. 1861–67.

William Cobbett described early-19th-century London, in *Rural Rides*, as "the great wen . . . the metropolis of empire". Trafalgar Square was created by Act of Parliament in 1826, as a symbol of city, nation, and empire, at the junction of Charing Cross Road and Whitehall. The medieval Royal Mews were demolished to make room for the new National Gallery of Art, designed by William Wilkins; the open space to the south was terraced and paved. The architect of the square, Sir Charles Barry, tried to block construction of Nelson's Column, fearing it would overwhelm the space. His concern for artistic integrity is touching in the light of everything that has happened to the square since then.

Trafalgar Square was never completed, though it achieves a spurious sense of unity in period paintings. A watercolor of 1840 by Thomas Shepherd focuses on the three strongest features: Gallery, Column and St Martin's in the Fields, an early-18th-century masterpiece by James Gibbs. Henry Pether's moonlit view from the Gallery terrace in the mid 1860s shows the unplanned jumble of buildings along the south side, and, to the east, Northumberland House topped with the lion emblem of the Percy family. Landseer's lions were not installed at the base of the Column until 1867; Shepherd took the liberty of painting them in, years in advance.

The square is full of good things, but as a grand gesture it falls short. The view down Whitehall to the Houses of Parliament and the juxtaposition of column and spire can be dazzling. The historic monuments have been scrubbed, the exuberant fountains restored. The equestrian bronze of Charles I on its leprous stone pedestal is one of the finest in London. The future Charles III denounced a proposed addition to the National Gallery as "a monstrous carbuncle on the face of a well-loved friend",

165

and a new design was commissioned, from the American firm of Venturi, Rauch and Scott Brown, which may prove to be a more compatible neighbor.

A veil should be drawn over the rest. Too many roads feed into the square, destroying any sense of enclosure and creating a day-long traffic jam. Northumberland House was demolished in 1874, as was the reticent classical block in Shepherd's painting. Three sides are occupied by tawdry relics of empire – Canada, South Africa and Uganda House – and by recent construction of stunning mediocrity. Admiralty Arch (1911), leading to the Mall, has no grandeur. Vitality redeems the square: it has always attracted crowds of sightseers and pigeon fanciers, protesters and revelers. But the view from the ill-kempt central enclosure, looking out over a sea of metal at a shabby backdrop, is lowering to the spirits.

Milan's main square, though imperfect, has more panache. The Piazza del Duomo was created in the 1860s as part of a grand design by Giuseppe Mengoni of Bologna. He won a competition (last of a series that began in 1838) for "a rectangular plaza to be enclosed by a portico with a free-standing building on the west side, and an arcade to connect the plaza with that of La Scala." The arcade became the Galleria Vittorio Emanuele II, greatest of 19th-century shopping malls,

Milan's Piazza del Duomo was designed to celebrate Italian unification and to enhance the great cathedral, whose west front was finally completed on the orders of Napoleon.

named for the first king of united Italy, whose statue graces the square. The Galleria celebrates a new nation and the ascendancy of the bourgeoisie. It is a fusion of art and engineering, a secular counterweight to the cathedral, an indoor version of the piazza, and a favorite gathering place for opera lovers and businessmen, shoppers and streetwalkers. Mark Twain declared: "I should like to live in it all my life."

Its presence energizes the piazza, which would otherwise be no more than what it was before 1860: a forecourt to the cathedral. Nothing could compete with this glorious white marble confection, begun on the initiative of Gian-Galeazzo Visconti in 1386 and finished, by order of Napoleon, in 1809. Mengoni intended to create a unified frame of palatial façades, with porticoes and rooftop trophies – pompous, undistinguished, but effective as a foil. Wide streets linked the piazza to the city, but the vistas were enclosed. A subsidiary plaza opened out of the south-east corner, set at an angle to the Palazzo Reale.

The plan was only partially realized. The cruciform Galleria, with its soaring glass vaults and grand entrance arch, was accounted a triumph. The free-standing building to the west was built more plainly than Mengoni intended, and is now covered in neon advertisements. The south side grew piecemeal, and was rebuilt in 1937 in stripped classical style, with porticoed pavilions framing a street that is aligned on the entrance to the Galleria. Like so much fascist-era building, it is unloved and shabby. The piazza has a geometrically patterned pavement which helps pull together the disparate elements. And the city intends to restore the symmetry of Mengoni's plan by constructing a free-standing arcade and sculpture gallery, designed by Ignazio Gardella, to screen the west side.

The Piazza del Duomo taps the energy of Italy's most sophisticated city, its capital of business and fashion. Traffic has been restricted to the west side to protect the cathedral, and the square is full of walkers and watchers. The latter sit around the edges of the steps as though in the tiers of the Teatro La Scala; the walkers have the

A shady portico (left) links the Galleria, Milan's grand 19th-century shopping arcade, to the Piazza del Duomo (above). Both are favorite places for strolling and people-watching.

confident step of people who know they are worth watching. Buoyed by this spectacle, by the incomparable backdrop of the cathedral, and by a distant glimpse of Leonardo da Vinci on his pedestal in the Piazza della Scala, it is easy to forgive the piazza's flaws. Italy's inherited sense of space and proportion, and its delight in vistas were still alive a hundred years ago.

From Milan to Moscow is a huge leap, in politics, climate, and culture, and Red Square appears to differ in every important way from the Piazza del Duomo. And yet, there are fascinating similarities, not least in the way the Russian square was replanned in the 19th century. Tsar Alexander I, who had triumphed over Napoleon and transformed the center of St Petersburg, also reshaped the crucible of Russian history. From the irregular marketplace at the foot of the Kremlin wall, he created a paved rectangle bounded by an exotic church and a glass-vaulted shopping arcade, to serve as the central focus for a growing city.

The Russian name for Red Square – Krasnaya Ploshchad – can also be translated as "beautiful", but for most of its history it was simply an expanse of raw ground. Much of the present 1,280 × 430 foot square was occupied by a wide moat and later by earth bastions that protected the Kremlin. This fortified enclosure, once the entire city, was founded when Moscow became the capital of Russia in the 14th century. In the late 15th century it began to think of itself as the bastion of orthodoxy, the successor to Rome and Constantinople. Architects were summoned from Italy to rebuild the Kremlin, which is why its swallow-tail battlements resemble those of northern Italian fortresses.

St Basil's marked a departure from foreign styles. Constructed in the 1560s to celebrate victory over the Tartars at Kazan, it was intended as a symbol of Holy Russia triumphing over evil. Russian architects designed it on the model of traditional wooden churches, in which one spire rises from a cluster of lower spires and cupolas, like a copse surrounding a tall old fir tree. Church and Kremlin walls were whitewashed in the 17th century to conform with tradition; since then, the original red brick of the walls has been revealed, and St Basil's has been repainted as brightly as a Russian doll.

The open space fronting these monuments has its own rich history. As Arthur Voyce recounts, it was the scene of Tartar attacks, popular risings and mass executions. Religious processions culminated in that of Palm Sunday, when the Patriarch rode an ass from the Cathedral of the Assumption to St Basil's in tribute to Christ's entry into Jerusalem; his mount was led by the Tsar, magnificently attired. From a low tribune, Ivan the Terrible confessed his misdeeds before the people and promised to reform. Crowds gathered to listen to the town crier and the reading of edicts, and to watch Peter the Great wielding the executioner's axe at the Lobnoye Mesto (place of the skull) — a round stone platform that can still be seen, in front of St Basil's.

A map of 1605 shows the Kremlin flanked by the Moskva river and its tributary, the Neglinnaya (which still flows underground), and by a moat on the third side. What is now Red Square appears as a vast forecourt to the fortress, stretching from river to river, and partially occupied by chapels and rows of traders. It was the main marketplace for the entire country. Unemployed priests offered their services to nobles; scribes sold religious texts and subversive literature; vendors peddled pirogi and kvass. Comedians, actors, and performing bears entertained the crowds; drunks reeled from taverns; prostitutes and beggars plied their trade.

Much of the vitality survived replanning into the present century. Maurice Baring described the Palm Sunday Fair of 1906 in *What I Saw in Russia*, "You can buy almost anything: birds, tortoises, goldfish, grass snakes, linoleum, carpets, toys, knives, musical instruments, books, music, cakes, lace, icons, Easter eggs, carved woodwork . . ." There was even an "American Bazaar", where everything was priced at 5 kopecks.

Many of the buildings around the space were destroyed in 1812 when the Russians set Moscow on fire to deny haven to the French troops. St Basil's would have disappeared, too, if Napoleon had had his way: he thought it a monstrosity and ordered it be demolished, but his officers were impatient to leave the city. Two years later, the architect Osip Ivanovich Bove replanned the space as an open parade ground, linked to wide boulevards and new squares. Old buildings and the earthworks along the Kremlin wall were removed, and the commercial buildings on the opposite side were redesigned with a portico and cupola to balance the dome of the Senate Building within the Kremlin.

In the 1880s, the Historical Museum was built by an English architect, in a clumsy pastiche of traditional Russian architecture, at the opposite end to St Basil's, sealing the space. GUM (New Trade Halls), with its three levels of galleries within a cathedral-like nave, replaced the old commercial stores. Since then, the only addition has been Lenin's Tomb, designed by Aleksey Shchusev in 1925–30 — a handsome stepped block of polished red and gray stone which serves as shrine and tribune.

The Bolsheviks walked into the Winter Palace in St Petersburg; they had to fight fiercely to seize the Kremlin from the Whites. For Moscow, not Peter's capital, remained the heart of Russia, and Red Square — together with the Kremlin — is its physical manifestation. Visitors are physically awed by Palace Square; Red Square

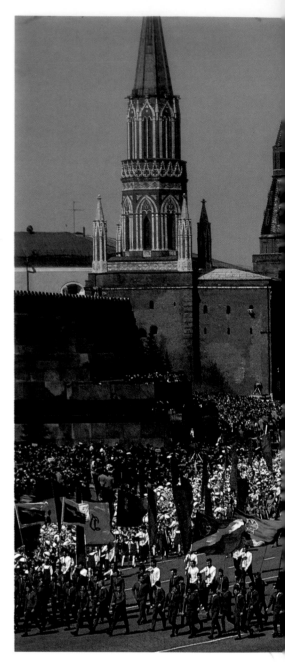

Lenin's Tomb, Senate Tower and the dome of the Senate building within the Kremlin.

has more than size to make you feel insignificant. Nobody runs or raises his voice. This is sacred ground; immaculate, tightly regulated, sometimes closed to all but invited guests. A long line waits to file past the embalmed body of Lenin (some say his wax effigy) in its crystal casket. Lesser saints of the Marxist pantheon are buried in the gardens behind the tomb.

The only cars permitted are those of top officials. Every year, on 1 May and 7 November, Soviet leaders and foreign dignitaries mount the tribune, as did the Tsars of old, to review a parade of military might and of broad masses marching together with banners unfurled. In November 1941, as the German army approached to within a few miles of Moscow, the troops that marched past Stalin continued on to the front.

Little happens that has not been authorized by high authority or meticulously planned. When Mathias Rust landed his light plane on this almost deserted runway it was an act as heretical as it was audacious. When, in 1988, Mikhail Gorbachev decided to telegraph to the world a thaw in Soviet–American relations and to impress his guest, he took President Reagan for an elaborately choreographed stroll through Red Square, with the Kremlin as backdrop. And everyone knew that glasnost was here to stay when Frank Sinatra was invited to sing "My Way" with the backing of the Red Army Choir. No plaza, not even St Peter's, offers a better stage or a more potent symbol.

May Day Parade through Red Square, reviewed by leaders atop Lenin's tomb. To the rear is the Historical Museum, designed in the 1880s by an English architect.

The Delights of the Poet, *painted by Giorgio de Chirico in 1913, anticipates the surreal emptiness of the piazzas that would be created in the planned communities of fascist Italy.*

Reinventing the Square

WHEN THE PLANS were revealed, Lewis Mumford called it "the sorriest failure of imagination and intelligence in modern American architecture." A Broadway revue joked that John D. Rockefeller, Jr., had tried to give it away to his father. Cartoonists and editorial writers joined in the chorus. As Ira Gershwin wrote, a few years later: "They all laughed at Rockefeller Center/Now they're fighting to get in."

New York would seem incomplete without Rockefeller Center. Its sunken plaza is a must-see on every visitor's list, whether for a summery lunch beside the Prometheus fountain, or a look at the Christmas tree and the skaters whirling on the ice. New Yorkers go out of their way to walk around it and linger for an outdoor concert. Radio City Music Hall is the grandest theater in America, and the Rainbow Room, high atop the RCA Building, is the epitome of elegance and class.

Little of this was foreseen in 1928, when John D. Rockefeller, Jr., leased three blocks of mid Manhattan (Fifth to Sixth Avenue, 48th to 51st Street) from Columbia University. The Metropolitan Opera was interested in moving from Broadway and 39th Street to a more dignified site; Rockefeller dreamed of building a new opera house and public square as the prestigious centerpiece of a commercial development. It seemed a good idea at the time. Architect Raymond Hood described how things were done in this "period of opulence and extravagance. There was plenty of money everywhere, and it was spent freely on . . . buildings, private homes, wives, children and steam yachts . . . When it came to the exterior of a building we reminded [the owner] — at his expense, of course — of his civic obligations and told him he must do his duty toward the silhouette of New York."

The stock market crash of 1929 put an abrupt end to extravagance. Walter Karp describes how the Opera Board withdrew from the project; the Empire State Building and other new offices stood empty. Rockefeller had spent millions on rent and land acquisition; he decided that the only way out of his predicament was to create a uniquely appealing complex to lure those few tenants whose fortunes were surviving the Depression. The gamble paid off. The Radio Corporation of America agreed to lease the central tower and two large theaters, transforming a millionaire's folly into a bastion of democracy, science and progress. A team of architects, led by Raymond Hood, Harvey Wiley Corbett and Wallace K. Harrison, created the design that so appalled Mumford, then a better one. A $1 million art program was begun, with the theme, "New Frontiers and the March of Civilization."

As the project evolved, the public square that was to have served the opera house became a sunken plaza that focused attention on the slender, sheer-sided RCA Tower, rising 800 feet from the street. Its shape changed from round to oval to rectangular as it assumed its new role: as entrance to a subterranean shopping concourse. John Wenrich's 1932 rendering shows one version of the concept, with multi-level terraces and a schematic fountain. Rockefeller and his director of development, John R. Todd, pushed the architects to create a complex as functional as it was dramatic. Low buildings and the Channel Gardens were designed to lure shoppers from the smart stores along Fifth Avenue, 900 feet through the block to the theaters and subway on Sixth — which was then a scruffy thoroughfare, lined with speakeasies and overshadowed by an elevated railway.

They succeeded too well: there was so much to admire at ground level that few ventured into the sunken plaza. The underground luxury shops were soon replaced by restaurants. An ice rink, tried out as an experiment at Christmas 1936, became a winter fixture from 1939 on. A year-round program drew the crowds: carols around the Christmas tree, an Easter fashion parade, concerts and floral displays, boxing matches and civic rallies were among the early attractions. Social historian Frederick Lewis Allen, writing in *Harper's* in 1938, described the plaza on a warm afternoon as resembling "a shipboard scene, full of animation, and sunlight, and a sense of holiday." Rockefeller Plaza preserved the spirit of the Jazz Age through the Depression as successfully as did the Fred Astaire and Ginger Rogers musicals on the screen of Radio City Music Hall.

Recently named a National Historic Landmark, the Center is as fresh as ever. The sunken plaza is the symbolic heart of New York. Here, you can experience the spatial drama of the complex: an axial Beaux Arts complex that has been compressed and made abstract, like a cubist sculpture. The plaza should seem oppressive, so extreme is the plot-height ratio. But the architects knew what they were doing. Setbacks and the smaller buildings to the east admit a flood of sunlight at noon, and breezes to set the flags snapping.

The plaza makes the pent-up energy of the Center and the city accessible and exhilarating. The avenues are bruising; here, except during the gridlock of Christmas, there is room to breathe and space to sit. The fountain could be dismissed as an oversized tree ornament (a writer in the 1930s WPA Guide to New York called it "Leaping Looie"). The inscription from Isaiah over the RCA portal — "Wisdom and Knowledge Shall Be the Stability of Thy Times" — would seem more apt for a high school auditorium than the headquarters of a broadcasting network. Diego Rivera tactlessly included a portrait of Lenin in his lobby mural; when he refused to delete it, his fresco was removed, and a safer, duller work took its place.

None of this diminishes the experience: Rockefeller Center is theater, not art, and living theater of an excellence this century has yet to match. It was a new kind of urban space, and it demonstrates that the square is still a valid concept, despite the fragmentation of its traditional functions.

"Nowadays plazas seldom harbor great popular festivities, and they see less and less daily use . . . in our day plazas are, at most, used as parking lots." That was written a hundred years ago by Camille Sitte in Vienna. He continued: "Many

Rockefeller Center, New York, in John Wenrich's 1932 rendering. First conceived in 1928 as a prestige development, it was designed in the early years of the Depression as an innovative complex that would compete effectively in a glutted market.

The sunken plaza at the heart of Rockefeller Center (rendering by John Wenrich, opposite above) evolved from the dream of a public square that would set off a new opera house. On a warm autumn day lunch can be enjoyed out of doors.

Christmas in Rockefeller Plaza (opposite below). The skating rink has been a popular winter attraction since 1939.

175

attempts have been made in modern times to revive ancient city planning with its forumlike public squares . . . [all have] remained on paper."

Medieval squares served every need of a community that had nowhere else to go. Even then, prosperity was intensifying segregation by class and interest. In the centuries that followed, market halls and malls, barracks, theaters, sports stadia and recreation grounds expropriated the plaza's useful activities; parks served leisure needs. Today, in most countries, a majority of the population enjoys unprecedented mobility and freedom of choice. People have left the city and its squares for suburbia.

Against these odds, many squares have continued to flourish, others have made death-bed recoveries, and new ones are being built, even in countries that have no tradition of shaped public space. The human compulsion to gather together has been reinforced by the power of an idea. Goals differ widely. Squares have been created or restored to give identity to a city or neighborhood, often through a distinctive design or art work; to preserve a link with the past; to bring greenery to the heart of the urban jungle; to set off important buildings; and to persuade the pedestrian that he is not an endangered species.

The plaza for mass assembly is an idea that continues to seduce dictators and democracies. It is a tradition as old as the agora, and as manipulative as Baroque Rome. Most 20th-century examples are merely colossal, lacking artistry and imagination. Megalomaniac rulers have seen them as tools with which to awe the masses and compel their submission. For Adolf Hitler, a frustrated architect, they were a special indulgence. Troost's improvement of the Königsplatz in Munich was a first modest step towards the Hitler Platz that was proposed for several major German cities.

To celebrate his anticipated conquest of Europe, Hitler dreamed of a new Berlin, rebuilt on a gargantuan scale as the capital of a Greater Reich. Architect Albert Speer developed plans for a three-mile north-south axis, extending from a huge parade ground and triumphal arch to a great plaza and domed hall. The plaza was to occupy the site of Berlin's Platz der Republik, formerly the Königsplatz, which had been laid out by Karl Friedrich Schinkel a hundred years before. Other architects had planned to enclose it with buildings; Speer designed a two-level Grosse Platz, four times the area of Red Square, dominated by the 950-foot-high dome of the Great Hall, and flanked by the Fuehrer's Palace, Chancellery, Parliament and Military High Command.

According to a recent study by Stephen Helmer, Hitler ordered Speer to outdo Haussmann (who had replanned Paris) and demanded that work proceed at "American tempo" for completion by 1950. War intervened and nothing of the plaza was built. But it is possible to imagine its terrifying banality – from the detailed renderings, and from the ruins of the Zeppelinfeld in Nuremberg, which Speer designed for the annual party rallies. And for an echo of the robotic spirit of those parades, you had only to cross the border to East Berlin and watch the militia goose-stepping down Unter den Linden for a ceremonial changing of the guard until that relic of the Nazi past was abolished in 1989.

The Grosse Platz embodied the spirit of totalitarian regimes: what George Orwell described in *1984* as "a boot stamping on a human face – for ever." The

classical forms were divorced from the humanist spirit that gave them meaning; they stood not for the heritage of Rome, but a rejection of modernism. Stalin and Mussolini shared Hitler's petit-bourgeois fear of the new, seeking reassurance in bombastic classical or nationalistic forms. Moscow was replanned as a city of towering monuments, great axes and squares, but there were no funds to build them. Fascist Italy had longer than the Third Reich to build; the surreal emptiness of the piazzas in its planned towns was anticipated in the paintings of Giorgio de Chirico, a decade before the Duce seized power.

What Hitler and Stalin dreamed of, Mao Zedong realized. On 1 October 1949, six months after the communists had entered Beijing, he proclaimed the People's Republic from the balcony of Tiananmen (Gate of Heavenly Peace), which gave its name to the new central square. The crowd was larger than any emperor had addressed. For the tenth anniversary of the revolution, the square was extended even further, south to the Quianmen, enclosing an area equivalent to 94 football fields, twice the size of Speer's Grosse Platz. Buildings in a local version of stripped classical style, each a quarter of a mile long, were built on the east and west sides to house the Museum of the Chinese Revolution and the Great Hall of the People. At the center was erected the Monument to the People's Heroes.

What makes this dubious achievement so remarkable is that China had no tradition of public squares. Before the revolution, Beijing was a linear, grid-planned city, designed like Versailles to emphasize the supreme authority of the emperor. It comprised three concentric walled enclosures: the palace, inner and outer cities, with a processional way linking the palace with the Temple of Heaven to the south. There was a small open space before the Tiananmen, where demonstrations were held during the republic, but this was insignificant beside the palace courtyards. Mao cleverly inserted his vast plaza along the imperial axis, as a symbolic confirmation of his legitimacy, but the model, in form and function, was Moscow's Red Square. On 1

Megalomaniac fantasy. Albert Speer's proposal for a great hall and square in Berlin was commissioned by Hitler, who wanted to rebuild the city as the capital of Nazi-dominated Europe. Rendering from the Speer Archives.

Sunday afternoon in early spring in Beijing's great square. Visitors climb the steps to the central monument; in the background is the Tiananmen gate with its portrait of Mao.

Flying a kite before the Museum of the Revolution in Tiananmen Square.

May, three-hour parades of flag-waving cadres and children with balloons roll past the reviewing stands on both sides of the gate. Every flagstone in the square is numbered to organize mass rallies of up to a million workers and peasants. In *China Diary*, Stephen Spender describes the portrait of Mao on the gate, "superimposed on 600 years of history, looking like a postage stamp affixed to a huge crimson envelope addressed to the future."

But the Great Helmsman seems increasingly remote from contemporary China. His embalmed body lies in a crystal coffin, like Lenin's, in the huge mausoleum that occupies the south half of the square. Viewing hours are limited, and the Chinese who spend their free Sundays here seem more intent on having a good time than kowtowing to the past. Children fly kites, proud parents photograph babies, young couples sit, arm in arm, on the steps of the Heroes' Monument. The pink-faced guards nudge them gently, they move, and then return like pigeons to another perch. The cheerful ebullience of the Chinese subverts even this vast and solemn space, turning it into a medieval town square — for a community of ten million. Martial law put the square off limits to pedestrians, but it is hard to imagine that it will remain empty for long.

A million Chinese jammed Tiananmen Square in Beijing in May 1989, demanding democratic rights and defying the government's threats of a crackdown.

179

Schematic model of Shah and Nation Square, planned in the 1970s as the centerpiece of a new city center for Teheran. The project, inspired by Western models, was never realized.

Gigantism seems to be a contagious disease. Lucio Costa's inhuman plan for Brasilia includes a Plaza of the Three Powers that induces as strong a feeling of agoraphobia (*Platzangst* in German) as the huge open square in Chandigarh, the new capital of the Punjab that Le Corbusier designed. French architects were even hired to design a concrete caricature of St Peter's and its piazza in the remote inland capital of the Ivory Coast.

One of the grandest Third World follies was never built. In the mid 1970s, the Shah of Iran decided to commission a new city center for Teheran. Called the Shahestan Pahlavi, it was to be located on an undeveloped hilly site to the north of the broken-down old city, and was meant to be a worthy symbol of the Shah's enlightened rule and the country's material progress. Llewelyn-Davies International won the competition, and project director Jaquelin Robertson designed a lucid axial grid with a ceremonial plaza at its center. Inspired by the Maidan in Isfahan and covering a similar 19 acres, the Shah and Nation Square comprised a parade ground and public garden on each side of a traffic intersection that linked the main north-south boulevards. Around the square were deployed the same public institutions that were built along Vienna's Ringstrasse a hundred years before: city hall, museums, prime minister's office, ministry of foreign affairs, theater and royal library.

The vision was Western and secular. Peter the Great had the skill and ruthlessness to impose his will on a primitive country; the Shah did not. Robertson and his colleagues created a brilliant scheme that solved the practical problems, respected the topography, and drew inventively on the Persian building tradition. A 40-foot-high free-standing loggia, enhanced with colored tilework and a water course, created a shady walkway with shops and food kiosks to animate the perimeter of the square. Along the top were a promenade and a succession of little open-air enclosures with fountains and arbors where families might picnic. And yet, in this fanatically Moslem country, the entire development contained no mosque. Had the Shah survived, the project would have been realized, but it would probably have enjoyed greater esteem abroad than at home.

Even Mexico seems to have lost its touch in the creation of civic plazas. Guadalajara's Plaza de Armas is one of the finest squares in the country, an appropriate setting for the eclectic cathedral and 17th-century Gobierno. In recent years, the city decided that this plaza and the half-block cathedral square were insufficient. Colonial buildings were demolished and new structures erected to create a cruciform pattern of squares flanking the cathedral and linking it with the handsome Teatro Delgado.

By themselves, they offer a pleasing variety of prospects; even the barren Plaza de la Liberación, which roofs an underground garage, has urbane qualities. The cruciform plan has a distinguished precedent in the four plazas that flank the cathedral of Santiago de Compostela in Spain. But this is just a prelude to the broad axis that extends half a mile past the theater to the handsome Hospicio Cabanas, a 19th-century orphanage turned arts center. Intimidatingly long and empty, this promenade diminishes the landmarks it is meant to enhance. The commercial buildings are unhappily reminiscent of Mussolini's tepid classicism — and their stores seem to be going out of business. The so-called Plaza Tapatia, bridging a highway, is an ill-proportioned, unenclosed space, overpowered by an abstract sculpture in the

In Guadalajara, Mexico, the bare Plaza de la Liberación und a new garden square have been added to the original block and a half of urban space to create an open cross around the cathedral.

fountain, and unprotected by the dwarf trees in planters. Even the entertainers, imported to perform on an open stage, look out of place.

Boston's City Hall Plaza, commonly known as Government Center, epitomizes the failings of 1960s "urban renewal". The new City Hall, a competition-winning paraphrase of late Le Corbusier, sits in the midst of a vast windswept plaza, created by the ruthless destruction of old buildings. Intended as a showcase of government, a symbol of unity in a racially and socially fragmented city, it serves instead to highlight the problems. If the architects looked to Chandigarh for inspiration, the sloping expanse of brick paving seems to have been modeled on Siena's Campo. There are a few essential differences. The loggias around City Hall are too dark and windy to offer protection from the harsh climate. The space is three or four times as large as the Campo; there are no outdoor cafés; and, on a bleak day, with the uncleared litter flying, it has more in common with Tiananmen than Tuscany. Only on New Year's Eve, or when the Red Sox have won the pennant is there a sufficient crowd to justify the space – and for such rare occasions, Boston Common would suffice.

Washington D.C. narrowly escaped a similar fate. The President's Council on Pennsylvania Avenue, established in 1962, shared the obsession of previous planners to create grand vistas and open spaces to set off the capital's monuments. The Avenue had become shabby, but it was full of handsome though neglected buildings, like the Romanesque Old Post Office and the Edwardian Willard Hotel. The Council, in its 1964 report, proposed that these be swept away to achieve a stylistic uniformity, and to clear the ground for a National Square. The language bears quoting: "As Pennsylvania Avenue approaches the White House grounds, its ceremonial difficulties increase. Here it fails altogether in its role of leading the citizen *from* Capitol *to* White House with firm conclusive effect." They proposed, as a terminal feature, a White House Gate, "strong enough to command respect", and continued, "In order to be effective the White House Gate must be sweepingly visible, and this demands that it be framed by a large open space in front. A square is what this means."

The square would have been 800 × 900 feet (slightly smaller than the Place de la Concorde) with a central fountain 150 feet across, framed by a patterned pavement and shade trees. As in Boston, it was designed to impress; practical uses were tagged on for those less moved by the imperatives of Beaux Arts planning. Happily it was stillborn. Critics lampooned the project as "the largest frying pan in America", and as "Nixon's Red Square". Preservationists rallied to save and recyle the Willard Hotel and Post Office; the plan for a National Square was dropped in favor of smaller plazas that straddle the Avenue. A city already awash in public open space curbed those who wanted to add more.

Like the plaza builders of Guadalajara and Boston, the Council was well-intentioned, if misguided. The dictator has no such principles, but often his showpiece can be used as a weapon against him. He can coerce or truck in the broad masses to demonstrate their spontaneous enthusiasm for his regime, but the more he exploits the space, the more it enhances the significance of protest.

The Plaza de Mayo in Buenos Aires has been a barometer of Argentine politics since 1945, when a mob of several hundred thousand gathered before the presidential palace to affirm its support for Colonel Perón in his challenge to the military rulers. For thirty years, the square was a rallying point for the Peronistas; so much so that a poster appeared, on the very eve of the 1976 coup against the government of Isabel Perón, showing the disembodied faces of Juan and Eva looking down from heaven upon a crowd of their supporters. During the reign of terror that followed, the only effective protest against the junta came from the mothers of the "disappeared" — las Madres de la Plaza de Mayo — who fearlessly rallied in the square to demand news of their loved ones. Their silent reproach was strengthened by the prestige and high visibility of the plaza. During this time, the square was landscaped to deter mass assembly — just as the Zócalo in Mexico City had been paved to permit it.

During the euphoria of the Russian Revolution, the poet Mayakovsky declared: "Let us make the streets our brushes, the squares our palettes." For decades, the

The Plaza de Mayo, Buenos Aires, is shown in this campaign poster as a rallying point for Peronistas. During military dictatorships it has served as a forum for protest.

Party determined who would paint the town red. When the controls were relaxed, thousands flocked to the squares of Tiblisi and Yerevan, Riga and Tallinn to air their grievances. The *New York Times* reported in August 1988 on "the crowds that collect each weekend in Moscow's Pushkin Square. The square has become a sort of people's park, where people stand in clusters around the poet's statue and take passionate sides on issues that used to be debated only in much more discreet locations."

The squares of St Petersburg were the cradle of the communist revolution. History may record the explosion in Tiananmen Square in spring 1989 as the symbol of its death agony. Tens of thousands had demonstrated there in 1976, protesting the abrupt removal of Zhou Enlai's funeral wreaths — an unprecedented outburst that hastened the end of the Cultural Revolution and the disgrace of Mao's clique. In May 1989, as many as a million crowded in to support the students' hunger strike. The square became a city within the city. Protestors waved red banners, acclaimed the visiting Soviet leader, sang the Internationale and erected a heroic statue: Marxist rituals that expressed their enthusiasm for democratic reforms. For six weeks they commanded a worldwide audience and paralyzed the will of their rulers. The bloody crackdown recalled the cossack charge against the peasants in Palace Square, half a world and three-quarters of a century away.

And then, in one East European country after another, the dam burst. In June, Solidarity swept Poland's communists aside. Later that month, in Hungary, Imre Nagy, the disgraced leader of the 1956 uprising, was given a state funeral in Budapest's Heroes Square. East German protests were beaten down until, to stem mass flight, the Berlin Wall was opened up in early November. As the human tide surged through, it rediscovered the long-lost Potsdamer Platz and Leipziger Platz, historic squares that may one day be restored as symbols of unity. A week later, it was Prague's turn to match action and symbol. Wenceslas Square is the hub of the modern city, a broad boulevard, closed off at one end by the National Museum. Here students tried to block the tanks in 1968 — and Jan Palac immolated himself in protest against the invasion. It is surveyed by the equestrian statue of Bohemia's patron saint. And so it was here that a quarter of a million demonstraters assembled, spontaneously, every day for a week. Smaller demonstrations had been clubbed into submission. Now, an entire people had mustered, and the rulers — who owed their authority to Soviet tanks — collapsed like puppets whose master had dropped the strings.

In Romania it happened within a few seconds when workers, summoned to Bucharest's Palace Square to cheer Nicolae Ceausescu's brutal repression of a provincial uprising, spontaneously booed. The dictator recoiled in shock, the image was carried live on national television and it spurred the people to action. Ceausescu fled, the army defeated his security forces, and Palace Square became the forum of a people struggling to be free. It was an appropriate end to a year of revolution.

"Small is Beautiful" (the title of a book by E.F. Schumacher) was a popular slogan in the 1970s, and it is certainly true that the most rewarding of contemporary squares have been modest in scale and organically related to their site and purpose. Many have been designed as (or to frame) works of art. The most ambitious such

program was launched in Barcelona in 1979, on the initiative of a socialist mayor, Narcis Serra, to strengthen the identity of a city that had suffered during the Franco years for its defiance in the Civil War. It continued through the mid 1980s under his successor, Pasqual Maragall.

The goal was to restore to old districts and create in new ones what critic Robert Hughes called "a sense of the city as a hive of places with particular flavors and local allegiences, rather than a monotonous sprawl of housing and business buildings." Open spaces throughout the city were to be rehabilitated as neighborhood squares and parks, each with a distinctive character that would respond to local needs and strengthen the sense of place.

A team of urbanists, architects and historians, headed by Oriol Bohigas and, later, by Josep Acebillo, did the research and design; local and foreign artists were commissioned to create new work in collaboration with the architects. Old downtown squares were the first to be remodeled; techniques developed there were applied to open and undefined spaces. To date, two hundred new squares, parks and street improvements have been completed. They comprise an eclectic mixture of progressive and historicist designs, with sculpture that animates or merely occupies its allotted space.

Reactions from critics and neighbors have been mixed. Bohigas defended his preference for austere designs: "The traditional square in European cities, particularly Mediterranean cities, has always had a hard surface. It is a place to walk, to dance, to barter, to love, to *be*." Some of the squares strive too hard to be monumental. The Parc de l'Espanya Industrial attempts to define its linear site along a busy street with a row of stylized lighting towers and a vast expanse of bleachers, which seem to have been airlifted in from a sports stadium. The Placa dels Paisos Catalans is located on a more intractable site, bordering the Sants railroad station. It is anchored by a high canopy and undulating arcade of pierced steel that offer only token shade – an unprotected row of wood benches, and a fountain that seems too delicate to stand up to the assertive commercial buildings all around.

Far more inviting – and intensively used – are the smaller spaces away from the center. Iron and brick from old railroad buildings have been employed to create a

Barcelona's Placa de la Palmera, before and after it was improved. American artist Richard Serra created two concrete arcs to separate the active from the passive areas of this popular working-class square.

temple-like enclosure in the Parc del Clot — as a reminder of the site's former use, a setting for Bryan Hunt's bronze, *The Rite of Spring*, and a favorite play sculpture for kids. Richard Serra, whose *Tilted Arc* outraged the users of a New York plaza, integrated his contribution with the design of the Placa de la Palmera, which serves as the lungs for a working-class neighborhood. Serra's two concrete arcs are appropriate for the context of raw high rise apartments, withstand hard use, and deftly separate a playing field from a cobbled promenade, kiosk and benches. On one side, fathers play football with their sons, and mothers chat on the bleachers while their kids frolic in the sand; on the other, lovers and the elderly can find a peaceful retreat. A similar mix of uses is compressed into the tiny triangular Placa de Navas.

New Orlean's Piazza d'Italia also attempts to be a useful art work and to define a neighborhood — with mixed results. Its greatest difficulty has been finding its neighbors; the city commissioned the project in 1975 as a monument/gathering place for the city's Italian community, but few live near the piazza. Only in the last few years has this warehouse district begun to attract homesteaders of any ethnic persuasion. As the city's economy slumped, the commercial development that was intended to pay for its upkeep and generate activity failed to materialize. For ten years, the Piazza deteriorated, was vandalized, and became a refuge for derelicts.

Barcelona has created or rebuilt small squares all over the city to achieve a stronger sense of place, both in neighborhoods and downtown. This temple-like enclosure in the Parc del Clot is half artistic shrine, half playground.

A raised triangular enclosure separates a sand pit from shaded benches in the Placa de Navas of Barcelona (right); as in the Placa de la Palmera, an architectural feature is used to define areas with differing functions.

186

Two views of the Piazza d'Italia and its fountain in New Orleans. The square was created in 1975–78 by Charles Moore and others as a tribute to the city's Italian community and the centerpiece for a projected commercial development in the warehouse district. It was restored in 1988 after a long period of neglect.

Just as it was being written off as a hopeless case, the new director of the Contemporary Arts Center, Adolfo Nodal, rallied public support, and developers expressed renewed interest. In a twist worthy of the movies, Orleans Parish Criminal Sheriff Charles C. Foti, Jr., rode to the rescue, deploying the best talent behind bars to restore the broken stone and fountains. Someone overheard him say: "Three of them guys was so good, I'll never let 'em go."

The Piazza was designed by Charles Moore, with Ron Filson and the local architectural firm of August Perez, as a playful ensemble of pavilions, colonnades and gateways surrounding a cobbled circle, and a fountain that spills out as exuberantly as the Trevi over a stylized relief of the Italian peninsula. Materials and motifs are scrambled with reckless abandon: neon highlights stainless-steel capitals, marble is applied to stucco, water spouts from masks of Moore's face.

When it was completed, in 1978, everyone had a strong opinion. Paul Goldberger of the *New York Times* hailed it as "boundlessly good-natured . . . a joyous embrace of the classical tradition." Older Italians hated the neon; a few liberals were upset by what they felt was an ethnic slur, as though authentic Corinthian columns were sacred to Italians. The controversy helped fuel interest, and the Piazza fulfills Moore's vision on the rare occasions when there's a crowd and the fountains are working. But he was too optimistic in supposing that a brittle art work would wear well as a public plaza. Its future is still in the balance. The Sheriff has pledged to stay on the job, the CAC to bring in musicians. Developers are exploring the possibility of building the upscale hotel and restaurant that are now ten years overdue.

Arata Isozaki, Japan's leading contemporary architect, was luckier than Moore: the civic center he planned for Tskuba, a new town 40 miles north of Tokyo, was fully built and is well maintained. But it shares the Piazza's problem: too few users. As the community is built up, it should generate more traffic, but the two-level plaza will still have a struggle to win acceptance, for the Japanese have no tradition of urban squares. Markets and other public activities take place on the street. Even parks are treated as linear space: a Japanese will follow a prescribed route to enjoy the vistas that compose well from a sequence of fixed points.

Japanese cities are jammed with people and buildings: a Westerner grows claustrophobic and longs for the release of open space; residents retreat to tiny bars or private courtyards. Even Tokyo, a city of 14 million, is structured and scaled like a succession of villages. Its downtown towers rise sheer from the street; around and below are labyrinths of shopping passages. There is a scatter of parks, but most of the open space in the city is occupied by the Emperor's private garden, shrines, temples and cemeteries. There are many reasons for this. Land is in short supply and frighteningly expensive; the Japanese have been a rural people for most of their history, and, during the long feudal era, peasants were discouraged from moving around or assembling together. History and circumstance help explain why most Japanese show little respect for urban public space, while cherishing whatever is private or exclusive; and why they feel uncomfortable sitting out in public.

Thus Isozaki's plaza should perhaps be regarded more as an art work and a symbol of Tskuba than as a town square in the Western sense. A hotel tower, bank,

and concert hall define two sides of a raised podium, located midway along a landscaped main axis. The other two sides of the podium are open, but the space is defined by a paved grid, reserved for the use of pedestrians and cyclists. Steps lead down past fountains to an oval piazza that serves as an entrance to shops and public buildings. Its star-patterned paving was inspired by the Campidoglio in Rome, but its center is occupied not by a statue, but by a hole into which water flows.

The architect has tried to compensate for the monotony of the city — a planned development for scientists and technologists — by creating a center that is dense, layered and prismatic. He has collected and condensed fragments of other cities, building a collage of rusticated stone, sleek mosaic and shiny metal. Quotations from other architects mingle with references to Japanese tradition. A golden shawl wrapped around a sculptured tree alludes to the Greek legend of Daphne, who was transformed into a laurel to elude the pursuing Apollo.

Tskuba's civic center is a tour de force of wit, erudition, and sheer inventiveness, impeccably executed, and well suited to an intellectual community. It also embodies the spirit of contemporary Japan, flexing its muscles and flaunting its wealth, creating a distinctive hybrid of East and West which may become the strongest current in world architecture. Isozaki has continued to lead the way, incorporating porticoed "Renaissance" and "Baroque" squares in a Tokyo residential development that also includes an imaginative recreation of Shakespeare's Globe Theatre.

Emilio Ambasz has proposed two urban plazas which, if built, could be as poetic and challenging as Isozaki's. The more audacious of the two is intended for the center of Houston, Texas: a geometric water garden that would serve as an image for the city and an oasis for the office towers, theaters, galleries and restaurants that surround it. Houston Center Plaza draws on the tradition of Islamic gardens, from Lahore to Granada (which use water and greenery to create an earthly paradise), and the sculptured topiary of the Baroque. It is also inspired by the plan of Houston: the plaza contains a grid of vine-covered trellises (the city) surrounding a square pool (the plaza).

Looking down on the two-level plaza of Tskuba City, Japan (left), part of the civic center which was designed by Arata Isozaki for this new scientific community, 40 miles north of Tokyo. The architect has combined quotations from Western architecture (notably the Campidoglio in Rome) and Japanese spatial concepts to create an innovative urban space (right).

Plan and overview of Houston
Center Plaza: a proposal by
Emilio Ambasz for a cool oasis
at the heart of a high-rise
commercial development in
downtown Houston, Texas. It
was inspired by Islamic water
gardens and the city's grid plan.

Section through another Ambasz
proposal (opposite above), this
time for a radical reshaping of
the Plaza Mayor in Salamanca,
Spain. It would substitute for the
present cobbled expanse a
stepped-down, tree-filled space
with community spaces below.

Proposed improvements by
Benjamin Thompson &
Associates for Rotterdam's
Theater Square (opposite below).

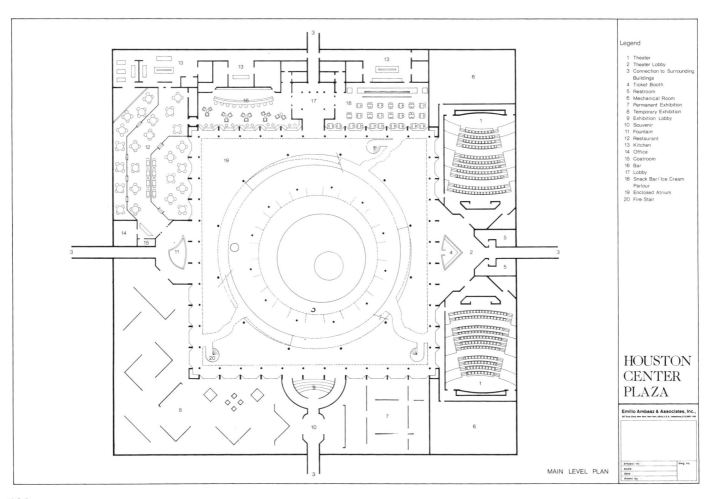

MAIN LEVEL PLAN

HOUSTON CENTER PLAZA

Emilio Ambasz & Associates, Inc.,

Legend

1 Theater
2 Theater Lobby
3 Connection to Surrounding Buildings
4 Ticket Booth
5 Restroom
6 Mechanical Room
7 Permanent Exhibition
8 Temporary Exhibition
9 Exhibition Lobby
10 Souvenir
11 Fountain
12 Restaurant
13 Kitchen
14 Office
15 Coatroom
16 Bar
17 Lobby
18 Snack Bar/Ice Cream Parlour
19 Enclosed Atrium
20 Fire Stair

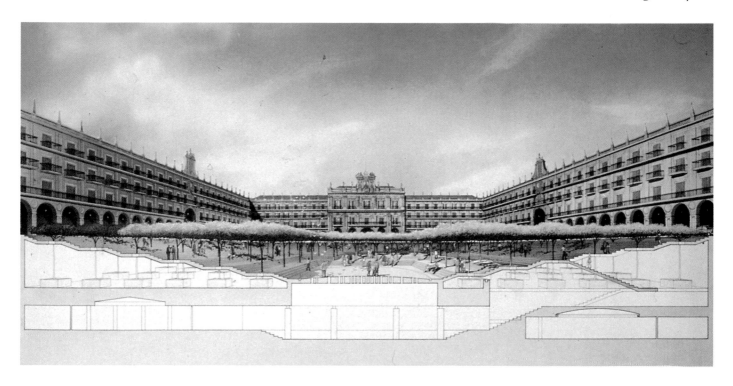

Sensuality infuses the abstract. The space steps down from the street, and the taller trellises towards the center serve as shady gazebos with benches and fragrant flowers. The square "pool" with its hollow center is a canopy of translucent blue fibreglass, over which water flows and cascades into the cylindrical courtyard below. Three irregular fissures at the edges of this structure (a reference to the city's incomplete development) lead down to the courtyard and public spaces within the buildings. From the courtyard, machines generate a cloud of water vapor that creates rainbows from sunlight and diffuses colored laser beams at night. Additional nozzles atop the trellises emit a cool spray that mingles with the scent of jasmine and jacaranda, and produce a soothing hiss.

All this sounds, in the context of Houston, as precious and improbable as Versailles must have seemed before it was built. But we depend on poets and visionaries to advance civilization. Before its economy slumped, Houston was busily transforming itself from frontier town to cultural center, hiring the finest architects to create showcases for the arts. It is hard to imagine booted entrepreneurs and elegant Texan ladies leaving their air-conditioned retreats to sit in a misty gazebo, but perhaps the plaza could be advertised as a spa, refreshing to the complexion and guaranteed to tone the muscles. People would line up.

Ambasz is philosophical: "There are two months in spring and fall when Houston's climate is delightful; the rest of the year is horrible. But you can inhabit the plaza mentally, year round, and it creates a graphic design to look down on from the four 60-storey office towers." Most corporate plazas are crushed by the towers they serve. Ambasz believes that "Stature is a feature of spiritual dimension, not of physical size." In this plaza he has achieved that dimension.

Another Ambasz proposal that still hangs in the balance is a transformation of a classic European square: the Plaza Mayor of Salamanca (described on pages 78–81). The city council decided that it needed shade from summer heat and shelter from winter cold, and commissioned Ambasz to replan the space. He proposed a sunken garden with honey locust trees stepping down to a central square, with a social and cultural center below. The trees would increase in height as they step down, maintaining what the architect calls "a metaphorical ground cover of leafy clouds" at about the level of the present expanse of pavement. At the center, light would shine up through a circular grating from the subterranean dance hall.

Ambasz claims that his plaza would be cool in summer and hold the heat in winter; and that this, and the social attractions (cinema, child-care center, meeting spaces), would lure people down the steps. He insists that most of the opposition comes from non-residents — like "the landowners who live in Madrid, occasionally visit their properties in Castile, and who feel that, if their tenants want gardens, they can wait until they reach paradise." He recalls that the "traditionally Castilian hard surfaces" were restored in recent times; the plaza of Salamanca was planted with trees in the last century.

It is hard to predict how well such an innovative design would work. Does Salamanca need so radical a solution? There are shady public gardens within a few blocks of the plaza. Is it necessary to build underground, when most of the new amenities could be incorporated within existing structures at a fraction the cost?

Houston's high humidity and suffocating heat drive people off the streets, and in consequence they have been abandoned to marginal uses and users; Salamanca's hum with life all year round. The arcades provide shade, the cafés warmth and shelter. The ecology of the Spanish plaza is a precious survival; the architectural ensemble of Salamanca's is enhanced by the contrast between cobbled paving and softly modeled façades.

Ambasz has a magic touch, as he demonstrated in the sunken spaces of the Botanical Gardens in San Antonio, Texas. His plan for Salamanca is seductive – on paper. But once an architect has completed a project, others have to make it work. If it is built, Houston's plaza will be intensively supervised and maintained by its parent corporation. Can the city of Salamanca do the same?

The squalor of Les Halles in Paris, the Piazza d'Italia, and so many other new urban spaces all over the world suggest that municipalities lack the funds, skills or commitment to care properly for unconventional plazas. And, as Rockefeller Plaza and Tskuba show, given a choice between walking down and watching from the perimeter, most people choose the passive option. The hard, exposed Spanish plaza may not be ideal, but it is extraordinarily inclusive, democratic and flexible. It works.

Nothing works in Rotterdam's Theater Square, a 280 × 480 foot civic plaza, created during post-war reconstruction. The bare deck of an underground parking lot separates a theater and concert hall, with low-rise residential buildings between; people hurry across on their way to somewhere else. The celebration of Rotterdam's 650th anniversary in 1990 provided an incentive for improvement, and the city invited Benjamin Thompson & Associates, of Cambridge, Massachusetts, to submit a proposal for animating the space.

It was an inspired choice. Benjamin and Jane Thompson had designed the hugely successful "festive marketplaces" for the Rouse Company which helped regenerate the inner cities of Boston and Baltimore. Working against the clock, they proposed a "City Garden" that would combine art and entertainment, shopping and eating, sitting and playing in a setting as colorful and exuberant as a world's fair. The main organizing element was an open-sided, glass-canopied promenade running diagonally across the space, and along the route that a majority of pedestrians already followed. This walkway was flanked by kiosks and innovative art works, and broadened at the center to shelter a performance space. Cafés and restaurants were to occupy one of the triangular spaces beyond, a market the other. The Thompsons used a Matisse print in their model to suggest how the pavement could be integrated with the structural fireworks above. Lighting and sail-like canopies were built in so that the space would function well at night and in bad weather.

This exotic cocktail appeared to be as radical a departure from European tradition as from the decorative revivalism of the Rouse markets. But it drew from both in seeking to generate excitement with a crowded, urbane, multi-purpose space – on a site that is a sterile abstraction, ordained by planners and devoid of spontaneity. And to protect it from municipal inertia, private owners and tenants were to be responsible for maintenance. Just as approval seemed assured, the project fell victim to local political disputes. A similar fate blighted another imaginative proposal.

Freedom Plaza, Washington D.C., with a mock-up of the Capitol echoing the real Capitol at the end of Pennsylvania Avenue. Review committees stripped the vertical elements from this imaginative 1978 design by Venturi, Rauch and Scott Brown.

"Washington is no place to carry out inventions", declared Alexander Graham Bell. His comment is one of thirty-nine that are carved in stone on Freedom (formerly Western) Plaza, astride Pennsylvania Avenue in Washington D.C. The firm of Venturi, Rauch and Scott Brown soon learned how truly Bell spoke as their bold plan to frame views and recreate L'Enfant's vision of a link between Capitol and White House was stripped of the vertical elements that gave it point. They thought it would be judged on artistic merit, unaware that politics is the only game in town, and forgetting that L'Enfant himself was dismissed for being too demanding.

Their concept, unveiled in 1978 and dedicated in 1980, comprised a walk-on map of L'Enfant's plan for the surrounding area, paved with yard-wide streets of white marble, and city blocks of black granite. Two 86-foot marble pylons would have framed the view down the Avenue to the Treasury and the park to the south of the White House. The architects saw the image as "picturesque . . . a Romantic scene of a Classical portico in a rural landscape . . . And it is a symbol of American pragmatism, perhaps — framed in a baroque plan and developed not with the authority of a prince but through the vagaries of checks and balances." At each end of the plaza there were to be models: a 20-foot Capitol and a 6-foot White House, conceptually restoring the axis that the Treasury Building now interrupts.

In contrast to the authoritarian rigor of the plan for a National Square, this was a modestly scaled, playful scheme. But one does not play on sacred ground. Mayor Marion Barry saw the pylons as a reminder of Federal authority impertinently close to the District Building, and demanded they be eliminated. The Fine Arts Commission considered the models Disneyesque and removed them. That left nothing to catch the eye of a passing motorist or a pedestrian on the far side of the Avenue. And the square is hemmed in by the whimsically landscaped Pershing Park and a brimming pool to the west, and by planters around the Pulaski statue to the east. As realized, the plaza is all too clearly a symbol of checks and balances.

A similar concept of defining space and evoking the past has been applied in the north Argentine city of Cordoba, where the façades of colonial buildings are "mirrored" in the paving of the Plaza de Armas and along a pedestrian street. More radical and inventive is the Campo of Santa Severina, an ancient Calabrian hill town in the toe of Italy. It is an irregular space extending along the ridge of a hill from cathedral to castle. The town, having decided the square should be resurfaced

The Campo of the southern Italian hill town of Santa Severina. The new pavement was designed by Giuseppe Patane and Alessandro Anselmi to unify the irregular space and give the remote community a better sense of itself.

Warsaw's Old Town Market Square was systematically destroyed by the Nazis in 1944, along with the rest of the Polish capital, in reprisal for the October uprising. Vintage prints inspired the reconstruction of its façades.

artistically, commissioned a local architect, Giuseppe Patane, to execute the task with Alessandro Anselmi from Rome. Together they created a design, of white travertine on dark porphyry cobbles, that enhances and ornaments the space. An elongated oval extends down the main axis of the piazza; within it is a compass that indicates the different winds that blow across this exposed site. Lines branch out like ripples on still water, and the theme is echoed in the undulating walls of a tiny garden to one side.

Most Italian towns have preserved their squares unchanged; north of the Alps, huge sums have been spent to restore them to what they were before neglect or the devastation of war. The reconstruction of Warsaw began with the Old Town Market Square, a symbol of the city's resilience and a vital link to its historic past. It was a task almost as challenging as bringing a corpse back to life. For there was nothing left but rubble and a few skeleton walls; the Nazis had demolished the entire city, with explosives and flamethrowers, as a reprisal for the mass uprising of October 1944. No city, not even Berlin, was so systematically ruined; and there was no American assistance, for Poland had become a Soviet satellite. The Poles did it entirely by themselves, brick by brick, recreating the square as it appeared in 18th-century prints.

The square – called *rynek* (ring) in Polish because the space formerly encircled a cluster of buildings, as in Cracow and Poznań – was the nucleus of the old town established in the 14th century. Recurrently devastated by fire, most of the buildings that survived until 1944 were 16th-century in origin, but many had newer façades and all were sadly run-down. The decision was made not to restore 19th-century additions, but to update the interiors. Work on the square was completed in 1953, and it was given a facelift in 1988.

Like Williamsburg, it is too perfect to be entirely convincing. As you admire the brightly painted, richly ornamented façades, with their Renaissance garlands and masks, graffiti and *trompe l'oeil* facets, you wonder whether this is a two-dimensional illusion, like a movie set. You discover the substance in the Gothic cellars and stuccoed parlors, in poster and record stores, and the cozy restaurants that continue to flourish through the economic crisis. Paintings are hung for sale on a fence; old women sell piles of ripe cherries in season; there are outdoor cafés and horse-drawn carriages for hire.

The old town that surrounds the square has been completely rebuilt. Narrow streets and tight corner openings dramatize the experience of walking into this outdoor room. It belongs to every Pole: a place in which to dream of better times and to refresh the spirits after the insidious ugliness of the new city. The visionaries who planned the re-creation in the cruel winter of 1945 understood how essential the old town was to a people who had lost everything but pride.

The Germans who rebuilt their cities from rubble were more pragmatic: masterpieces were recreated or restored, new construction filled the spaces between. Dresden was the great exception. The East German authorities decided to make the old town a cultural showpiece, and to score political points – since it had been needlessly destroyed at the end of the war by an Anglo-American raid. The

The Zwinger Palace and Theater Square of Dresden as they appeared before the devastating air raid of February 1945. The East German authorities have skilfully reassembled the fragments, but the exuberant spirit is gone.

Theaterplatz has been reconstructed as a magnificent stage set, flanked by Gottfried Semper's neo-Renaissance opera house, the art gallery he designed to enclose the courtyard of the Baroque Zwinger Palace, the cathedral and the royal castle.

When the square was laid out in the mid 19th century, Semper proposed that the Zwinger be extended towards the Elbe to help define the irregular space and to frame the opera house. Instead, the two spaces are sharply contrasted: the courtyard a refined and symmetrical enclosure, the square dynamic and open. Its mood is sombre and detached from the life of the city. Each building stands alone, an artistic treasure reassembled like the fragments of an ancient sculpture in a museum. Blackened by fire or pollution, they seem to be in mourning. Turn the corner, and you see what they are mourning for. Beyond the monumental center, the new construction is as drab and shoddy as that of Warsaw.

East Berlin has made a more successful recovery. No one pretends that the prewar city was a period gem, and so the contrast between old and new is less dispiriting. The authorities have worked marvels in restoring Baroque and neo-classical landmarks; their finest achievement is perhaps the Platz der Akademie, formerly called the Gendarmenmarkt for its 18th-century guardhouse.

The Gendarmenmarkt in Berlin as it appeared before 1944. It has now been restored and renamed Academy Square. Twin cathedrals and Schinkel's Neo-classical theater are deployed on a two-block rectangle, as precisely as soldiers on a parade ground.

Improvised space in West Berlin: outdoor summer theater in the Breitscheidplatz.

As in Dresden, older buildings flank a space that became a square with the construction of a theater in the 19th century. But here the effect is quite different. The Saxon capital had a southern exuberance, which makes its present depression all the sadder. Berlin was, and in the east remains, Prussian – brisk, regimented, severe. Three impressive buildings are deployed on a huge cobbled rectangle like squads of soldiers on a parade ground; you can almost imagine an officer ordering them to march away. The French and German cathedrals, built in the early 18th century to a similar design, provide vertical emphasis; between them is Schinkel's Schauspielhaus (1818–21, now occupied by concert halls), a superb neo-classic temple, with lions guarding a massive flight of steps and an Ionic portico. Across the street from the space they frame is the plain façade of the Academy for which the square is named. But the buildings are also framed *by* the square, and the perimeter has been sensitively landscaped with trees, benches and lamps.

West Berlin has nothing to compare with this; until the early 19th century only country towns and the Charlottenburg Palace lay beyond the Brandenburg Gate. Most of its older squares are residential retreats or traffic hubs. The Potsdamer Platz, once the busiest, is no more; but even in its heyday it lacked architectural distinction. West Berlin's most popular square, the Breitscheidplatz, has been newly improvised from the space around the battered hulk of the Kaiser Wilhelm Church. It is little more than an island squeezed by the convergence of the Kurfürstendamm and Budapesterstrasse, an apt metaphor for a beleaguered city, and it is bordered by banal commercial façades. But people look in, not out: to the terraced U-Bahn entry, a splendid fountain and a sidewalk café. It has become a place for outdoor art shows and theater: a focus for the young and rebellious on the site of prewar Berlin's celebrated literary cafés.

Even before the war, German cities led the way in creating pedestrian zones, according to Suzanne and Henry Lennard; Copenhagen and Amsterdam followed, and every major European community now has at least one. On city streets, it has proved a mixed blessing. It is pleasant to wander freely in cleaner air, but too many pedestrian thoroughfares resemble parched streams, cluttered with debris. A monotonous repetition of trashy clothes, fast food and gift-wrapped junk, with pop music blasting from speakers, can provoke nostalgia for the bad old days. Traffic-free squares have stimulated greater diversity, appealing to, but not exclusively for, the young.

Paris offers a lively range of pedestrian zones. None is more animated than the Beaubourg Forum, a large cobbled rectangle that slopes down to the base of the

View over the Place Igor Stravinsky and the Paris skyline from the roof of the Pompidou Center. The square unifies disparate buildings and contains a witty fountain designed by Niki de Saint-Phalle and Jean Tinguely.

Beaubourg Forum, a cobbled expanse framed by old houses and the colorful geometry of the Pompidou Center, has become the most popular square in Paris, a mecca for the young.

Pompidou Center. As in Berlin, the city's most popular gathering place succeeds because of its location and associations – a lesson that planners should heed. The Louvre is chiefly patronized by foreigners; the Pompidou is a museum, library and cultural center for artists, students, and, above all, for Parisians. The Forum draws its public from that shrine; it is a medieval town square in its rude vitality and communal spirit. This is found space, sandwiched between traditional and avant-garde buildings – a blank canvas for performance art. Fire-eaters and mimes, jazz musicians and poets, acrobats and con artists find an eager audience. Ventilation shafts poke up from the underground garage as though from a sunken cruise liner.

Leading out of its south-east corner is the Place Igor Stravinsky, the Pompidou's formal forecourt. It encloses an art work – the Rites of Spring Fountain, designed by Niki de Saint-Phalle and Jean Tinguely – whose primary colors and clanking mechanisms affectionately mock the constructivist monumentality of the Center. The splashing water is an irresistible lure to children of all ages, and it draws together an odd assortment of buildings: Pompidou, the flamboyant Gothic church of St Merri, and an older structure whose café tables spill out beneath a canopy of trees. Enclosing the fourth side is IRCAM, a center for contemporary music that has recently been built up from its subterranean studios.

Parisians cherish their neighborhood *places*. The Square des Innocents, a few blocks from the Pompidou, has become a popular place to hang out. Its handsome Renaissance fountain, once used by local butchers and fishmongers, has been scrubbed and the space around improved with steps and geometrical paving, trees and benches. The Café Costes, designed by Philippe Starck, serves as a spectators' gallery. Over on the Left Bank, the Place St Sulpice combines the same basic elements – central fountain, trees and paving – but it remains tranquil and

unimproved. Annette Insdorf, a professor of film at Columbia University, recalls the year she lived in the neighborhood, and went to this square every day to write. "It was cheaper and less distracting than a café," she explains. "But it was chilly in Fall and so I would keep moving through the afternoon, from bench to bench, chasing the sun."

Throughout Europe, a similar pattern of improving the old and improvising the new demonstrates the enduring appeal of the square. In London, Covent Garden has enjoyed a spectacular renewal since the flower and produce markets were relocated in 1974. The great 19th-century market buildings were happily preserved; the cobbled space around is again called the Piazza. Scarlet buses and subway trains of the London Transport Museum now occupy the Flower Market; boutiques and wine bars flourish where cauliflowers and cabbages were once sold. Weekend crowds enjoy entertainment as varied as Punch and Judy, reggae, or the solo violin of a music student earning her rent.

Neon artist Stephen Antonakos lives in New York but returns to his family home in the south of Greece every year to enjoy the social life of the *plateia*, the square that serves as the hub of community life. Typically, a church and town hall, post office, grocery store and cafés abut the space. An old tree shades the benches; in hill villages and on the islands, the *plateia* often commands a sweeping view. Money from the tourist trade has been spent to pave and improve these spaces, and to strengthen the sense of community — even in places where the population is declining. The space is more important than the buildings; these *plateies* have been created piecemeal, examples of what Bernard Rudofsky described as "architecture without architects".

In Italy, centuries of the finest architecture are being restored and traffic turned away to enhance the appeal of the square for residents and visitors alike. They are no longer an essential part of daily life, but old idioms linger on in everyday speech: *far la piazza* (to hold a meeting or play outdoors), *mettere una cosa in piazza* (to disseminate information) and *sfidare la piazza* (to express contempt for ordinary people). Historical spectacles, however anachronistic, sustain memories of a communal past.

That past is still alive in the rural areas of Appenzell in Switzerland. Once a year, in April, able-bodied men gather in town squares to elect local judges and political officials, and to approve laws. Even today, they may walk for hours to attend this solemn ceremony, dressed in traditional red-and-white costumes, and carrying daggers and swords that are family heirlooms. As many as 12,000 men (no women allowed) assemble in the square of Herisau. Seven councillors take their seats on a platform, church bells ring, and everyone joins in an oath. Votes are taken by a show of hands; only rarely is an officer or a measure rejected. Conviviality in local taverns is the natural sequel to this survival of medieval democracy.

European immigrants carried such traditions to the American colonies, and the town meeting survives — indoors — in the rural communities of New England. Outdoors is another matter. "The open piazza is seldom appropriate for an American city today," declared Robert Venturi in 1965. "The piazza, in fact, is 'un-

Voting for public officials in the town square of Herisau, Switzerland.

American'. Americans feel uncomfortable sitting in a square: they should be working at the office or home with the family looking at television, or perhaps at the bowling alley." This is a tongue-in-cheek version of the Puritan view that idleness is a sin, loiterers are anti-social, and leisure should be put to productive or active use. Preachers no longer say these things to their flock, but the feeling persists.

Historically, the United States has been unreceptive to squares. Civic planning has always run a poor second to private speculation. Land is a commodity to be exploited, and decorative space yields no tangible return. During the years of expansion, the uninterrupted grid was a metaphor and a mechanism for rapid growth; the street led to the horizon and a new field to mine or farm or build over. Squares were something immigrants left behind when they jumped into the melting pot, and even if they had craved them, they would have had no chance of creating such spaces in the overcrowded warrens of the inner city. So the street stood in for the *Platz*, the *piazza* and the *ploshchad*: that was the American way. And for leisure there was the park, the saloon and the beer garden. Families and friends congregated around the front stoop, much as New Yorkers hang out at weekends on the giant stoop of the Metropolitan Museum of Art on Fifth Avenue.

The American journalist Lincoln Steffens visited the Soviet Union in 1919 and declared: "I have seen the future, and it works." We have experienced that future, and feel that it has failed us. There is a prevalent mood of escapism from present and future, a yearning for an imagined past. At Disneyland and its clones, there is a town plaza with a soda fountain and drug store, bijou theater, hatter and railroad station, a horse-drawn tram and a band playing Sousa marches. Was any American town square as neatly composed, as satisfying inclusive? It seems unlikely: this is not the way we were, but how we wish it had been!

"The magnificent plaza right outside your home will remind you of places like Venice or Paris", promised an advertisement for a recent housing project in Manhattan. It sounded implausible – where were the gondolas? – but the important thing is that developers and theme parks are now packaging for mass consumption an idea that was long the preserve of an effete élite. Architects would spend a sabbatical year in Italy and return home breathlessly declaring that they had seen the past, and it worked. They dreamed of recreating the squares they had admired abroad. Over the past decade millions more Americans have traveled through Europe and some have come to share the vision. As city streets become impassable on foot or by car, the square's attractions grow.

Restoration was one possibility, as Savannah demonstrated. In 1958, New Haven planned to level 19th-century Wooster Square to make way for a transportation center. Italian residents organized a community association and enlisted the support of Yale, their rich neighbor. The city was persuaded to change its mind and to offer grants and expert advice to homeowners, on condition they restore the square to its original appearance. Baltimore renovated Union Square, the long-time home of H.L. Mencken.

New York and other major cities have established business improvement districts, assessing tenants and property owners for additional taxes to fund local improvements, which are supervised by elected boards and carried out by non-

profit corporations. Large companies with a stake in a neighborhood have made outright grants and have encouraged employees to pitch in. In Manhattan, assessments have improved Union Square; Metropolitan and New York Life insurance companies have pledged support to restore badly decayed Madison Square, and private contributions are paying for the renewal of Grand Army Plaza.

New squares come in three flavors – markets, corporate plazas and gardens – though few of the markets are true squares. Americans have made shopping their national religion and the mall a non-denominational place of worship. Just as the churches of the Counter Reformation borrowed the gorgeous decor, dramatic lighting and illusionistic techniques of the theater to induce religious ecstasy, so have malls taken their cue from Disneyland, which is programmed to draw people through the maze while giving them little jolts of pleasure. Within the climate-controlled labyrinth of the covered mall, the graphics, colors, placement of escalators, and easy-listening music all conspire to induce a feeding frenzy.

There are some who see the mall as a new kind of town square: a safe, comfortable haven in which teenagers can hang out with their friends, and the elderly can participate vicariously in the bustle. It plays that socially useful role, but

Nostalgia for an imaginary past: the town plaza in Southern California's Disneyland.

such unproductive activities are tolerated, not encouraged. The kids who come to stare may stay to shop or see a movie; the old folk keep out of the way. Security will pounce on anyone who sings, runs, flies a kite, romps with a dog, plays ball or makes a speech. The mall's relation to the traditional square resembles that of Disneyland to the real world: a colorful counterfeit, unnaturally clean, carefully censored and devoid of surprise. Which is just the way it should be, since Disney and the malls are in the business of fantasy.

The new breed of outdoor shopping center is a hybrid of mall and square. The Rouse Company led the way, inaugurating the first of its "festive marketplaces" in Boston in 1976. At their best, they imaginatively recycled historic buildings, created attractive urban plazas and reanimated inner city districts. The visual style and mix of decorative boutiques rapidly became a cliché, and James Rouse left the company he founded, but the original is still a joyful place.

Faneuil Hall Marketplace in Boston remains the most successful of these ventures because it built on solid foundations. Like Covent Garden in London, this was the main city market for over a century. Benjamin Thompson & Associates remodeled and made tasteful additions to the three brick-and-granite market halls. These powerful early-19th-century buildings anchor the space around and give dignity and a sense of enclosure to the cobbled plazas. It is a felicitious conjunction of old and new, commercial and public space. At 9 a.m. on a Sunday morning, Boston's expensive City Hall Plaza appears blighted; a block away the marketplace buzzes expectantly, as the stores and cafés open their doors, and the first pilgrims arrive to worship at the shrine of Our Lady of Perpetual Abundance. In the late 1960s, Benjamin Thompson was one of the few with the vision of "bringing people and vitality back into the city", and it was he who persuaded Rouse to build it.

Lively outdoor shopping plazas now flourish in Jackson, Wyoming, in Lake Forest, Illinois, and in all parts of the United States. Horton Plaza, designed by the Jerde Partnership in downtown San Diego, clusters its tenants along a curving, multi-level open-air street, which opens up to a succession of varied plazas. Entertainers perform in these spaces; the architecture is an elaborate stage set that evokes a Mediterranean hill town. It seems tame beside a real Mediterranean market, or the Viktualienmarkt in Munich, but it marks a dramatic advance on the plastic cocoon of the suburban mall.

Cities have always dramatized the contrast between the haves and have-nots, but they seem now to be returning to 18th-century extremes of private wealth and public squalor. Most of the new "public" urban spaces are privately owned and maintained. Corporate plazas and atriums are less an enlightened gift to the city, in the tradition of Carnegie and Rockefeller, than a response to planning incentives that permit a building to rise higher if it is set back behind a plaza. The initiative was well-intended, for downtown business districts had become as tight-packed as medieval walled cities.

The response of most developers has been cynical or inept. Manhattan has as many corporate plazas as there are holes in an Emmenthal cheese and a majority are just that — holes in the urban fabric. A cramped, undistinguished space on East 51st Street bears a plaque, stating: "This urban plaza has four trees, 171 linear feet of

Faneuil Hall Marketplace, Boston, 1978. Solid old buildings enclose and dignify the public space around the first and most successful of the Rouse Company's "festive marketplaces".

seating, and other features that meet or exceed the minimum requirements of the City of New York." Many plazas are inaccessible and inhospitable; they break up the street line, and they permit the overbuilding that worsens the congestion of those streets.

A few excel. The atrium of the IBM Building on Madison Avenue, designed by Edward Larrabee Barnes, is a serene oasis, a grove of bamboo trees canopied with glass, offering generous views of the street. Visitors can order a coffee and doughnut, and move the chairs around to create their own groupings. Equally fine is the Winter Garden in Battery Park City: a sumptuous, columned marble hall looking out over the Hudson.

Liberty Plaza, one of a linear sequence of corporate plazas in Lower Manhattan created in the 1960s and 1970s as part of a city incentive scheme that allows developers to build higher if they provide recreational public spaces.

The Seagram Building was designed by Mies van der Rohe and Philip Johnson in 1958, with a broad plaza facing onto Park Avenue. The architects never dreamed that anyone would sit there, but on fine days the parapets of the reflecting pools are jammed with office workers brown-bagging their lunch. William Whyte filmed them for his Street Life Project, and concluded that Seagram's drew the crowds because of its shallow steps, broad ledges at different heights, water and shade. The sense of enclosure and handsome architecture also helped; Mies's tower faces the Florentine Renaissance Harvard Club across the avenue, and trees border the sides.

In the financial district of Lower Manhattan, there is an impressive sequence of corporate plazas that extends from the raised Chase Manhattan plaza, with its sculptured arch by Jean Dubuffet, to the World Trade Center. Along the way, a tilted red cube by Isamu Noguchi anchors the travertine forecourt of the Marine Midland Bank, a sleek black tower looking onto Broadway. Across the street is the finest of these spaces — Liberty Plaza — which is defined by massive bollards, and by steps at both ends. Delicate plane trees contrast with the industrial-strength black steel benches. Steps lead up to the five-acre plaza of the World Trade Center, an unrelievedly bleak expanse of paving, where the individual feels crushed by the pompous fountain sculpture, overscaled arcades and scale-less 110-storey towers.

Downtown Chicago has a sequence of plazas along Dearborn Street, each with its blue-chip art work: a Picasso construction in Daley Plaza; an Alexander Calder in front of the Federal Building; a ceramic wall by Marc Chagall in the First National Bank Plaza, a two-level space that draws a lively crowd for its lunchtime programs. These bare spaces pale beside the inventiveness of the six-acre plaza that Dan Kiley designed for the Allied Bank Tower in Dallas. The 60-storey tower was designed by Henry Cobb of I.M. Pei and Partners as a sleek, faceted glass pinnacle; the garden was described in *Places* magazine as "a world of Magritte strangeness . . . a fantasy of waterfalls, isolated trees and bubbling geysers." The plaza serves as an outdoor lobby to the building; from above, the tower seems to be emerging from the water that covers 70 per cent of the space.

It exemplifies a trend towards urban plazas that freely interpret the natural world. Landscape architect Lawrence Halprin pioneered such spaces, beginning in Portland, Oregon, in the late 1960s. His designs for the Lovejoy and Ira Keller Fountains were inspired by waterfalls in the High Sierras and were intended as performance spaces. Halprin's wife, Anna, is a dancer and choreographer, and he designed Lovejoy for "sculpture shows, concerts, dance events with dancers all over *and* arriving to center space from above, down stairs, around the fountain." Working with Charles Moore, who wrote his doctoral dissertation on the uses of water in architecture, he turned Lovejoy into an exuberant cascade, splashing over concrete ledges — more a spectacle than a stage.

Wells Fargo Plaza, a decorative but little-used bank forecourt, which opens onto Flower Street in downtown Los Angeles.

209

The Ira Keller Fountain proved more versatile. Dancers can leap from one platform to another in counterpoint to the falling water, which fills Auditorium Square and distracts from its mediocre buildings. The two fountains are half a mile apart, and to connect them, Halprin designed a pocket park and parallel pedestrian paths: a sequence of spaces he described as "choreography for the urban dance." Together with Moore he submitted a proposal for Pioneer Square, an extension of the axis, but the city inexplicably selected an inferior design.

For Seattle, Halprin created a water garden to bridge a freeway, with a fall that drowned the roar of traffic. In downtown Los Angeles, he has designed a mile-long sequence of urban spaces, extending from the Court in the Wells Fargo Center to South Hope Park. It begins with Bunker Hill Steps: a broad staircase, bisected by a water course and punctuated by broad terraces, that sweeps around the 1017-foot-high First Interstate World Center. The route is planned to continue on through a garden square to the west of the restored Central Library, and along a landscaped South Hope Street, connecting old and new, prosperous and depressed.

That is Halprin's greatest achievement: to weave together the varied strands of the cities he works in. The most seductive of these tapestries to date is Levi's Plaza

The Ira Keller Fountain fills Auditorium Square in Portland, Oregon. Lawrence Halprin, inspired by his experience of natural waterfalls in the High Sierras, designed this and another Portland fountain so that they could be used by dancers.

Halprin designed the two-acre
Levi's Plaza in his home town of
San Francisco. The square and
adjoining park form a broad
axis, framed by low buildings,
which creates a visual link
between the Bay and Telegraph
Hill. Water splashes over a
rough-hewn block of granite.
Terraces and benches
accommodate the lunch-time
crowd.

and Park in San Francisco, the city this Brooklyn expatriate has made his home. The site runs west to east, from the foot of Telegraph Hill towards the Bay, and is flanked by low-rise brick offices. The principal tenant is Levi Strauss, whose jeans are a symbol of the rugged West, and the project was designed to restore a feeling of community to this fast-expanding family firm.

The two-acre plaza and three-acre park are separated by a street, but continuous paving emphasizes the visual axis that frames the steep hill and the landmark Coit Tower. Halprin described the plaza as "a great rug": an expanse of exposed aggregate with granite cross-grids creating a pattern of 35-foot-square triangles. Grass berms and trees enclose the space; to the north water splashes over a huge, rough-hewn block of carnelian granite; benches and ledges accommodate the lunchtime crowd. Beyond the fountain, café tables extend into the plaza. The park is more sheltered and irregular, with a winding stream, trees and rocks creating a distinctive Northern California flavor.

In the United States, much more has been spent on creating new spaces than on maintaining the old. The contrast between corporate initiative and civic inertia, private wealth and public squalor, is evident at the heart of booming Los Angeles. Pershing Square occupies a city block at the boundary between the new high-rise office corridor and the decaying, but architecturally distinguished, downtown to the east. It could be a bridge; instead, it has become a divide — an unsightly, crime-ridden

SITE Projects of New York won a competition to transform Pershing Square in downtown Los Angeles with this proposal for an undulating, landscapeed grid.

expanse of straggly trees and battered turf that is shunned even by the homeless. Created in 1866, it flourished as an urban park until it was torn up in 1951 to build an underground fallout shelter and parking garage. Cosmetic improvements failed, and concerned citizens formed a management association to do what the city could not. They researched needs, consulted users and, in 1986, held an open competition for the redesign of the square.

SITE Projects of New York won with a plan that combined versatility and poetry. They were inspired by the view of Los Angeles from the air — a flat grid of streets that buckles as it collides with the hills to the north and east. SITE proposed a "magic carpet" that would create a microcosm of the city, a sense of place where none existed, and a magnet to draw in a variety of users. The hills were to be hollow vaults that would arch over the ramps to the underground garage, concealing the ditch that now discourages people from using the square. They would also house services, canopy restaurants and a performance space, and give people the pleasure of climbing slopes — as in SITE's popular Highway 66 at the 1986 Vancouver Exposition. The paving grid would accommodate modular kiosks, arbors, planting, and seating.

The design was enthusiastically received, and the city's Community Redevelopment Agency pledged $6 million towards the cost of construction. But the management association failed to raise funds and build support. Three years later, a new association of local property owners was formed and agreed to pay its share of the costs only if the design and designer were changed. Most contended that SITE's scheme was too costly to build and too elaborate to maintain — though the winning team was never given an opportunity to answer its critics or to flesh out its proposal. And, because the city authorities are unwilling to assume responsibility, a group of businessmen has made itself the client for public space.

There is another, fiercely debated issue: how much "design" is appropriate in a heavily trafficked urban space? Is SITE's scheme too elaborate: a tourist attraction more than an integral part of the urban fabric? James Wines, the firm's principal, argues that the buildings surrounding Pershing Square are incoherent, and that a bold design was needed to reverse decades of neglect, a position that the jury and many leading Angelenos supported. It now seems unlikely that their opinion — or SITE's expertise in creating people-places — will be put to the test.

Boston, true to its reputation, has adopted a more conservative stance. In 1966–70, Copley Square was redesigned as a sunken, hard-surfaced plaza. The city authorities delayed completion and reduced the budget; a good design was fatally compromised and deteriorated rapidly. The city realized its mistake and selected Dean Abbot, of Clarke and Rapuano, to develop a scheme that returns to basics: brick paths at street level, lawns and seasonal flowers, a larger fountain, more benches and moveable chairs. Shade trees give a sense of enclosure, but reveal the Public Library and Trinity Church — the finest of the buildings flanking this urbane space. The authorities have also promised improvements to City Hall Plaza: outdoor cafés in summer, a "steam feature" in winter, and more trees.

At the heart of Boston's business district, a private corporation headed by Robert Weinberg is creating Post Office Square and a huge underground garage to

Aerial view of the site for Post Office Square in the business district of Boston. The four-acre space is tightly enclosed by towers; the plan is to put the parking underground and create a properly understated Bostonian garden.

replace an ugly parking structure. The site is a crossroads; Museum Wharf, Faneuil Hall Market, City Hall, the Aquarium and prestigious stores are a few blocks away. The four-acre space is tightly enclosed by a rich diversity of towers: the 1930s *moderne* post office and telephone company, a classic hotel, and a dramatically cutaway red granite bank. It took four years to secure the site and build a coalition to support and finance the development. The New York office of Skidmore, Owings and Merrill wrote the program, and educated the clients by taking them on field trips to other urban squares. It conducted a limited design competition, based on the clients' preference for "a comfortable public room, with a lawn and trees", a proper Bostonian plaza.

Craig Halvorsen's design uses trees to conceal the ramps to the underground parking garage, and fountains to mute traffic noise. Low walls separate the garden from the busy streets; there are multiple points of entry to encourage pedestrians to use it as a short cut. But will people brave the traffic? Weinberg laughs: "This is the city of Sacco and Vanzetti. True Bostonians look away from oncoming cars — it's considered unsporting to hit someone who isn't looking!"

Two of mid-Manhattan's most civilized pocket plazas employ a similar strategy: Paley Park and Greenacre Park are decompression chambers that achieve their effects with the simplest materials. Both were donated to the city in the late 1960s — the first by William Paley of CBS; the second by Jean Mauzé, daughter of John D. Rockefeller, Jr. Each occupies a vacant site, walled by buildings on three sides, with a gate that opens to the sidewalk. Trees, fountain and paving define the space. At Paley Park, just off crowded Fifth Avenue, people pull their chairs up to the waterfall that covers the back wall and immerse themselves in its soothing roar. In contrast to the street-wise spectators in the Seagram Plaza, they tend to lunch or read with the self-absorbed detachment that protects New Yorkers like armor.

"It takes real work to create a lousy space," remarked William Whyte. His analysis of time-lapse film of Manhattan plazas exploded many of the myths that architects and planners live by. He observed that access and choice of where to sit determine success more than shape, size or design. He noted that people are the big attraction; that they cluster together as close to the action as possible and have an instinctive sense of spacing. He concluded that "the best way to handle undesirables is to make the place attractive to everyone else," rather than rail it off.

Paley Park: a decompression chamber in mid-Manhattan, donated by the Chairman of CBS in 1967. The soothing roar of the waterfall blankets the sound of traffic.

A legacy of Whyte's research was the Project for Public Spaces, a non-profit corporation established in 1975. Dubbed "the space doctors", PPS has improved the quality of public spaces all over the United States as consultants and planners. They emphasize the need to involve users and link plazas with the surrounding area — the importance of security, preventive maintenance and a good mix of uses. PPS Director Fred I. Kent notes that "a group of children can turn a vacant concrete lot into a lively playground; adults need help."

In Phoenix, PPS helped transform the Civic Plaza from what Kent called "the world's emptiest space" into the Arizona Solar Oasis. The concept of a learning center for desert living, which would demonstrate solar technology and the conservation of resources, was originated by the University of Arizona's Environmental Research Laboratory. Architect Richard Larry Medlin was selected to design it, and PPS was brought in to develop a detailed design/use program, drawing on the recommendations of six local advisory groups. Three artists worked with Medlin on the design to create a fountain and natural lighting effects.

Together they are transforming the concrete deck of a parking garage into a desert landscape and a sheltered basin, cooled by water and solar energy. In summer, Phoenix is one of the hottest places on earth, and Medlin has set himself the goal of reducing outdoor temperatures of 120°F. to the high 80s, without electricity. When it is completed, in 1991, the Oasis should create a sense of place and community in a fragmented city, besides serving as an educational resource, visitor attraction and a link between the cultural and convention centers.

Phoenix is a special case, but all these recent American plazas respond thoughtfully to the history and culture, physical character and user needs of their sites. The most hopeful augury for the future of squares — in Europe and the Americas — is not their proliferation but their social relevance. In the 1960s a priority of urban planners was "a plaza in every pot"; as Jane Jacobs observed at that time, "open spaces are venerated as savages venerate magic fetishes." She pointed out that they were not a panacea for urban decay, that they took their character from the neighborhood; and if neglected they would drag down the surrounding area. Thanks to her criticism and to the space doctors of PPS, cities and corporations seem to be learning from past failures.

Clients can draw on the vision of artists and architects, and a growing body of expert research. Toni Sachs Pfeiffer studied the patterns of human behavior in Frankfurt, Germany, and found that people crave a place in which they can sit or stand without getting in each other's way. Adolfo Nodal insists that varied programing is essential to draw a lively audience. Emilio Ambasz believes that a plaza should stimulate a sense of belonging and have a good sense of enclosure. Lawrence Halprin argues that urban spaces should offer excitement and calm but in different locations — providing a choice between a Times Square and a Paley Park.

"A city must be designed so as to make its people at once secure and happy," declared Aristotle, more than 2300 years ago. Squares can make a contribution to both goals. They are as varied as the people who created and use them, as different as the places in which they are found. Each community and era strives to balance form and function, and both continue to evolve. Architect Kevin Lynch concluded

that squares define cities, helping to organize them into a coherent pattern in which the parts can be recognized.

The one essential ingredient is people. Around 1850, Robert Browning contrasted life in the city and in a country villa:

> "Had I but plenty of money, money enough and to spare,
> "The house for me, no doubt, were a house in the city square.
> "Ah, such a life, such a life, as one leads at the window there."

What makes the square so rewarding is that you need neither money nor a room with a view to enjoy it. You can walk around, every day of the year, and observe or participate in the life of the city, in much the same way as our ancestors did. Squares change, but in essence they remain the same.

Model of the Arizona Solar Oasis in the civic plaza of Phoenix, due for completion in 1991. Architect Richard Larry Medlin worked with artists and researchers to create a showcase for desert living on what had been bare concrete slab.

217

Bibliography

BASIC READING

Birth of Modern City Planning,
  Camillo Sitte (New York 1986;
  translation, with new
  introduction by C.R. and C.C.
  Collins, of Sitte's *City Planning
  According to Artistic Principles,*
  Vienna 1889)
Cities, Lawrence Halprin
  (Cambridge, MA, 1972)
Cities and People, Mark Girouard
  (New Haven/London 1985)
The City in History, Lewis
  Mumford (San Diego 1961)
Design of Cities, Edmund Bacon
  (New York/London 1967)
*Europäische Stadt-Plätze: Genius und
  Geschichte,* Heinz Coubier
  (Cologne 1985)
Histoire de l'Urbanisme, Pierre
  Lavedan (Paris 1926–52)
History of Architecture, Spiro
  Kostof (Oxford/New York
  1985)
*International History of City
  Development,* E.A. Gutkind.
  (Eight-volume survey of
  European cities. New York/
  London 1964–72)
*Matrix of Man: an Illustrated
  History of Urban Environment,*
  Sibyl Moholy-Nagy (New
  York 1968)
Le Piazze, edited by Franco Borsi
  and Geno Pampaloni (Italian
  text. Novara 1975)
Les Places de l'Europe (Paris 1984)
Plazas: a Bibliography, Mary Vance
  (Monticello, IL, 1981)
Plazas of Southern Europe (Tokyo
  1980)
Space, Time and Architecture,
  Sigfried Giedion (Cambridge,
  MA/London 1941)
Towns and Buildings, Steen Eiler
  Rasmussen (Cambridge, MA,
  1951)

*Town and Square: from the Agora
  to the Village Green,* Paul
  Zucker (New York 1959)
*Urban Design in Western Europe:
  Regime and Architecture, 900–
  1900,* Wolfgang Braunfels
  (Chicago 1988)
Urban Open Spaces (New York
  1979)
Urban Space, Jere Stuart French
  (Dubuque, IA, 1983)

1. VARIATIONS ON A THEME

Isfahan: *Maidan: Problem &
  Remedy* (London: *Architectural
  Review,* May, 1976)
Jerusalem: *Western Wall* (Milan:
  Architettura, June, 1978)
Greek Agora: *Forum et Agora:
  Ancêtres de la Plaza Mayor?,*
  Roland Martin (*Forum et Plaza
  Mayor dans le Monde
  Hispanique,* symposium at
  Casa de Velasquez, Madrid;
  French translation published
  Paris 1978)
Roman Forum: *The Roman Forum
  and Roman Memory,* Diane
  Favro (Cambridge, MA. *Places,*
  volume 5, number 1)
Prague: *Architektura CSR,* May
  1988

2. MEDIEVAL HUBS

Cento Città, Paul Hofmann (New
  York 1988)
Medieval Cities, Howard Saalman
  (New York 1968)
Siena: *La Terra in Piazza,* Alan
  Dundes and Alessandro Falassi
  (Los Angeles 1975; English-
  language account of the Palio.
  See also: *Palio,* Alessandro
  Falassi, Guiliano Catoni; Milan
  1983)
Telč: *Pamet Mest: Mestske*

*Pamatkove Rezervace v Ceskych
  Zemich* (Prague 1975.
  Illustrated descriptions with
  plans and English summary of
  35 historic Czechoslovak cities)
Bastides: *La Place dans les Bastides
  Mediévales,* Charles Higounet
  (*Plazas et Sociabilité en Europe et
  Amérique Latine:* symposium at
  Casa de Velasquez, Madrid.
  Paris 1982)
Venice: *Venetian Life,* William
  Dean Howells (Boston 1878)
Livable Cities, Suzanne Crowhurst
  Lennard and Henry Lennard
  (New York 1987)

3. CLASSICAL IDEALS

*Architectural Principles in the Age of
  Humanism,* Rudolf Wittkower
  (London 1952)
Renaissance City, Giulio C. Argan
  (New York 1969)
Ten Books of Architecture, Leone
  Battista Alberti (London 1955).
  First published as *De re
  aedificatoria,* 1452
Pienza: *Pienza: the Reward of
  Patience,* Murray Kempton
  (*House & Garden,* December
  1987)
Vigevano: *Studies in Italian
  Renaissance Architecture,*
  Wolfgang Lotz (Cambridge,
  MA, 1977)
Spain: *La Plaza Mayor dans
  l'Urbanisme Hispanique,* Bruno
  Vayssiere and Jean-Paul Le
  Flem; *Le Concept de la Plaza
  Mayor en Espagne depuis le 16e
  siècle,* Antonio Bonet Correa
  (*Forum et Plaza Mayor dans le
  Monde Hispanique:* symposium
  at Casa de Velasquez; Paris
  1979). Also: *España: Republica
  de Trabajadores,* Ilya Ehrenburg
  (Madrid 1932)

Spanish Netherlands: *Les Places comme Décor de la Vie Urbaine dans les Pays-Bas Méridionaux à l'Epoque Espagnole*, Pierre Deyon (*Plazas et Sociabilité en Europe et Amérique Latine*, v. supra)

Paris: *French Architecture*, Pierre Lavedan (London 1979)
La Place Vendôme, F. de Saint-Simon (Paris 1982)

London: *The History of the Squares of London*, E. Beresford Chancellor (London 1907)
Town Planning in London, Donald Olsen (New Haven 1964/1982)
Survey of London (University of London; vol. 20 Trafalgar Square, 1940; vol. 29 St James's Square, 1960; vol. 36 Covent Garden, 1970)
Londoners, Celina Fox (London/New York 1987)
London: the Unique City, Steen Eiler Rasmussen (Cambridge, MA, 1934/1982)

Bath: *Heavenly Mansions*, John Summerson (New York 1963)

4. NEW WORLD

America by Design, Spiro Kostof (New York 1987)
Central Courthouse Square in the American County Seat, Edward T. Price (New York: *Geographical Review*, January 1968)
Landscapes, J.B. Jackson (Amherst, MA, 1970)
The Making of Urban America, J.W. Reps (Princeton 1965)
Mexican Architecture of the 16th Century, George Kubler (Westport, CT, 1972)
Mexico City, Robert Payne (New York 1968)
On Common Ground, Ronald Lee Fleming & Lauri A. Halderman (Cambridge, MA, 1982)
La Plaza Mayor en Amérique Espagnole, François Chevalier

(*Forum et Plaza Mayor dans le Monde Hispanique*, v. supra)
The Public Faces of Architecture: Civic Culture and Public Space, edited by Nathan Glazer and Mark Lilla (New York 1987)
Spanish City Planning in North America, Dora P. Couch, Daniel J. Garr, Axel I. Mundingo (Cambridge, MA, 1982). Includes new translation of the Laws of the Indies.
Town Planning in Frontier America, J.W. Reps (Princeton 1969)
Savannah: *Historic Savannah* (Historic Savannah Foundation, 1968)
Savannah Revisited, Mills Lane (Savannah 1973)

5. URBAN THEATER

Experiencing Architecture, Steen Eiler Rasmussen (Cambridge, MA, 1962)
Salzburg: *Salzburg in alten Ansichten* (Salzburg 1963). Historic prints of the city.
Rome: *Companion Guide to Rome*, Georgina Masson (London 1965)
Il Campidoglio di Michelangelo (Milan 1965)
Rome 1748: facsimile of great plan by Giambattista Nolli (Highmount, NY, 1984)
The Trevi Fountain, John A. Pinto (New Haven 1986)
Lisbon: *Portugal and Madeira*, Sacheverell Sitwell (London 1954)
Copenhagen: *Fyrste & Hest: Rytterstatuen på Amalienborg* (Copenhagen 1976)

6. ENLARGING THE BOUNDS

Paris: *Monumens Erigés en France à la Gloire de Louis XV*, Pierre Patté (Paris 1763)
De la Place Louis XV à la Place de la Concorde (Paris 1982)
Rome: *La Piazza del Popolo*,

Giorgio Ciucci (Rome 1974)
Leningrad: *The Architectural Planning of St Petersburg*, I.A. Egerov (Columbus 1969)
Munich: *Der Königsplatz, 1812–1988* (Munich 1988)
Moscow: *Moscow Kremlin*, Arthur Voyce (Berkeley 1954)

7. REINVENTING THE SQUARE

The Death and Life of Great American Cities, Jane Jacobs (New York 1961)
Discovering the Vernacular Landscape, J.B. Jackson (New Haven 1984)
Emilio Ambasz (New York: Museum of Modern Art, 1989). Illustrated exhibition catalogue
Experiencing Places, Tony Hiss (*The New Yorker*, June 22 & 29, 1987)
Image of the City, Kevin Lynch (Cambridge, MA, 1960)
Lawrence Halprin: Changing Places (San Francisco Museum of Modern Art, 1986). Illustrated exhibition catalogue, with essays by Charles Moore and others on Halprin's projects and philosophy.
On the Rise, Paul Goldberger (New York 1983)
Politics of Park Design, Galen Cranz (Cambridge, MA, 1982)
The Return of Public Space, James Sanders (New York: *Architectural Record*, April 1985)
Social Life of Small Urban Spaces, William Whyte (Washington D.C.: The Conservation Foundation, 1980)
Rockefeller Center: *The Center: History and Guide to Rockefeller Center*, Walter Karp (New York 1982)
New York 1930, Robert Stern, Gregory Gilmartin, Thomas Mellins (New York 1987)
Berlin: *Hitler's Berlin*, Stephen

Helmer (Ann Arbor 1985)
Albert Speer: Architecture 1932–42, Leon Krier (Brussels 1985)
Teheran: *Shahestan Pahlavi* (London 1976)
Boston: *City Hall Boston*, James Marston Fitch (London: *Architectural Review*, June 1970)
Copley Square (New York: *Architectural Forum*, October 1970)
Washington, D.C.: *Report of the President's Council on Pennsylvania Avenue* (Washington, D.C.: US Government Printing Office, 1964). See also *Report of Pennsylvania Avenue Development Corporation*, 1974
Venturi, Rauch and Scott Brown Buildings and Projects, Stanislaus von Moose (New York 1987)
Western Plaza (New York: *Progressive Architecture*, May 1979, October 1981)
Barcelona: *Barcelona: Spaces and Sculptures (1982–86)* (Ajuntament de Barcelona & Joan Miró Foundation, 1987)
New Orleans: *Piazza d'Italia* (Cambridge, MA. *Places* vol. 1, number 2, 1984)
Tskuba New Town: *Arata Isozaki, 1976–84* (Tokyo 1985)
Cordoba: *Reverting to Plazas and Streets* (Milan: *Lotus*, number 39, 1983)
Santa Severina: *Sulla Piazza di Santa Severina* (Milan: *Abitare*, October 1987)
Warsaw: *Poland*, Marc E. Heinc (New York 1987)
Greece: *Agoras and Plateias*, Margaret Tallet (London: *Architectural Review*, September, 1968)
New Haven: *Wooster Square Design*, Mary Hommann (New Haven Redevelopment Agency, 1965)

Photographic Acknowledgments

Color illustration numbers are in *italic*

Peter Aaron 211 b; Aer Foto, Milan 48; Alinari 23 tl, 52 b, 69, 134 b; Emilio Ambasz and Associates, New York, *190 t, 191 t*; courtesy the Archaeological Institute of America 31 tl; © J. H. Aronson 1972, Highmount, NY 53, 132 tr; Associated Press 179; Austrian National Tourist Office 130 b; Ajuntament de Barcelona 185 tl, 185 tr, *186 b*; Belgian National Tourist Office, New York (Wagner International Photos Inc.) 83 b; Besançon: Musée des Beaux-Arts et Archéologie/photo Charles Choffet *150 tl*; APT, Bologna 52 t; Brussels: Musées Communaux 82; Budapest: Museum of Fine Arts *71 b*; © Norman F. Carver 61; Ville de Charleville-Mézières 86; Frances Clarke 77; courtesy of Cooper, Robertson and Partners, New York/photo Tim Street-Porter 180; Dresden: Sächsische Landesbibliothek, Abt. Deutsche Fotothek 197, 198; Florence: Museo dell'Angelico/photo Scala *71 t*; Mäddel Fuchs 203; courtesy of Fundacion Universo 21/photo Michael Calderwood 181; Studio Gavirati, Gubbio *14 tr*; German National Tourist Office 21; Glasgow Art Gallery and Museum 75; Archiv der Kur- und Fremdenverkehrsgesellschaft, Goslar-Hahnenklee 42; Grassi, Siena 32; © Arthur Griffin, Winchester, Mass. 123 t; courtesy Lawrence Halprin Associates, San Francisco 210, 211 b; Hanover: Niedersächsisches Landesmuseum 137 r; Historic Urban Plans, Ithaca, New York 74, 100 tl, 120; KLM Aerocarto 41; Koblenz: Bundesarchiv 177 tl, 177 tr; Landslides © 1982, Boston 123 b, 214; Leningrad: State Russian Museum *159*; London: British Library 144, British Museum 93 tl, 93 tr, Museum of London *94*, 164, 165; Los Angeles County Museum of Art/photo Peter Brenner *26*; APT, Mantua/Toni Lodigiani *51 b*; Bildarchiv Foto Marburg 163 b; Arxiu Mas 79 t; Mas 79 b; Richard Larry Medlin 217; courtesy Office of the President of Mexico 101; Piotr Mikucki, Warsaw 196 r; State Historical Society of Missouri, Columbia 119 b; courtesy of Charles W. Moore, Austin, Texas 187 b; National Trust, Petworth House Collection/photo A.C. Cooper *131*; © New Orleans Historic Collection, Museum/Research Center 115 t; New-York Historical Society, NY 121; New York: The Metropolitan Museum of Art, The Elisha Whittelsey Collection 31 tr; courtesy Nuremberg Tourist Office 15; Oxford: Ashmolean Museum 76 t; Paris: Bibliothèque Nationale 43 t, Bibliothèque Nationale/photo Giraudon 8, Musée Carnavalet/photo Bulloz 88, Musée Carnavalet/photo Giraudon *151*, Musée Carnavalet/© Spadem 1987 89, Sorbonne, ms.1501, pl.22/photo Jean-Loup Charmet 87; Giuseppe Patane, Santa Severina 195; courtesy of Pennsylvania Avenue Development Corporation, Washington, DC 182 r; Prague: Narodni Galerie/photo Milan Posselt *18*; Private Collection, Mexico City/photo Mirek Switalski 98; Archivio e Studio Folco Quilici *35 tr, 50, 55, 66 t*, 135, *155 br*, 166; Rennes: Musée de Bretagne (Collections photographiques Musée de Bretagne) 90 b; courtesy Rockefeller Group *174, 175 tl, 175 tr, 175 b*; Rome: Biblioteca Vaticana 134 b, Museo dell'Arte Moderna 76 b, Museo di Roma/photo Oscar Savio 136, 153, Museo di Roma/photo Scala *154*; courtesy of the Essex Institute, Salem, Mass./photo Mark Sexton 119 t; Stadtverkehrsbüro, Salzburg 128; Scala *34 br, 51 t*, 76 b; Emil Schulthess, Zürich 171; © Ronald Sheridan 27 t; © H. Silvester/Rapho 110; courtesy SITE projects, New York 212; courtesy S.O.M. 214; © Saul Steinberg/photo Pace Gallery, New York 2–3; Süddeutscher Verlag, Munich 162 b; TAF, Barcelona 80; Benjamin Thompson and Associates, Cambridge, Mass./photo Tom Bernard 191 b; Unichrome (Bath) Ltd. 97 bl; Venturi, Rauch and Scott Brown, Philadelphia/photo Tom Bernard 194; Provincia di Vicenza-Assessorato al Turismo, Vicenza 12; Villeneuve-Rapho 152; H. Roger Viollet 43 b; Kamil Wartha, Prague 17; Warsaw City Archives 196 l; Washington, DC: Library of Congress 124, 126, 127; © Whittelsey Foundation Inc. 30; Baron Wolman, Mill Valley, Calif. 27 b; Collection of Mr and Mrs Leonard C. Yaseen 172

R. Ackermann, *The Repository of Arts*, 1812 *91*; P.X. Coste, *Monuments modernes de la Perse*, 1867 25; C. Heath, *Picturesque Annual*, 1836 168; Giambattista Noli, *Rome 1748*, facsimile of Great Plan, Highmount, NY, 1984 137 l, 141, 155 l; Pierre Patte, *Monuments érigés en France à la gloire de Louis XV*, 1765 148; G.B. Piranesi, *Vedute di Roma*, c. 1748–1778 140; S.E. Rasmussen, *Towns and Buildings*, University Press of Liverpool, 1951 146; A. Ricard de Montferrand, *Plans et détails de monument consacré à la memoire de l'Empereur Alexandre*, Paris 1836 157; G. Zocchi, *Scelta di XXIV Vedute*, 1754 73 r; G. Zocchi, *Scelta di XXV Vedute*, 1756 73 l

Plans drawn by John Kaine 38, 39, 58, 64, 70, 142

Other illustrations photographed or collected by the author

Index